THE

PHYSICAL GEOGRAPHY

OF

THE SEA.

BY M. F. MAURY, LL.D.,
LIEUT. U. S. NAVY.

THIRD EDITION, ENLARGED AND IMPROVED.

NEW YORK:
HARPER & BROTHERS, PUBLISHERS,
329 & 331 PEARL STREET,
FRANKLIN SQUARE.
1855.

Entered, according to Act of Congress, in the year one thousand eight hundred and fifty-five, by

HARPER & BROTHERS,

in the Clerk's Office of the District Court of the Southern District of New York.

AS

A TOKEN OF FRIENDSHIP, AND A TRIBUTE TO WORTH,

This Volume is Dedicated to

GEORGE MANNING,

OF NEW YORK.

WASHINGTON OBSERVATORY, *December*, 1854.

INTRODUCTION.

§ I. The primary object of "The Wind and Current Charts," out of which has grown this Treatise on the Physical Geography of the Sea, was to collect the experience of every navigator as to the winds and currents of the ocean, to discuss his observations upon them, and then to present the world with the results on charts for the improvement of commerce and navigation.

II. Accordingly, when this object was made known, and an appeal was addressed to mariners, there was a flight up into the garrets, and a ransacking of time-honored sea-chests in all the maritime communities of the country for old log-books and sea journals.

III. It was supposed that the records therein contained as to winds and weather, the sea and its currents, would afford the information requisite for such an undertaking.

IV. By putting down on a chart the tracks of many vessels on the same voyage, but at different times, in different years, and during all seasons, and by projecting along each track the winds and currents daily encountered, it was plain that navigators hereafter, by consulting this chart, would have for their guide the results of the combined experience of all whose tracks were thus pointed out.

V. Perhaps it might be the first voyage of a young navigator to the given port, when his own personal experience of the winds to be expected, the currents to be encountered by the way, would itself be blank. If so, there would be the wind and current chart. It would spread out before him the tracks of a thousand vessels that had preceded him on the same voyage, wherever it might be, and that, too, at the same season of the year. Such a chart, it was held, would show him not only the tracks of the vessels, but the experience also of each master as to the winds and currents by the way, the temperature of the ocean, and the variation of the needle. All this could be taken in at a glance, and thus the young mariner instead of groping his way along until the lights of experience should come to him by the slow teachings of the dearest of all schools, would here find, at once, that he had already the experience of a thousand navigators to guide him on his voyage. He might, therefore, set out upon his first voyage with as much confidence in his knowledge as to the winds and currents he might expect to meet with, as though he himself had already been that way a thousand times before.

VI. But, to show the tracks of these vessels on a chart, a line had to be drawn for each one; now this, for so many, and all in black or blue, and on the same sheet of paper too, would present, it was perceived, a mass of lines in inextricable confusion. Moreover, after these tracks were projected, there would be no room left for the name of the month to show when each one was made, much less for any written account of the winds and currents daily encountered by each vessel of the multitude. After the tracks were projected, there would, it was found after trial, be barely room left on the chart to write the name of the vessel, much less the direction and set of the winds and currents.

VII. An appeal, it was consequently decided, should be taken to the most comprehensive sense of the five, and it was thereupon resolved to address all those tracks, and winds, and currents, with their strength, set, and direction—in short, all this experience, knowledge, and information—to the eye, by means of colors and symbols.

VIII. The symbols devised with this view were a comet's tail for the wind, an arrow for currents, Arabic numerals for the temperature of the sea, Roman for the variation of the needle, continuous, broken, and dotted lines for the month, and colors for the four seasons.

IX. A continuous line was used to show that the track was made during the first month; a broken, the second; and a dotted line, the last month of each season: black standing for the winter, green for spring, red for summer, and blue for autumn.

X. The comet's tail, and the arrow, and the numerals, were also in colors, according to the seasons. The force and direction of the wind were indicated by the shape and position of this tail; while the flight and length of the arrows designated the velocity and set of the currents.

XI. Thus the eye was successfully addressed; for, by a mere glance at the chart, the navigator saw in a moment from what quarter he might expect to find the wind in any part of the sea to prevail for any month; and he thus had to guide him across the pathless ocean, not theory or conjecture, nor the faint glimmerings of any one man's experience, but the entire blaze and full flood of light which the observations of all the navigators that had preceded him could shed.

XII. Thus, while the young ship-master, with these charts before him, would be immediately lifted up and placed on a footing with the oldest sea-captains in this respect, the aged might see in these charts also the voyages made in their young days spread out before them. There, on the chart, was the ship's name, her track, the year; and, by the color and fashion of the line (§ IX.), the month might be told. There, on that day, in that latitude and longitude, these charts would remind the old sailor that he had encountered a terrible gale of wind; there, that he had been beset with calms; how here, with fair winds and a smooth sea, he had made a glorious run. Here, he had first encountered the trades; and there, lost them. At this place, he had met with a "hawsing current." Here, the winds were squally with rain; and there, it was he had been beset with fogs; here, with thunder-storms. All this was seen on paper, and so represented as to recall the reality vividly to mind.

XIII. Such a chart could not fail to commend itself to intelligent ship-masters, and such a chart was constructed for them. They took it to sea, they tried it, and to their surprise and delight they found that, with the knowledge it afforded, the remote corners of the earth were brought closer together, in some instances, by many days' sail. The passage hence to the equator alone was shortened ten days. Before the commencement of this undertaking, the average passage to California was 183 days; but with these charts for their guide, navigators have reduced that average, and brought it down to 135 days.

XIV. Between England and Australia, the average time going, without these charts, is ascertained to be 124 days, and coming, about the same; making the round voyage one of about 250 days on the average.

XV. These charts, and the system of research to which they have given rise, bid fair to bring that colony and the mother country nearer by many days, reducing, in no small measure, the average duration of the round voyage.*

XVI. At the meeting of the British Association of 1853, it was stated by a distinguished member—and the statement was again repeated at its meeting in 1854—that in Bombay, whence he came, it was estimated that this system of research, if extended to the Indian Ocean, and embodied in a set of charts for that sea, such as I have been describing, would produce an annual saving to British commerce, in those waters alone, of one or two millions of dollars;† and in all seas, of ten millions.‡

XVII. A system of philosophical research, which is so rich with fruits and abundant with promise, could not fail to attract the attention and commend itself to the consideration of the seafaring community of the whole civilized world. It was founded on observation; it was the result of the experience of many observant

* The outward passage, it has since been ascertained, has been reduced to 97 days on the average.

† . . . "Now let us make a calculation of the annual saving to the commerce of the United States effected by those charts and sailing directions. According to Mr. Maury, the average freight from the United States to Rio Janeiro is 17.7 cts. per ton per day; to Australia, 20 cts.; to California, also, about 20 cts. The mean of this is a little over 19 cents per ton per day; but to be within the mark, we will take it at 15, and include all the ports of South America, China, and the East Indies.

"The sailing directions have shortened the passages to California 30 days, to Australia 20, to Rio Janeiro 10. The mean of this is 20, but we will take it at 15, and also include the above-named ports of South America, China, and the East Indies.

"We estimate the tonnage of the United States engaged in trade with these places at 1,000,000 tons per annum.

"With these data, we see that there has been effected a saving for each one of these tons of 15 cents per day for a period of 15 days, which will give an aggregate of $2,250,000 saved per annum. This is on the outward voyage alone, and the tonnage trading with all other parts of the world is also left out of the calculation. Take these into consideration, and also the fact that there is a vast amount of foreign tonnage trading between these places and the United States, and it will be seen that the annual sum saved will swell to an enormous amount."—*Extract from Hunt's Merchant's Magazine, May*, 1854.

‡ See Inaugural Address of the Earl of Harrowby, President of the British Association at its twenty-fourth meeting. Liverpool, 1854.

men, now brought together for the first time and patiently discussed. The results tended to increase human knowledge with regard to the sea and its wonders, and therefore they could not be wanting in attractions to right-minded men.

XVIII. As we went on with our labors in this field, it was found that the flight into the garret and the dive into the sea-chests for old logs (§ II.) were not sufficient. The old records thence turned up proved to be only outcroppings to the rich vein which had been struck; but the indications which they gave of hidden treasure were unmistakable to the nautical mind of the world. It was found necessary to go deeper, and to observe more minutely than our ancestors of the sea had done.

XIX. Accordingly, it was deemed advisable to make an exhibit of what had been obtained from the old sea-chests. This was done, and presented to mariners in the shape of a set of "Track Charts" for the North Atlantic Ocean.

XX. On those charts all the tracks that could be collected at that time from the old sea-journals were projected, and one was surprised to see how they cut up and divided the ocean off into great turnpike-looking thoroughfares. There was the road to China: it, and the road to South America, to the Pacific around Cape Horn, to the East around the Cape of Good Hope, and to Australia, were one and the same until the navigator had left the North, crossed the equator, and passed over into the South Atlantic. Here there was, in this great highway, a fork to the right, leading to the ports of Brazil. A little farther on you came to another on the left: it was the road by which the Cape of Good Hope was to be doubled. There was no finger-board or other visible sign to guide the wayfarer, but, nevertheless, all turned off at the same place. None missed it.

XXI. This outward road to India and the gold fields of Australia was, as it passed through the South Atlantic, a crooked one, but the road home from the Cape was straight, for the winds along it were fresh and fair.

XXII. But the outward-bound route through the North Atlantic, from the United States especially, was most curious and crooked. It seemed, on the chart, to be as well beaten, and almost as well defined, as any Indian trail through the wilderness. First it struck across the Atlantic until it reached the Cape de Verd Islands on the other side; then it took a turn, and came back on this side again, reaching the coast of Brazil in the vicinity of Cape St. Roque. Here there was another turn, and another recrossing of the broad ocean, striking this time for the Cape of Good Hope, but bending far away to the right before that turning point was reached.

XXIII. Thus the great highway from the United States to the Cape of Good Hope nearly crossed the Atlantic, it was discovered, three times. The other parts of the ocean by the wayside were blank, untraveled spaces. All the vessels that sailed went by one road and returned by the other. Now and then there was a sort of a country cross-road, that was frequented by robbers and bad men as they passed on their voyage from *Africa* to the *West Indies* and back. But all the rest of the ocean on the wayside, and to the distance of hundreds of miles on either hand, was blank, and seemed as untraveled and as much out of the way of the haunts of civilized man as are the solitudes of the wilderness that lie broad off from the emigrants' trail to Oregon. Such was the old route.

XXIV. Who were the engineers that laid out these highways upon the sea, and why did traders never try short cuts across the blank spaces? There was neither rock, nor shoal, nor hidden danger of any sort to prevent; why did not traders, therefore, seek to cut off these elbows in the great thoroughfares, and, instead of crossing the Atlantic three times on their way to the Cape of Good Hope (§ XXII.), cross it only once, as they did coming home?

Who, it was repeated, were the hydrographic engineers concerned in the establishing of this zigzag route?

XXV. Inquiry was instituted, and, after diligent research, it was traced, by *tradition*, to the early navigators and the chance that directed them. When they set sail from Europe, seeking a passage to the East *via* the Cape of Good Hope, they passed along down by the Cape de Verd Islands, and then, as they approached the equator, the winds forced them over toward the coast of Brazil. Thus a track was made, and the route to the East laid out.

XXVI. As one traveler in the wilderness follows in the trail of another, so, it was discovered, did the trader on the high seas follow in the wake of those who had led the way.

The pioneer goes and returns: "Which way did you go? How lies the route? Give us your sailing directions," say his followers.

XXVII. He that is questioned can speak only of the route by which *he* went and came. He knows of no others; and this, therefore, he commends to his followers, and they to those who come after them; and thus, in many cases, the route from place to place across the sea was, it was ascertained, handed down from sailor to sailor by tradition, or as legend, and very much in the same way that the overland route of the first emigrants to California continued to be followed season after season.

XXVIII. Among other things, these legends told of the most sweeping currents to the north of St. Roque, along the coast of Brazil. The vessel, said they, that should fall so far to leeward of that cape and coast as to come within the influence of these currents, was almost sure to be beset, and her crew to be cast upon an iron-bound coast amid the horrors of shipwreck.

XXIX. Now these investigations have proved that there is no current there worth the name, and no danger to be apprehended when it is encountered, and so mariners now allude to these currents as the "bugbear" of St. Roque.

XXX. Nevertheless, impressed with these legends and traditions, the early navigators of this country, when they first commenced to double the Cape of Good Hope on trading voyages, thought it most prudent to make the best of their way to the route from Europe, which had been often tried and was well known. They aimed to fall in with this route about the Cape de Verd Islands. The winds there threw them back on this side of the Atlantic, upon the coast of Brazil, and so they had to cross the ocean again to reach the Cape of Good Hope. But every body said that was the way, and it was so written down in the books. Hence the zigzag route (§ XXII.), and the supposed necessity, on the outward voyage to India, of crossing the Atlantic Ocean three times instead of once.

XXXI. The results of the first chart, however (§ XIII.), though meagre and unsatisfactory, were brought to the notice of navigators; their attention was called to the blank spaces, and the importance of more and better observations than the old sea-chests generally contained was urged upon them.

XXXII. They were told that if each one would agree to co-operate in a general plan of observations at sea, and would send regularly, at the end of every cruise, an abstract log of their voyage to the National Observatory at Washington, he should, for so doing, be furnished, free of cost, with a copy of the charts and sailing directions that might be founded upon those observations.

XXXIII. The quick, practical mind of the American ship-master took hold of the proposition at once. To him the field was inviting, for he saw in it the promise of a rich harvest and of many useful results.

XXXIV. So, in a little while, there were more than a thousand navigators engaged day and night, and in all parts of the ocean, in making and recording observations according to a uniform plan, and in furthering this attempt to increase our knowledge as to the winds and currents of the sea, and other phenomena that relate to its safe navigation and physical geography.

XXXV. To enlist the service of such a large corps of observers, and to have the attention of so many clever and observant men directed to the same subject, was a great point gained: it was a giant stride in the advancement of knowledge, and a great step toward its spread upon the waters.

XXXVI. Important results soon followed, and great discoveries were made. These attracted the attention of the commercial world, and did not escape the notice of philosophers every where.

XXXVII. The field was immense, the harvest was plenteous, and there was both need and room for more laborers. Whatever the reapers should gather, or the merest gleaner collect, was to inure to the benefit of commerce and navigation—the increase of knowledge—the good of all.

XXXVIII. Therefore, all who use the sea were equally interested in the undertaking. The government of the United States, so considering the matter, proposed a uniform system of observations at sea, and invited all the maritime states of Christendom to a conference upon the subject.

XXXIX. This conference, consisting of representatives from France, England and Russia, from Sweden and Norway, Holland, Denmark, Belgium, Portugal, and the United States, met in Brussels, August 23, 1853, and recommended a plan of observations which should be followed on board the vessels of all friendly nations, and especially of those there present in the persons of their representatives.

XL. Prussia, Spain, the free city of Hamburg, the republics of Bremen and Chili, and the empires of Austria and Brazil, have since offered their co-operation also in the same plan.

XLI. Thus the sea has been brought regularly within the domains of philosophical research, and crowded with observers.

XLII. In peace and in war these observations are to be carried on; and, in case any of the vessels on board of which they are conducted may be captured, the abstract log—as the journal which contains these observations is called—is to be held sacred.

XLIII. Baron Humboldt is of opinion that the results already obtained from this system of research are sufficient to give rise to a new department of science, which he has called the Physical Geography of the Sea. If so much have already been accomplished by one nation, what may we not expect in the course of a few years from the joint co-operation of so many?

XLIV. Rarely before has there been such a sublime spectacle presented to the scientific world: all nations agreeing to unite and co-operate in carrying out one system of philosophical research with regard to the sea. Though they may be enemies in all else, here they are to be friends. Every ship that navigates the high seas with these charts and blank abstract logs on board may henceforth be regarded as a floating observatory, a temple of science. The instruments used by every co-operating vessel are to be compared with standards that are common to all; so that an observation that is made any where and in any ship, may be referred to and compared with all similar observations by all other ships in all other parts of the world.

But these meteorological observations which this extensive and admirable system includes will relate only to the sea. It is a pity. The plan should include the land also, and be universal. It is now proposed to have another and general meteorological congress; and the initiatory steps, by way of counsel, for calling it together, have been taken, both in England and on the Continent. It is to be hoped that this country will not fail to co-operate in such a humane, wise, and noble undertaking as is this. It involves a study of the laws which regulate the atmosphere, and a careful investigation of all its phenomena.

XLV. Another beautiful feature in this system is, that it costs nothing additional. The instruments that these observations call for are such as are already in use on board of every well-conditioned ship, and the observations that are required are precisely those which are necessary for her safe and proper navigation.

XLVI. As great as is the value attached to what has been accomplished by these researches in the way of shortening passages and lessening the dangers of the sea, a good of higher value is, in the opinion of many seamen, yet to come out of the moral, the educational, influence which they are calculated to exert upon the seafaring community of the world. A very clever English shipmaster, speaking recently of the advantages of educational influences among those who intend to follow the sea, remarks:

"To the cultivated lad there is a new world spread out when he enters on his first voyage. As his education has fitted, so will he perceive, year by year, that his profession makes him acquainted with things new and instructive. His intelligence will enable him to appreciate the contrasts of each country in its general aspect, manners, and productions, and in modes of navigation, adapted to the character of coast, climate, and rivers. He will dwell with interest on the phases of the ocean, the storm, the calm, and the breeze, and will look for traces of the laws which regulate them. All this will induce a serious earnestness in his work, and teach him to view lightly those irksome and often offensive duties incident to the beginner."* Sentiments which can not fail to meet with a hearty response from all good men, whether ashore or afloat.

XLVII. Never before has such a corps of observers been enlisted in the cause of any department of physical science as is that which is now about to be engaged in advancing our knowledge of the physical geography of the sea, and never before have men felt such an interest with regard to this knowledge.

* "The Log of a Merchant Officer; viewed with reference to the Education of young Officers and the Youth of the Merchant Service. By Robert Methren, commander in the Peninsular and Oriental Company, and author of the 'Narrative of the Blenheim Hurricane of 1851.'" London: John Weale, 59 High Holborn; Smith, Elder & Co., Cornhill; Ackerman & Co., Strand. 1854.

Under this term will be included a philosophical account of the winds and currents of the sea; of the circulation of the atmosphere and ocean; of the temperature and depth of the sea; of the wonders that are hidden in its depths; and of the phenomena that display themselves at its surface. In short, I shall treat of the economy of the sea and its adaptations—of its salts, its waters, its climates, and its inhabitants, and of whatever there may be of general interest in its commercial uses or industrial pursuits, for all such things pertain to its PHYSICAL GEOGRAPHY.

XLVIII. The object of this little book, moreover, is to show the present state, and, from time to time, the progress of this new and beautiful system of research, as well as of this interesting department of science; and the aim of the author is to present the gleanings from this new field in a manner that may be interesting and instructive to all, whether old or young, ashore or afloat, who desire a closer look into "the wonders of the great deep," or a better knowledge as to its winds, its adaptations, or its Physical Geography.*

* There is an old and very rare book which treats upon some of the subjects to which this little work relates. It is by Count L. F. MARSIGLI, a Frenchman, and is called NATURAL DESCRIPTION OF THE SEAS. The copy to which I refer was translated into Dutch by Boerhaave in 1786.

The French count made his observations along the coast of Provence and Languedoc. The description only relates to that part of the Mediterranean. The book is divided into four chapters: the first, on the bottom and shape of the sea; the second, of sea water; the third, on the movements of sea water; and the fourth, of sea plants.

He divides sea water into surface and deep-sea water; because, when he makes salt from surface water (not more than half a foot below the upper strata), this salt will give a red color to blue paper; whereas the salt from deep-sea water will not alter the colors at all. The blue paper can only change its color by the action of an acid. The reason why this acid (iodine?) is found in surface and not in deep-sea water is: it is derived from the air; but he supposes that the saltpetre that is found in sea water, by the action of the sun's rays and the motion of the waves, is deprived of its coarse parts, and, by evaporation, embodied in the air, to be conveyed to beasts or plants for their existence, or deposed upon the earth's crust, as it occurs on the plains of Hungary, where the earth absorbs so much of this saltpetre vapor.

Donati, also, was a valuable laborer in this field. His inquiries enabled Mr. Trembley[a] to conclude that there are, "at the bottom of the water, mountains, plains, valleys, and caverns, just as upon the land."

But by far the most interesting and valuable book touching the physical geography of the Mediterranean is Admiral Smyth's last work, entitled "THE MEDITERRANEAN; A MEMOIR, PHYSICAL, HISTORICAL, AND NAUTICAL. By Rear-admiral WILLIAM HENRY SMYTH, K.S.F., D.C.L.," &c. London: John W. Parker and Son. 1854.

[a] Philosophical Transactions.

CONTENTS.

CHAPTER I.

THE GULF STREAM.

CHAPTER II.

INFLUENCE OF THE GULF STREAM UPON CLIMATES.

CHAPTER III.

THE ATMOSPHERE.

CHAPTER IV.

RED FOGS AND SEA DUST.

CHAPTER V.

ON THE PROBABLE RELATION BETWEEN MAGNETISM AND THE CIRCULATION OF THE ATMOSPHERE.

CHAPTER VI.

CURRENTS OF THE SEA.

CHAPTER VII.

THE OPEN SEA IN THE ARCTIC OCEAN.

CHAPTER VIII.

THE SALTS OF THE SEA.

CHAPTER IX.

THE EQUATORIAL CLOUD-RING.

CHAPTER X.

ON THE GEOLOGICAL AGENCY OF THE WINDS.

CHAPTER XI.

THE DEPTHS OF THE OCEAN.

CHAPTER XII.

THE BASIN OF THE ATLANTIC.

CHAPTER XIII.

THE WINDS.

CHAPTER XIV.

THE CLIMATES OF THE OCEAN.

CHAPTER XV.

THE DRIFT OF THE SEA.

CHAPTER XVI.

STORMS.

CHAPTER XVII.

ROUTES.

CHAPTER XVIII.

A LAST WORD.

APPENDIX.

EXPLANATION OF THE PLATES.

PLATE I. (p. 70) is a diagram to illustrate the circulation of the atmosphere (Chap. III.). The arrows and bands within the circumference of the circle are intended to show the calm belts, and prevailing direction of the wind on each section of those belts. The arrows exterior to the periphery of the circle—which is a section of the earth supposed to be made in the plane of the meridian—are intended to show the direction of the upper and lower strata of winds in the general system of atmospherical circulation; and also to illustrate how the air brought by each stratum to the calm belts there ascends or descends, as the case may be; and then, continuing to flow on, how it crosses over in the direction in which it was traveling when it arrived at the calm zone.

PLATES II. and III. (p. 207) are drawings of Brooke's Deep-sea Sounding Apparatus, for bringing up specimens of the bottom (§ 438).

PLATE IV. (p. 230) is intended to illustrate the extreme movements of the isotherms 50°, 60°, 70°, &c., in the Atlantic Ocean during the year. The connection between the law of this motion and the climates of the sea is exceedingly interesting.

PLATE V. is a section taken from one of the manuscript charts at the Observatory. It illustrates the method adopted there for co-ordinating for the Pilot Charts the winds as reported in the abstract logs. For this purpose the ocean is divided into convenient sections, usually five degrees of latitude by five degrees of longitude. These parallelograms are then subdivided into a system of engraved squares, the months of the year being the ordinates, and the points of the compass being the abscissæ. As the wind is reported by a vessel that passes through any part of the parallelogram, so it is assumed to have been at that time all over the parallelogram. From such investigations as this the Pilot Charts (§ 558) are constructed.

PLATE VI. illustrates the position of the channel of the Gulf Stream (Chap. I.) for summer and winter. The diagram A shows a thermometrical profile presented by cross-sections of the Gulf Stream, according to observations made by the hydrographical parties of the United States Coast Survey. The elements for this diagram were kindly furnished me by the superintendent of that work. They are from a paper on the Gulf Stream, read by him before the American Association for the Advancement of Science at its meeting in Washington, 1854. Imagine a vessel to sail from the Capes of Virginia straight out to sea, crossing the Gulf Stream at right angles, and taking the temperature of its waters at the surface and at various depths. This diagram shows the elevation and depression of the thermometer across this section as they were actually observed by such a vessel.

The black lines *x*, *y*, *z*, in the Gulf Stream, show the course which those threads of warm waters take (§ 55). The lines *a*, *b* show the computed drift route that the unfortunate steamer San Francisco would take after her terrible disaster in December, 1853.

Plate VII. is intended to show how the winds may become geological agents. It shows where the winds that, in the general system of atmospherical circulation, blow over the deserts and thirsty lands in Asia and Africa (where the annual amount of precipitation is small), are supposed to get their vapors from; where, as surface winds, they are supposed to condense portions of it; and whither they are supposed to transport the residue thereof through the upper regions, retaining it until they again become surface winds.

Plate VIII. shows the prevailing direction of the wind during the year in all parts of the ocean, as derived from the series of investigations illustrated on Plate VII. It also shows the principal routes across the seas to various places. Where the cross-lines representing the yards are oblique to the keel of the vessel, they indicate that the winds are, for the most part, ahead; when perpendicular or square, that the winds are, for the most part, fair. The figures on or near the diagrams representing the vessels show the average length of the passage in days.

The arrows denote the prevailing direction of the wind; they are supposed to fly *with* it; so that the wind is going as the arrows point. The half-bearded and half-feathered arrows represent monsoons (§ 462), and the stippled or shaded belts the calm zones.

In the regions on the polar side of the calms of Capricorn and of Cancer, where the arrows are flying both from the northwest and the southwest, the idea intended to be conveyed is, that the prevailing direction of the wind is between the northwest and the southwest, and that their frequency is from these two quarters in proportion to the number of arrows.

Plate IX. is intended to show the present state of our knowledge with regard to the drift of the ocean, or, more properly, with regard to the great flow of polar and equatorial waters, and their channels of circulation as indicated by the thermometer (§ 528). Further researches will enable us to improve this chart. The most favorite places of resort for the whale—*right* in cold, and *sperm* in warm water—are also exhibited on this chart.

Plate X. exhibits the actual path of a storm, which is a type (§ 72) of the West India hurricanes. Mr. Redfield, Colonel Reid, and others, have traced out the paths of a number of such storms. All of this class appear to make for the Gulf Stream; after reaching it, they turn about and follow it in their course (§ 75).

Mr. Piddington, of Calcutta, has made the East India hurricanes, which are similar to these, the object of special, patient, and laborious investigation. He calls them *cycloins*, and has elicited much valuable information concerning them, which may be found embraced in his "Sailor's Horn-book," "Conversations about Hurricanes," and numerous papers published from time to time in the Journal of the Asiatic Society.

Plates XI. and XII. speak for themselves. They are orographic for the North Atlantic Ocean, and exhibit completely the present state of our knowledge with regard to the elevations and depressions in the bed of the sea; Plate XII. exhibiting a vertical section of the Atlantic, and showing the contrasts of its bottom with the sea-level in a line from Mexico across Yucatan, Cuba, San Domingo, and the Cape de Verds, to the coast of Africa, marked A on Plate XI.

PHYSICAL GEOGRAPHY OF THE SEA.

CHAPTER I.

THE GULF STREAM.

The Gulf Stream, § 1.—Its Color, 2.—Its Cause, 3–7.—Dr. Franklin's Theory, 8.—The Sargasso Sea, 13.—The Trade-wind Agency refuted, 14.—Galvanic Properties of Gulf Stream Waters, 26.—Initial Velocity, 30.—Agents that make Water in one part of the Sea heavier than in another, 31.—Temperature of the Gulf Stream, 37.—It is Roof-shaped, 39.—Why the Drift Matter of the Gulf Stream is sloughed off to the right of its Course, 42.—Course of the Gulf Stream, 47.—Currents run along arcs of Great Circles, 49.—The Course of Currents counter to the Gulf Stream, 52.—The Force derived from Changes of Temperature, 53.—Limits of the Gulf Stream for March and September, 54.—Streaks of Warm and Cool Water in it, 55.—A Cushion of Cold Water between the Bottom of the Sea and the Waters of the Gulf Stream, 56.—It runs up hill, 57.

1. THERE is a river in the ocean. In the severest droughts it never fails, and in the mightiest floods it never overflows. Its banks and its bottom are of cold water, while its current is of warm. The Gulf of Mexico is its fountain, and its mouth is in the Arctic Seas. It is the Gulf Stream. There is in the world no other such majestic flow of waters. Its current is more rapid than the Mississippi or the Amazon.

2. Its waters, as far out from the Gulf as the Carolina coasts, are of an indigo blue. They are so distinctly marked, that their line of junction with the common sea-water may be traced by the eye. Often one half of the vessel may be perceived floating in Gulf Stream water, while the other half is in common water of the sea; so sharp is the line, and such the want of affinity between those waters, and the reluctance, on the part of those of the Gulf Stream to mingle with the common water of the sea.

3. What is the cause of the Gulf Stream has always puzzled

philosophers. Modern investigations and examinations are beginning to throw some light upon the subject, though all is not yet clear.

4. Early writers maintained that the Mississippi River was the father of the Gulf Stream. Its floods, they said, produce it; for its velocity, it was held, could be computed by the rate of the current of the river.

5. Captain Livingston overturned this hypothesis by showing that the volume of water which the Mississippi River empties into the Gulf of Mexico is not equal to the one thousandth part of that which escapes from it through the Gulf Stream.

6. Moreover, the water of the Gulf Stream is salt—of the Mississippi, fresh; and those philosophers (§ 4) forgot that just as much salt as escapes from the Gulf of Mexico through this stream, must enter the Gulf through some other channel from the main ocean; for, if it did not, the Gulf of Mexico, in process of time, unless it had a salt bed at the bottom, or was fed with salt springs below—neither of which is probable—would become a fresh-water basin.

7. The above quoted argument of Captain Livingston, however, was held to be conclusive; and upon the remains of the hypothesis which he had so completely overturned, he set up another, which, in turn, has been upset. In it he ascribed the velocity of the Gulf Stream as depending "on the motion of the sun in the ecliptic, and the influence he has on the waters of the Atlantic."

8. But the opinion that came to be the most generally received and deep-rooted in the mind of seafaring people was the one repeated by Dr. Franklin, and which held that the Gulf Stream is the escaping of the waters that have been *forced* into the Caribbean Sea by the trade-winds, and that it is the pressure of those winds upon the water which forces up into that sea a head, as it were, for this stream.

9. We know of instances in which waters have been accumulated on one side of a lake, or in one end of a canal, at the expense of the other. But they are rare, sudden, and partial, and for the most part confined to sheets of shoal water where the ripples are proportionably great. As far as they go, the pressure of the trade-winds may *assist* to give the Gulf Stream its initial velocity, but is it of itself adequate to such an effect? To my mind,

the laws of Hydrostatics, as at present expounded, appear by no means to warrant the conclusion that it is, unless the aid of other agents also be brought to bear.

Admiral Smyth, in his valuable memoir on the Mediterranean (p. 162), mentions, that a continuance in the Sea of Tuscany of "*gusty gales*" from the southwest has been known to raise its surface no less than twelve feet above its ordinary level. This, he says, occasions a strong surface drift through the Strait of Bonifaccio. But in this we have nothing like the Gulf Stream; no deep and narrow channel-way to conduct these waters off like a miniature river even in the sea, but a mere surface flow, such as usually follows the piling up of water in any pond or gulf above the ordinary level. The Bonifaccio current does not flow like a river in the sea across the Mediterranean, but it spreads itself out as soon as it passes the Straits, and, like a circle on the water, loses itself by broad spreading as soon as it gets to sea.

10. Supposing the pressure of the waters that are *forced* into the Caribbean Sea by the trade-winds to be the *sole* cause of the Gulf Stream, that sea and the Mexican Gulf should have a much higher level than the Atlantic. Accordingly, the advocates of this theory require for its support "a great degree of elevation." Major Rennell likens the stream to "an immense river descending from a higher level into a plain." Now we know very nearly the average breadth and velocity of the Gulf Stream in the Florida Pass. We also know, with a like degree of approximation, the velocity and breadth of the same waters off Cape Hatteras. Their breadth here is about seventy-five miles against thirty-two in the "Narrows" of the Straits, and their mean velocity is three knots off Hatteras against four in the "Narrows." This being the case, it is easy to show that the depth of the Gulf Stream off Hatteras is not so great as it is in the "Narrows" of Bemini by nearly 50 per cent., and that, consequently, instead of *descending*, its bed represents the surface of an inclined plane from the north, *up* which the lower depths of the stream *must* ascend. If we assume its depth off Bemini to be two hundred fathoms, which are thought to be within limits, the above rates of breadth and velocity will give one hundred and fourteen fathoms for its depth off Hatteras. The waters, therefore, which in the Straits are below the level of the Hatteras depth, so far from descending, are actually forced up

an inclined plane, whose submarine ascent is not less than ten inches to the mile.

The Niagara is an "immense river descending into a plain." But instead of preserving its character in Lake Ontario as a distinct and well-defined stream for several hundred miles, it spreads itself out, and its waters are immediately lost in those of the lake. Why should not the Gulf Stream do the same? It gradually enlarges itself, it is true; but, instead of mingling with the ocean by broad spreading, as the "immense rivers" descending into the northern lakes do, its waters, like a stream of oil in the ocean, preserve a distinctive character for more than three thousand miles.

11. Moreover, while the Gulf Stream is running to the north from its supposed elevated level at the south, there is a cold current coming down from the north; meeting the warm waters of the Gulf midway the ocean, it divides itself, and runs by the side of them right back into those very reservoirs at the south, to which theory gives an elevation sufficient to send out entirely across the Atlantic a jet of warm water said to be more than three thousand times greater in volume than the Mississippi River. This current from Baffin's Bay has not only no trade-winds to give it a head, but the prevailing winds are unfavorable to it, and for a great part of the way it is below the surface, and far beyond the propelling reach of any wind. And there is every reason to believe that this polar current is quite equal in volume to the Gulf Stream. Are they not the effects of like causes? If so, what have the trade-winds to do with the one more than the other?

12. It is a custom often practiced by seafaring people to throw a bottle overboard, with a paper, stating the time and place at which it is done. In the absence of other information as to currents, that afforded by these mute little navigators is of great value. They leave no tracks behind them, it is true, and their routes can not be ascertained. But knowing where they were cast, and seeing where they are found, some idea may be formed as to their course. Straight lines may at least be drawn, showing the shortest distance from the beginning to the end of their voyage, with the time elapsed. Captain Beechey, R. N., has prepared a chart, representing, in this way, the tracks of more than one hundred bottles. From it, it appears that the waters from every quarter of the Atlantic tend toward the Gulf of Mexico and

its stream. Bottles cast into the sea midway between the Old and the New Worlds, near the coasts of Europe, Africa, and America, at the extreme north or farthest south, have been found either in the West Indies, or within the well-known range of Gulf Stream waters.

Of two cast out together in south latitude on the coast of Africa, one was found on the island of Trinidad; the other on Guernsey, in the English Channel.

In the absence of positive information on the subject, the circumstantial evidence that the latter performed the tour of the Gulf is all but conclusive.

Another bottle, thrown over off Cape Horn by an American master in 1837, has been recently picked up on the coast of Ireland. An inspection of the chart, and of the drift of the other bottles, seems to *force* the conclusion that this bottle too went even from that remote region to the so-called *higher* level of the Gulf Stream reservoir.

13. Midway the Atlantic, in the triangular space between the Azores, Canaries, and the Cape de Verd Islands, is the Sargasso Sea. (Plate VI.) Covering an area equal in extent to the Mississippi Valley, it is so thickly matted over with Gulf weed (fucus natans), that the speed of vessels passing through it is often much retarded. When the companions of Columbus saw it, they thought it marked the limits of navigation, and became alarmed. To the eye, at a little distance, it seems substantial enough to walk upon. Patches of the weed are always to be seen floating along the Gulf Stream. Now, if bits of cork or chaff, or any floating substance, be put into a basin, and a circular motion be given to the water, all the light substances will be found crowding together near the centre of the pool, where there is the least motion. Just such a basin is the Atlantic Ocean to the Gulf Stream, and the Sargasso Sea is the centre of the whirl. Columbus first found this weedy sea in his voyage of discovery; there it has remained to this day; and certain observations as to its limits, extending back for fifty years, assure us that its position has not been altered since that time. This indication of a circular motion by the Gulf Stream is corroborated by the bottle chart and other sources of information. If, therefore, this be so, why give the endless current a higher level in one part of its course than another?

14. Nay, more; at the very season of the year when the Gulf Stream is rushing in greatest volume through the Straits of Florida, and hastening to the north with the greatest rapidity, there is a cold stream from Baffin's Bay, Labrador, and the coasts of the north, running to the south with equal velocity. Where is the trade-wind that gives the high level to Baffin's Bay, or that even presses upon, or assists to put this current in motion? The agency of winds in producing currents in the deep sea must be very partial. These two currents meet off the Grand Banks, where the latter is divided. One part of it underruns the Gulf Stream, as is shown by the icebergs which are carried in a direction tending across its course. The probability is, that this "fork" continues on toward the south, and runs into the Caribbean Sea, for the temperature of the water at a little depth there has been found far below the mean temperature of the earth, and quite as cold as at a corresponding depth off the Arctic shores of Spitzbergen.

15. More water can not run from the equator or the pole than to it. If we make the trade-winds cause the former, some other wind must produce the latter; but these, for the most part, and for great distances, are *submarine*, and therefore beyond the influence of winds. Hence it should appear that *winds* have little to do with the general system of aqueous circulation in the ocean.

The other "fork" runs between us and the Gulf Stream to the south, as already described. As far as it has been traced, it warrants the belief that it, too, runs *up* to seek the so-called *higher* level of the Mexican Gulf.

16. The power necessary to overcome the resistance opposed to such a body of water as that of the Gulf Stream, running several thousand miles without any renewal of impulse from the forces of gravitation or any other known cause, is truly surprising. It so happens that we have an argument for determining, with considerable accuracy, the resistance which the waters of this stream meet with in their motion toward the east. Owing to the diurnal rotation, they are carried around with the earth on its axis *toward the east* with an hourly velocity of one hundred and fifty-seven* miles greater when they enter the Atlantic than when they arrive off the Banks of Newfoundland. In consequence of the difference

* In this calculation the earth is treated as a perfect sphere, with a diameter of 7925·56 miles.

of latitude between the parallels of these two places, their rate of motion around the axis of the earth is reduced from nine hundred and fifteen* to seven hundred and fifty-eight miles the hour.

17. Therefore this immense volume of water, in passing from the Bahamas to the Grand Banks, meets with an opposing force in the shape of resistance, sufficient, in the aggregate, to retard it two miles and a half the minute, and this only in its eastwardly rate. If this resistance be calculated according to received laws, it will be found equal to several atmospheres. And by analogy, how inadequate must the pressure of the gentle trade-winds be to such resistance, and to the effect assigned them? If, therefore, in the proposed inquiry, we search for a propelling power nowhere but in the higher level of the Gulf, we must admit, in the head of water there, the existence of a force capable of putting in motion, and of driving over a plain at the rate of four miles the hour, all the waters, as fast as they can be brought down by three thousand such streams as the Mississippi River—a power, at least, sufficient to overcome the resistance required to reduce from two miles and a half to a few feet per minute the velocity of a stream that keeps in perpetual motion one fourth of all the waters in the Atlantic Ocean.

18. The facts, from observation on this interesting subject, afford us at best but a mere glimmer of light, by no means sufficient to make any mind clear as to a *higher level* of the Gulf, or as to the sufficiency of any other of the causes assigned for this wonderful stream. If it be necessary to resort to a higher level in the Gulf to account for the velocity off Hatteras, I can not perceive why we should not, with like reasoning, resort to a higher level off Hatteras also to account for the velocity off the Grand Banks, and thus make the Gulf Stream, throughout its circuit, a *descending* current, and, by the *reductio ad absurdum,* show that the trade-winds are not adequate to the effect ascribed.

19. When facts are wanting, it often happens that hypothesis will serve, in their stead, all the purposes of illustration. Let us, therefore, suppose a globe of the earth's size, having a solid nucleus, and covered all over with water two hundred fathoms deep;

* Or, 915·26 to 758·60. On the latter parallel the current has an east set of about one and a half miles the hour, making the true velocity to the east, and on the axis of the earth, about seven hundred and sixty miles the hour at the Grand Banks.

and that every source of heat and cause of radiation be removed, so that its fluid temperature becomes constant and uniform throughout. On such a globe, the equilibrium remaining undisturbed, there would be neither wind nor current.

20. Let us now suppose that all the water within the tropics, to the depth of one hundred fathoms, suddenly becomes oil. The aqueous equilibrium of the planet is thereby disturbed, and a general system of currents and counter currents is immediately commenced—the oil, in an unbroken sheet on the surface, running toward the poles, and the water, in an under current, toward the equator. The oil is supposed, as it reaches the polar basin, to be reconverted into water, and the water to become oil as it crosses Cancer and Capricorn, rising to the surface and returning as before.

21. Thus, *without wind*, we should have a perpetual and uniform system of tropical and polar currents. In consequence of diurnal rotation of the planet on its axis, each particle of oil, were resistance small, would approach the poles on a spiral turning to the east, with a relative velocity greater and greater, until, finally, it would reach the pole and whirl about it at the rate of nearly a thousand miles the hour. Becoming water and losing its velocity, it would approach the tropics by a similar, but inverted spiral, turning toward the west. Owing to the principle here alluded to, all currents from the equator to the poles should have an eastward tendency, and all from the poles toward the equator a westward.

22. Let us now suppose the solid nucleus of this hypothetical globe to assume the exact form and shape of the bottom of our seas, and in all respects, as to figure and size, to represent the shoals and islands of the sea, as well as the coast lines and continents of the earth. The uniform system of currents just described would now be interrupted by obstructions and local causes of various kinds, such as unequal depth of water, contour of shore-lines, &c.; and we should have at certain places currents greater in volume and velocity than at others. But still there would be a system of currents and counter currents to and from either pole and the equator. Now do not the cold waters of the north, and the warm waters of the Gulf, made specifically lighter by tropical heat, which we see actually preserving such a system of counter currents, hold, at least in some degree, the relation of the supposed water and oil?

23. In obedience to the laws here hinted at, there is a constant tendency of polar waters toward the tropics and of tropical waters toward the poles. Captain Wilkes, of the United States Exploring Expedition, crossed one of these hyperborean under-currents two hundred miles in breadth at the equator.

24. Assuming the maximum velocity of the Gulf Stream at five knots, and its depth and breadth in the Narrows of Bemini as before (§ 10), the vertical section across would present an area of two hundred millions of square feet moving at the rate of seven feet three inches per second. The difference of specific gravity between the volume of Gulf water that crosses this sectional line in one second, and an equal volume of water at the ocean temperature of the latitude, is fifteen millions of pounds. If these estimated dimensions (assumed merely for the purposes of illustration) be within limits, then the force per second operating here to propel the waters of the Gulf toward the pole is the equilibrating tendency due to fifteen millions of pounds of water in the latitude of Bemini.

25. In investigating the currents of the seas, such agencies should be taken into account. As a cause, I doubt whether this one is sufficient of itself to produce a stream of such great velocity as that of the Gulf; for, assuming its estimated discharge to be correct, the proposition is almost susceptible of mathematical demonstration, that to overcome the resistance opposed in consequence of its velocity would require a force at least sufficient to drive, at the rate of three miles the hour, ninety thousand millions of tons up an inclined plane having an ascent of three inches to the mile.* Yet the very principle from which this agent is derived is admitted to be one of the chief causes of those winds which are said to be the sole cause of this current.

26. The chemical properties, or, if the expression be admissible, the *galvanic* properties of the Gulf Stream waters, as they come from their fountains, are different, or, rather, more intense than they are in sea water generally.

In 1843 the Secretary of the Navy took measures for procuring a series of observations and experiments with regard to the corrosive effects of sea water upon the copper sheathing of ships. With patience, care, and labor, these researches were carried on

* Supposing there be no resistance from friction.

for a period of ten years; and it is said the fact has been established, that the copper on the bottom of ships cruising in the Caribbean Sea and Gulf of Mexico suffers more from the action of sea water upon it than does the copper of ships cruising in any other part of the ocean. In other words, the salts of these waters create the most powerful galvanic battery that is found in the ocean.

27. Now it may be supposed—other things being equal—that the strength of this galvanic battery in the sea depends in some measure upon the proportion of salts that the sea waters hold in solution.

If, therefore, in the absence of better information, this suggestion be taken as a probability, we may go a step farther, and draw the inference that the waters of the Gulf Stream, as they rush out in such volume and with such velocity into the Atlantic, have not only chemical affinities peculiar to themselves, but, having more salts, they are therefore specifically heavier than the sea water through which they flow in such a clear and well-defined channel.

28. The affinities of which I speak, and which are manifested in the reluctance of the Gulf Stream to mingle its waters with those of the ocean (§ 2), may be the resultant of their galvanic properties, higher temperature, and greater degree of saltness, all combined.

29. If the story told by the copper (§ 26) be taken to mean a higher point of saturation with salts, and, consequently, a greater specific gravity for the waters of the Gulf and Caribbean Sea than for the waters of the broad ocean at the same temperature, then we should have as a source for the initial velocity of the Gulf Stream, not, indeed, a higher level of the waters in the Gulf, but a greater density.

30. Now a greater density, implying, of course, a greater specific gravity, would serve, as well as a higher level, to impart an initial velocity, but with this difference: the heavier waters would, by reason of their greater pressure, be ejected through the most convenient aperture out into the ocean of lighter waters by a sort of *squirting* force. But what, it may be asked, should make the waters of the Mexican Gulf and Caribbean Sea salter than the waters of like temperature in those parts of the ocean through which the Gulf Stream flows?

31. There are physical agents that are known to be at work in different parts of the ocean, the tendency of which is to make the waters in one part of the ocean salter and heavier, and in another part lighter and less salt than the average of sea water. These agents are those employed by sea-shells in secreting solid matter for their structures, also of heat* and radiation, evaporation and precipitation.

32. In the trade-wind regions at sea (Plate VIII.), evaporation is generally in excess of precipitation, while in the extra-tropical regions the reverse is the case; that is, the clouds let down more water than the winds take up again; and these are the regions in which the Gulf Stream enters the Atlantic.

33. Along the shores of India, where experiments have been carefully made, the evaporation amounts to three fourths of an inch daily. Suppose it in the trade-wind region of the Atlantic to amount to only half an inch, that would give an annual evaporation of say fifteen feet. In the process of evaporation from the sea, fresh water only is taken up, the salts are left behind.

Now a layer of sea water fifteen feet deep, and as broad as the trade-wind belts of the Atlantic, and reaching across the ocean, contains an immense amount of salts.

34. The great equatorial current (Plate VI.) which sweeps from the shores of Africa across the Atlantic into the Caribbean Sea is a surface current; and may it not bear into that sea a large portion of those waters that have satisfied the thirsty trade-winds with saltless vapor? If so—and it probably does—have we not detected here the foot-prints of an agent that does tend to make the waters of the Caribbean Sea salter, and therefore heavier than the average of sea water?

It is immaterial, so far as the correctness of the principle upon which this reasoning depends is concerned, whether the annual evaporation from the trade-wind regions of the Atlantic be fifteen, ten, or five feet. The layer of water, whatever be its thickness, that is evaporated from this part of the ocean, is not all poured back by the clouds in the same place whence it came. But they take it and pour it down in showers upon the extra-tropical regions of the earth—on the land as well as in the sea—where, as a rule, more water is let down than is taken up into the clouds again.

* According to Doctor Marcet, sea water contracts down to 28°.

Suppose the excess of precipitation in these extra-tropical regions of the sea amounts to but twelve inches, or even to but two, it is twelve inches or two inches, as the case may be, of fresh water added to the sea in those parts, and which, therefore, tends to lessen the specific gravity of sea water there to that extent; and for the simple reason, that what is taken from one scale, by being put into the other, reduplicates the difference.

35. Now, that we may form some idea as to the influence which the salts left by the vapor that the trade-winds, northeast and southeast, take up from sea water, is calculated to exert in creating currents, let us make a partial calculation to show how much salt this vapor held in solution before it was taken up, and, of course, while yet in the state of sea water. The northeast trade-wind regions of the Atlantic embrace an area of at least three million square miles; and the yearly evaporation from it is (§ 33), we will suppose, fifteen feet. The salt that is contained in a mass of sea water covering to the depth of fifteen feet an area of three million square miles in superficial extent, would be sufficient to cover the British islands to the depth of fourteen feet. As this water supplies the trade-winds with vapor, it therefore becomes salter, and as it becomes salter, the forces of aggregation among its particles are increased, as we may infer from the fact (§ 27), that the waters of the Gulf Stream are reluctant to mix with those of the ocean.

Now, whatever be the cause that enables these waters to remain on the surface, whether it be from the fact just stated, and in consequence of which the waters of the Gulf Stream are held together in their channel; or whether it be from the fact that the expansion from the heat of the torrid zone is sufficient to compensate for this increased saltness; or whether it be from both of these influences together that these waters are kept on the surface, suffice it to say, we do know that they go into the Caribbean Sea (§ 34) as a surface current. The trade-winds, by their constant force, may assist to skim them off from the Atlantic, and push them along into the Caribbean Sea, whence, for causes unknown, they escape by the channel of the Gulf Stream in preference to any other.

36. In the present state of our knowledge concerning this wonderful phenomenon—for the Gulf Stream is one of the most mar-

velous things in the ocean—we can do little more than conjecture. But we have two causes in operation which we may safely assume are among those concerned in producing the Gulf Stream. One of these is in the increased saltness of its water after the trade-winds have been supplied with vapor from it; and the other is in the diminished quantum of salt which the Baltic and the North Sea contain. The waters of the Baltic are nearly fresh; they contain only about half as much salt as sea water does generally (§ 248).

Now here we have, on one side, the Caribbean Sea and Gulf of Mexico, with their waters of brine; on the other, the Baltic and the North Sea, with waters that are but little more than brackish. In one set of these sea-basins the water is heavy; in the other, it is light. Between them the ocean intervenes; but water is bound to seek and to maintain its level; and here, therefore, we unmask one of the agents concerned in causing the Gulf Stream. What is the influence of this agent—that is, how great is it, and to what extent does it go—we can not say; only it is at least one of the agents concerned. Moreover, speculate as we may as to all the agencies concerned in collecting these waters, that have supplied the trade-winds with vapor, into the Caribbean Sea, and then in driving them across the Atlantic, of this we may be sure, that the salt which the trade-wind vapor leaves behind in the tropics has to be conveyed away from the trade-wind region, to be mixed up again in due proportion with the other water of the sea—the Baltic included—and that these are the waters which we see running off through the Gulf Stream. To convey them away is one of the offices which, in the economy of the ocean, has been assigned to it.

37. As to the temperature of the Gulf Stream, there is, in a winter's day, off Hatteras and even as high up as the Grand Banks in mid ocean, a difference between its waters and those of the ocean near by of 20°, and even 30°. Water, we know, expands by heat, and here the difference of temperature may more than compensate for the difference of saltness, and leave, therefore, the waters of the Gulf lighter by reason of their warmth.

38. Being lighter and adhesive, they should therefore occupy a higher level than those through which they flow. Assuming the depth off Hatteras to be one hundred and fourteen fathoms, and allowing the usual rates of expansion for sea water, figures show

that the middle or axis of the Gulf Stream there should be nearly two feet higher than the contiguous waters of the Atlantic. Hence the surface of the stream should present a double inclined plane, from which the water would be running down on either side, as from the roof of a house. As this runs off at the top, the same weight of colder water runs in at the bottom, and so raises up the cold water bed of the Gulf Stream, and causes it to become shallower and shallower as it goes north.

39. That the Gulf Stream is roof-shaped, causing the waters on its surface to flow off to either side from the middle, we have not only circumstantial evidence to show, but observations to prove.

40. Navigators, while drifting along with the Gulf Stream, have lowered a boat to try the surface current. In such cases, the boat would drift either to the east or to the west, as it happened to be on one side or the other of the axis of the stream, while the vessel herself would drift along with the stream in the direction of its course; thus showing the existence of a shallow roof-current from the middle toward either edge, which would carry the boat along, but which, being superficial, does not extend deep enough to affect the drift of the vessel.

41. That such is the case (§ 38), is also indicated by the circumstance that the sea-weed and drift-wood which are found in such large quantities along the outer edge of the Gulf Stream, are never, even with the prevalence of easterly winds, found along its inner edge, and for the simple reason that to cross the Gulf Stream, and to pass over from that side to this, they would have to drift up stream, as it were; that is, they would have to stem this roof-current until they reached the middle of the stream. We never hear of planks, or wrecks, or of any floating substance which is cast into the sea on the other side of the Gulf Stream being found along the coasts of the United States. Drift-wood, trees, and seeds from the West India islands, are said to have been cast up on the shores of Europe, but never, that I ever heard, on the Atlantic shores of this country.

We are treating now of the effects of physical causes. The question to which I ask attention is, Why does the Gulf Stream slough off and cast upon its outer edge sea-weed, drift-wood, and all other solid bodies that are found floating upon it?

42. One cause has been shown to be in its roof-shaped current;

but there is another which tends to produce the same effect; and because it is a physical agent, it should not, in a treatise of this kind, be overlooked, be its action never so slight. I allude now to the effects (upon the drift matter of the stream) produced by the diurnal rotation of the earth.

43. Take, for illustration, a rail-road that runs north and south. It is well known to engineers, that when the cars are going north on such a road, their tendency is to run off on the east side; but when the train is going south, their tendency is to run off on the west side of the track—*i. e.*, always on the right-hand side. Whether the road be one mile or one hundred miles in length, the effect of diurnal rotation is the same, and the tendency to run off, as you cross a given parallel at a stated rate of speed, is the same, whether the road be long or short, the tendency to fly the track being in proportion to the speed of the trains, and not at all in proportion to the length of the road.

44. Now, *vis inertiæ* and velocity being taken into the account, the tendency to obey the force of this diurnal rotation, and to trend to the right, is proportionably as great in the case of a patch of sea-weed as it drifts along the Gulf Stream, as it is in the case of the train of cars as they speed to the north, along the iron track of the Hudson River railway, or the Great Western railway of England.

The rails restrain the cars and prevent them from flying off; but there are no rails to restrain the sea-weed, and nothing to prevent the drift-matter of the Gulf Stream from going off in obedience to this force. The slightest impulse tending to turn aside bodies moving freely in water is immediately felt and implicitly obeyed.

45. It is in consequence of this diurnal rotation that drift-wood coming down the Mississippi is so very apt to be cast upon the west or right bank. This is the reverse of what obtains upon the Gulf Stream, for it flows to the north; it therefore sloughs off to the east.

The effect of diurnal rotation upon the winds and upon the currents of the sea is admitted by all—the trade-winds derive their *easting* from it—it must, therefore, extend to all the matter which these currents bear with them, to the largest iceberg as well as to the merest sprig of grass that floats upon the waters, or the minutest organism that the most powerful microscope can detect among the impalpable particles of sea-dust. This effect of diurnal rotation will be frequently alluded to in the pages of this work.

46. In its course to the north, the Gulf Stream gradually trends more and more to the eastward, until it arrives off the Banks of Newfoundland, where its course becomes due east. These banks, it has been thought, deflect it from its proper course, and cause it to take this turn. Examination will prove, I think, that they are an effect, certainly not the cause. It is here that the frigid current already spoken of (§ 11), with its icebergs from the north, are met and melted by the warm waters of the Gulf. Of course the loads of earth, stones, and gravel brought down upon them are here deposited. Captain Scoresby, far away in the north, counted five hundred icebergs setting out from the same vicinity upon this cold current for the south. Many of them, loaded with earth, have been seen aground on the Banks. This process of transferring deposits for these shoals has been going on for ages; and, with time, seems altogether adequate to the effect described.

The deep sea soundings that have been made by vessels of the navy (Plate XI.) tend to confirm this view as to the formation of these Banks. The greatest contrast in the bottom of the Atlantic is just to the south of these Banks. Nowhere in the open sea has the water been found to deepen so suddenly as here. Coming from the north, the bottom of the sea is shelving; but suddenly, after passing these Banks, its depth increases by almost a precipitous descent for many thousand feet, thus indicating that the debris which forms the Grand Banks comes from the north.

47. From the Straits of Bemini the course of the Gulf Stream (Plate VI.) describes (as far as it can be traced over toward the British Islands which are in the midst of its waters) the arc of a great circle as nearly as may be, only the thread or axis of the Gulf Stream does not generally go quite as far north as the great circle would. Such a course as this is the course that a cannon ball, could it be shot from these straits to those islands, would take.

If it were possible to see Ireland from Bemini, and to get a cannon that would reach that far, the person standing on Bemini and taking aim, intending to shoot at Ireland as a target, would, if the earth were at rest, sight along the plane of a great circle, for the path of the ball would be in such a plane.

48. But there *is* diurnal rotation; the earth *does* revolve on its axis; and since Bemini is nearer than Ireland is to the equator, the gun would be moving in diurnal rotation faster than the target, and therefore the marksman, taking aim point blank at his target, would miss. He would find, on examination, that he had shot south of his mark. In other words, that the path actually described by the ball would be the resultant of this difference in the rate of rotation and the explosive force; the former, impelling to the east, would cause the ball to describe a great circle, but one with too much obliquity to pass through the target; like a ray of light from the stars, the ball would be affected by aberration.

It is the case of the passenger in the rail-road car throwing an apple, as the train sweeps by, to a boy standing by the wayside. If he throw straight at the boy, he will miss, for the apple, partaking of the motion of the cars, will go ahead of the boy, and for the very reason that the shot will pass in advance of the target, for both the marksman and the passenger are going faster than the object at which they aim.

49. Hence we may assume it as a law, that the natural tendency of all currents in the sea, like the natural tendency of all projectiles through the air, is to describe their curves of flight in the planes of great circles, departing therefrom—unless *forced* to depart by obstructions—only so much as the forces of diurnal rotation may impel.

50. The arc of a great circle is the shortest distance between any two points on the surface of a sphere. Light, heat, and electricity, running water, and all substances, whether ponderable or imponderable, seek, when in motion, to pass from point to point by the shortest lines practicable. Electricity may be turned aside from its course, and so may the cannon-ball or running water; but remove every obstruction, and leave the current or the shot free to continue on in the direction of the first impulse, or to turn aside of its own volition, so to speak, and straight it will go, and continue to go—if on a plane, in a straight line; if on a sphere, in the arc of a great circle—thus showing that it has no volition except to obey impulse, and the physical requirements to take the shortest way to its point of destination.

The waters of the Gulf Stream, as they escape from the Gulf (§ 36), are bound over to the British Islands, to the North Sea, and

Frozen Ocean (Plate IX.). Accordingly, they take (§ 47), in obedience to this physical law, the most direct course by which nature will permit them to reach their destination. And this course, as already remarked (§ 49), is nearly that of the great circle, and exactly that of the supposed cannon ball.

51. Many philosophers have expressed the opinion—indeed, the belief is common among mariners (§ 46)—that the coasts of the United States and the Shoals of Nantucket turn the Gulf Stream toward the east; but if the view I have been endeavoring to make clear be correct—and I think it is—it appears that the course of the Gulf Stream is fixed and prescribed by exactly the same laws that require the planets to revolve in orbits, the planes of which shall pass through the centre of the sun; and that, were the Nantucket Shoals not in existence, the course of the Gulf Stream, in the main, would be exactly as it is and where it is. The Gulf Stream is bound over to the North Sea and Bay of Biscay partly for the reason, perhaps, that the waters there are lighter than those of the Mexican Gulf (§ 36);* and if the Shoals of Nantucket were not in existence, it could not pursue a more direct route. The Grand Banks, however, are encroaching, and cold currents from the north come down upon it: they may, and probably do, assist now and then to turn it aside.

52. Now if this explanation as to the *course* of the Gulf Stream and its eastward tendency hold good, a current setting from the north toward the south should have a westward tendency. It should also move in a great circle (§ 49), or rather in the circle of trajection, calling thus the circle traced upon the earth which would be described by a trajectile moving through the air without resistance and for a great distance. Accordingly, and in obedience to the propelling powers, derived from the rate at which different parallels are whirled around in diurnal motion, we find the current from the north, which meets the Gulf Stream on the Grand Banks (Plate IX.), taking a south*westwardly* direction, as already described (§ 45). It runs down to the tropics by the side of the Gulf Stream, and stretches as far to the west as our own shores will allow. Yet, in the face of these facts, and in spite of this force, both Major Rennell and M. Arago make the coasts of the

* The waters of the Atlantic generally contain 5½ per cent. more of saline matter than those of the English Channel.—*M. Bouillon la Grange.*

United States and the Shoals of Nantucket to turn the Gulf Stream toward the east.

53. But there are other forces operating upon the Gulf Stream. They are derived from the effect of changes in the waters of the whole ocean, as produced by changes in their temperature from time to time. As the Gulf Stream leaves the coasts of the United States, it begins to vary its position according to the seasons; the limit of its northern edge, as it passes the meridian of Cape Race (Plate VI.), being in winter about latitude 40°–41°, and in September, when the sea is hottest, about latitude 45°–46°. The trough of the Gulf Stream, therefore, may be supposed to waver about in the ocean not unlike a pennon in the breeze. Its head is confined between the shoals of the Bahamas and the Carolinas, but that part of it which stretches over toward the Grand Banks of Newfoundland is, as the temperature of the waters of the ocean changes, first pressed down toward the south, and then again up toward the north, according to the season of the year.

To appreciate the extent of the force by which it is so pressed, let us imagine the waters of the Gulf Stream to extend all the way to the bottom of the sea, so as completely to separate, by an impenetrable liquid wall, if you please, the waters of the ocean on the right from the waters in the ocean on the left of the stream. It is the height of summer: the waters of the sea on either hand are for the most part in a liquid state, and the Gulf Stream, let it be supposed, has assumed a normal condition between the two divisions, adjusting itself to the pressure on either side so as to balance them exactly and be in equilibrium. Now, again, it is the dead of winter, and the temperature of the waters over an area of millions of square miles in the North Atlantic has been changed many degrees, and this change of temperature has been followed by a change in the specific gravity of those waters, amounting, no doubt, in the aggregate, to many hundred millions of tons, over the whole ocean; for sea water, unlike fresh (§ 31), contracts to freezing. Now is it probable that, in passing from their summer to their winter temperature, the sea waters to the right of the Gulf Stream should change their specific gravity exactly as much in the aggregate as do the waters in the whole ocean to the left of it? If not, the difference must be compensated by some means. Sparks are not more prone to fly upward, nor water to seek its level, than Nature is sure with her efforts to restore equilibrium in both sea and air whenever, wherever, and by whatever it be disturbed. Therefore, though the waters of the Gulf Stream do not extend to the bottom, and though they be not impenetrable to the waters on either hand, yet, seeing that they have a waste of waters on the right and a waste of waters on the left, to which (§ 2) they offer a sort of resisting permeability, we are enabled to comprehend how the waters on either hand, as their specific gravity is increased or diminished, will impart to the trough of this stream a vibratory motion, pressing it now to the right, now to the left, according to the seasons and the consequent changes of temperature in the sea.

54. Plate VI. shows the limits of the Gulf Stream for March and September. The reason for this change of position is obvious. The banks of the Gulf Stream (§ 1) are cold water. In winter, the volume of cold water on the American, or left side of the stream, is greatly increased. It must have room, and gains it by pressing the warmer waters of the stream farther to the south, or right. In September, the temperature of these cold waters is modified; there is not such an extent of them, and then the warmer waters, in turn, press them back, and so the pendulum-like motion is preserved.

55. The observations made by the United States Coast Survey indicate that there are in the Gulf Stream threads of warmer, separated by streaks of cooler water. See Plate VI., in which these are shown. Figure A may be taken to represent a thermometrical cross section of the stream opposite the Capes of Virginia, for instance; the top of the curve representing the thermometer in the threads of the warmer water, and the depressions the height of the same instrument in the streaks of cooler water between, thus exhibiting, as one sails from America across the Gulf Stream, a remarkable series of thermometrical elevations and depressions in the surface temperature of this mighty river in the sea.

56. As a rule, the hottest water of the Gulf Stream is at or near the surface; and as the deep sea thermometer is sent down, it shows that these waters, though still far warmer than the water on either side at corresponding depths, gradually become less and less warm until the bottom of the current is reached. There is reason to believe that the warm waters of the Gulf Stream are no-

where permitted, in the oceanic economy, to touch the bottom of the sea. There is every where a cushion of cool water between them and the solid parts of the earth's crust. This arrangement is suggestive, and strikingly beautiful. One of the benign offices of the Gulf Stream is to convey heat from the Gulf of Mexico, where otherwise it would become excessive, and to disperse it in regions beyond the Atlantic for the amelioration of the climates of the British Islands and of all Western Europe. Now cold water is one of the best non-conductors of heat, and if the warm water of the Gulf Stream was sent across the Atlantic in contact with the solid crust of the earth—comparatively a good conductor of heat—instead of being sent across, as it is, in contact with a cold, non-conducting cushion of cool water to fend it from the bottom, all its heat would be lost in the first part of the way, and the soft climates of both France and England would be as that of Labrador, severe in the extreme, and ice-bound.

57. But to return to the streaks and reservoirs of hot water below. The hottest water is the lightest; as it rises to the top, it is cooled both by evaporation and exposure, when the surface is replenished by fresh supplies of hot water from below. Thus, in a winter's day, the waters at the surface of the Gulf Stream off Cape Hatteras may be at 80°, and at the depth of five hundred fathoms—three thousand feet—as actual observations show, the thermometer will stand at 57°. Following the stream thence off the Capes of Virginia, one hundred and twenty miles, it will be found—the water-thermometer having been carefully noted all the way—that it now stands a degree or two less at the surface, while all below is cooler. In other words, the stratum of water at 57°, which was three thousand feet below the surface off Hatteras, has, in a course of one hundred and twenty or one hundred and thirty miles in a horizontal direction, ascended, vertically, six hundred feet; that is, this stratum has run up hill with an ascent of five or six feet to the mile.

58. In the case of boiling springs we perceive how all the ascending water comes up in one column; that there is no descent of surface water through that which is boiling up, but at the side of the bubbling. Moreover, in a cold winter's day, the water, as it boils up, is relatively warm; it smokes, grows cool, and the surface thermometer will stand highest where it is boiling, lowest

off a little way toward the verge of the fountain. Just so with these warmer and cooler streaks in the Gulf Stream. This warm water, in its ascent (§ 57) of five feet to the mile—suppose we are considering the streak which is the hottest, and is, also, the nearest to the American shore—represents the boiling in the fountain; the warm, ascending water rising up in one body, and the cooler and heavier water going off to the side in another body, to sink and take its place with the other waters of the stream according to gravity and temperature. See the streaks x, y, z, Plate VI.

59. Now, when these waters come to the top and cool, they are traveling with the current toward the north, and the effect of diurnal rotation is to turn them, as it turns any other drift (§ 45), to the eastward. They obey this influence to a certain extent, sinking down as they obey, in consequence of their greater specific gravity; beyond this sinking—*i. e.*, farther from the shore—is another rising-up place, each thread of the hot water being less and less warm, and each stream of cooler water more and more cool. The forces of diurnal rotation, operating upon the waters as they are successively sloughed off from each thread and streak alternately above and below, are quite enough to determine them to the east. A rod being poised on a point at one end, so as to stand alone, has no more tendency to fall to the east than to the west; but the smallest force, the slightest breath, will determine it either way. So with the forces of diurnal rotation, and these streaks of warm and cool water; the water that has been to the top and is cooled must give way to warmer water that is pressing up from below; it must flow either to the west or to the east, and diurnal rotation assists in determining it. When it sinks and reaches its proper level, it must again go to the east or to the west to get into the ascending column, and rise again to the surface in its proper turn. There is no more tendency for it to go to the west than to the east, and diurnal rotation, like the weight of the feather, is sufficient; it again plies its forces, and they are obeyed.

Taking all these facts and views into consideration, we are led to the conclusion with which we set out (§ 49), that it is the law of matter in motion, and not the Shoals of Nantucket, that controls the Gulf Stream in its course.

CHAPTER II.

INFLUENCE OF THE GULF STREAM UPON CLIMATES.

An Illustration, § 60.—Best Fish in cold Water, 65.—The Sea a Part of a grand Machine, 67.—*Influence of the Gulf Stream upon the Meteorology of the Sea:* It is a "Weather Breeder," 69.—Dampness of Climate of England due to it, 70.—The Pole of Maximum Cold, 71.—Gales of the Gulf Stream, 72.—The Wreck of the San Francisco, 73.—*Influence of the Gulf Stream upon Commerce and Navigation:* Used as a Land-mark, 77.—The first Description of it, 78.—Thermal Navigation, 81.

60. Modern ingenuity has suggested a beautiful mode of warming houses in winter. It is done by means of hot water. The furnace and the caldron are sometimes placed at a distance from the apartments to be warmed. It is so at the Observatory. In this case, pipes are used to conduct the heated water from the caldron under the superintendent's dwelling over into one of the basement rooms of the Observatory, a distance of one hundred feet. These pipes are then flared out so as to present a large cooling surface; after which they are united into one again, through which the water, being now cooled, returns of its own accord to the caldron. Thus cool water is returning all the time and flowing in at the bottom of the caldron, while hot water is continually flowing out at the top.

The ventilation of the Observatory is so arranged that the circulation of the atmosphere through it is led from this basement room, where the pipes are, to all other parts of the building; and in the process of this circulation, the warmth conveyed by the water to the basement is taken thence by the air and distributed over all the rooms. Now, to compare small things with great, we have, in the warm waters which are confined in the Gulf of Mexico, just such a heating apparatus for Great Britain, the North Atlantic, and Western Europe.

The furnace is the torrid zone; the Mexican Gulf and Caribbean Sea are the caldrons; the Gulf Stream is the conducting pipe. From the Grand Banks of Newfoundland to the shores of Europe is the basement—the hot-air chamber—in which this pipe is flared out so as to present a large cooling surface. Here the circulation of the atmosphere is arranged by nature; and it is such that the warmth thus conveyed into this warm-air chamber of mid-ocean is taken up by the genial west winds, and dispensed, in the most benign manner, throughout Great Britain and the west of Europe.

61. The maximum temperature of the water-heated air-chamber of the Observatory is about 90°. The maximum temperature of the Gulf Stream is 86°, or about 9° above the ocean temperature due the latitude. Increasing its latitude 10°, it loses but 2° of temperature; and, after having run three thousand miles toward the north, it still preserves, even in winter, the heat of summer. With this temperature, it crosses the 40th degree of north latitude, and there, overflowing its liquid banks, it spreads itself out for thousands of square leagues over the cold waters around, and covers the ocean with a mantle of warmth that serves so much to mitigate in Europe the rigors of winter. Moving now more slowly, but dispensing its genial influences more freely, it finally meets the British Islands. By these it is divided (Plate IX.), one part going into the polar basin of Spitzbergen, the other entering the Bay of Biscay, but each with a warmth considerably above the ocean temperature. Such an immense volume of heated water can not fail to carry with it beyond the seas a mild and moist atmosphere. And this it is which so much softens climate there.

62. We know not, except approximately in one or two places, what the depth or the under temperature of the Gulf Stream may be; but *assuming* the temperature and velocity at the depth of two hundred fathoms to be those of the surface, and taking the well-known difference between the capacity of air and of water for specific heat as the argument, a simple calculation will show that the quantity of heat discharged over the Atlantic from the waters of the Gulf Stream in a winter's day would be sufficient to raise the whole column of atmosphere that rests upon France and the British Islands from the freezing point to summer heat.

Every west wind that blows crosses the stream on its way to Europe, and carries with it a portion of this heat to temper there the northern winds of winter. It is the influence of this stream upon climate that makes Erin the "Emerald Isle of the Sea," and that clothes the shores of Albion in evergreen robes; while in the same latitude, on this side, the coasts of Labrador are fast bound in fetters of ice. In a valuable paper on currents,* Mr. Redfield states, that in 1831 the harbor of St. John's, Newfoundland, was closed with ice as late as the month of June; yet who ever heard of the port of Liverpool, on the other side, though 2° further north, being closed with ice, even in the dead of winter?

63. The Thermal Chart (Plate IV.) shows this. The isothermal lines of 60°, 50°, &c., starting off from the parallel of 40° near the coasts of the United States, run off in a northeastwardly direction, showing the same oceanic temperature on the European side of the Atlantic in latitude 55° or 60°, that we have on the western side in latitude 40°. Scott, in one of his beautiful novels, tells us that the ponds in the Orkneys (latitude near 60°), are not frozen in winter. The people there owe their soft climate to this grand heating apparatus, for drift-wood from the West Indies is occasionally cast ashore there by the Gulf Stream.

64. Nor do the beneficial influences of this stream upon climate end here. The West Indian Archipelago is encompassed on one side by its chain of islands, and on the other by the Cordilleras of the Andes contracting with the Isthmus of Darien, and stretching themselves out over the plains of Central America and Mexico. Beginning on the summit of this range, we leave the regions of perpetual snow, and descend first into the *tierra témplada*, and then into the *tierra caliente*, or burning land. Descending still lower, we reach both the level and the surface of the Mexican seas, where, were it not for this beautiful and benign system of aqueous circulation, the peculiar features of the surrounding country assure us we should have the hottest, if not the most pestilential climate in the world. As the waters in these two caldrons become heated, they are borne off by the Gulf Stream, and are replaced by cooler currents through the Caribbean Sea; the surface water, as it enters here, being 3° or 4°, and that in depth 40°† cooler than when it escapes from the Gulf. Taking only this dif-

* American Journal of Science, vol. xlv., p. 293.

† Temperature of the Caribbean Sea (from the journals of Mr. Dunsterville):
Surface temperature, 83° September; 84° July; 83°–86½° Mosquito Coast.
Temperature in depth, 48°, 240 fathoms; 43°, 386 fathoms; 42°, 450 fathoms; 43°, 500 fathoms.

ference in surface temperature as an index of the heat accumulated there, a simple calculation will show that the quantity of specific heat daily carried off by the Gulf Stream from those regions, and discharged over the Atlantic, is sufficient to raise mountains of iron from zero to the melting point, and to keep in flow from them a molten stream of metal greater in volume than the waters daily discharged from the Mississippi River. Who, therefore, can calculate the benign influence of this wonderful current upon the climate of the South? In the pursuit of this subject, the mind is led from nature up to the Great Architect of nature; and what mind will the study of this subject not fill with profitable emotions? Unchanged and unchanging alone, of all created things, the ocean is the great emblem of its everlasting Creator. "He treadeth upon the waves of the sea," and is seen in the wonders of the deep. Yea, "He calleth for its waters, and poureth them out upon the face of the earth."

In obedience to this call, the aqueous portion of our planet preserves its beautiful system of circulation. By it heat and warmth are dispensed to the extra-tropical regions; clouds and rain are sent to refresh the dry land; and by it cooling streams are brought from Polar Seas to temper the heat of the torrid zone. At the depth of two hundred and forty fathoms, the temperature of the currents setting into the Caribbean Sea has been found as low as 48°, while that of the surface was 85°. Another cast with three hundred and eighty-six fathoms gave 43° below against 83° at the surface. The hurricanes of those regions agitate the sea to great depths; that of 1780 tore rocks up from the bottom in seven fathoms, and cast them on shore. They therefore can not fail to bring to the surface portions of the cooler water below.

At the very bottom of the Gulf Stream, when its surface temperature was 80°, the deep sea thermometer of the Coast Survey has recorded temperatures as low as 38° Fahrenheit.

These cold waters doubtless come down from the north to replace the warm water sent through the Gulf Stream to moderate the cold of Spitzbergen; for within the Arctic Circle, the temperature at corresponding depths off the shores of that island is only one degree colder than in the Caribbean Sea, while on the coasts of Labrador the temperature in depth is said to be 25°, or 7° below the melting point of fresh water. Captain Scoresby relates, that on the coast of Greenland, in latitude 72°, the temperature of the air was 42°; of the water, 34°; and 29° at the depth of one hundred and eighteen fathoms. He there found a current setting to the south, and bearing with it this extremely cold water, with vast numbers of icebergs, whose centres, perhaps, were far below zero. It would be curious to ascertain the routes of these under currents on their way to the tropical regions, which they are intended to cool. One has been found at the equator two hundred miles broad and 23° colder than the surface water. Unless the land or shoals intervene, it no doubt comes down in a spiral curve, approaching the great circle.

65. Perhaps the best indication as to these cold currents may be derived from the fish of the sea. The whales first pointed out the existence of the Gulf Stream by avoiding its warm waters. Along our own coasts, all those delicate animals and marine productions which delight in warmer waters are wanting; thus indicating, by their absence, the cold current from the north now known to exist there. In the genial warmth of the sea about the Bermudas on one hand, and Africa on the other, we find, in great abundance, those delicate shell-fish and coral formations which are altogether wanting in the same latitudes along the shores of South Carolina. The same obtains in the west coast of South America; for there the cold current almost reaches the line before the first sprig of coral is found to grow.

A few years ago, great numbers of bonita and albercore—tropical fish—following the Gulf Stream, entered the English Channel, and alarmed the fishermen of Cornwall and Devonshire by the havoc which they created among the pilchards there.

It may well be questioned if our Atlantic cities and towns do not owe their excellent fish-markets, as well as our watering-places their refreshing sea-bathing in summer, to this stream of cold water. The temperature of the Mediterranean is 4° or 5° above the ocean temperature of the same latitude, and the fish there are very indifferent. On the other hand, the temperature along our coast is several degrees below that of the ocean, and from Maine to Florida our tables are supplied with the most excellent of fish. The sheepshead, so much esteemed in Virginia and the Carolinas, when taken on the warm coral banks of the Bahamas, loses its flavor, and is held in no esteem. The same is the case with other fish: when taken in the cold water of that coast, they have a delicious flavor and are highly esteemed; but when taken in the warm water on the other edge of the Gulf Stream, though but a few miles distant, their flesh is soft and unfit for the table. The temperature of the water at the Balize reaches 90°. The fish taken there are not to be compared with those of the same latitude in this cold stream. New Orleans therefore resorts to the cool waters on the Florida coasts for her choicest fish. The same is the case in the Pacific. A current of cold water from the south sweeps the shores of Chili, Peru, and Columbia, and reaches the Gallipagos Islands under the line. Throughout this whole distance, the world does not afford a more abundant or excellent supply of fish. Yet out in the Pacific, at the Society Islands, where coral abounds, and the water preserves a higher temperature, the fish, though they vie in gorgeousness of coloring with the birds, and plants, and insects of the tropics, are held in no esteem as an article of food. I have known sailors, even after long voyages, still to prefer their salt beef and pork to a mess of fish taken there. The few facts which we have bearing upon this subject seem to suggest it as a point of the inquiry to be made, whether the habitat of certain fish does not indicate the temperature of the water; and whether these cold and warm currents of the ocean do not constitute the great highways through which migratory fishes travel from one region to another.

Navigators have often met with vast numbers of young sea-nettles (medusæ) drifting along with the Gulf Stream. They are known to constitute the principal food for the whale; but whither bound by this route has caused much curious speculation, for it is well known that the habits of the right whale are averse to the warm waters of this stream. An intelligent sea-captain informs me that, two or three years ago, in the Gulf Stream on the coast of Florida, he fell in with such a "school of young sea-nettles as had never before been heard of." The sea was covered with them for many leagues. He likened them, in appearance on the water, to acorns floating on a stream; but they were so thick as to completely cover the sea. He was bound to England, and was five or six days in sailing through them. In about sixty days afterward, on his return, he fell in with the same school off the Western Islands, and here he was three or four days in passing them again. He recognized them as the same, for he had never before seen any like them; and on both occasions he frequently hauled up buckets full and examined them.

Now the Western Islands is the great place of resort for whales; and at first there is something curious to us in the idea that the Gulf of Mexico is the harvest field, and the Gulf Stream the gleaner which collects the fruitage planted there, and conveys it thousands of miles off to the hungry whale at sea. But how perfectly in unison is it with the kind and providential care of that great and good Being which feeds the young ravens when they cry, and caters for the sparrow!

66. The sea has its climates as well as the land. They both change with the latitude; but one varies with the elevation above, the other with the depression below the sea level. Each is regulated by circulation; but the regulators are, on the one hand, winds; on the other, currents.

67. The inhabitants of the ocean are as much the creatures of climate as are those of the dry land; for the same Almighty hand which decked the lily and cares for the sparrow, fashioned also the pearl and feeds the great whale. Whether of the land or the sea, they are all his creatures, subjects of his laws, and agents in his economy. The sea, therefore, we infer, has its offices and duties to perform; so may we infer, have its currents, and so, too, its inhabitants; consequently, he who undertakes to study its phenomena, must cease to regard it as a waste of waters. He must look upon it as a part of the exquisite machinery by which the harmonies of nature are preserved, and then he will begin to perceive the developments of order and the evidences of design which make it a most beautiful and interesting subject for contemplation.

68. To one who has never studied the mechanism of a watch, its main-spring or the balance-wheel is a mere piece of metal. He may have looked at the face of the watch, and, while he admires the motion of its hands, and the time it keeps, or the tune it plays, he may have wondered in idle amazement as to the character of the machinery which is concealed within. Take it to pieces, and show him each part separately; he will recognize neither design, nor adaptation, nor relation between them; but put them together, set them to work, point out the offices of each spring, wheel, and cog, explain their movements, and then show

him the result; now he perceives that it is all *one* design; that, notwithstanding the number of parts, their diverse forms and various offices, and the agents concerned, the whole piece is of *one* thought, the expression of *one* idea. He now perceives that when the main-spring was fashioned and tempered, its relation to all the other parts must have been considered; that the cogs on this wheel are cut and regulated—*adapted*—to the rachets on that, &c.; and his conclusion will be, that such a piece of mechanism could not have been produced by chance; the adaptation of the parts is such as to show it to be according to design, and obedient to the will of *one* intelligence. So, too, when one looks out upon the face of this beautiful world, he may admire the lovely scene, but his admiration can never grow into adoration unless he will take the trouble to look behind and study, in some of its details at least, the exquisite system of machinery by which such beautiful results are accomplished. To him who does this, the sea, with its physical geography, becomes as the main spring of a watch; its waters, and its currents, and its salts, and its inhabitants, with their adaptations, as balance-wheels, cogs and pinions, and jewels. Thus he perceives that they, too, are according to design; that they are the expression of One Thought, a unity with harmonies which One Intelligence, and One Intelligence alone, could utter. And when he has arrived at this point, then he feels that the study of the sea, in its physical aspect, is truly sublime. It elevates the mind and ennobles the man. The Gulf Stream is now no longer, therefore, to be regarded by such an one merely as an immense current of warm water running across the ocean, but as a balance-wheel—a part of that grand machinery by which air and water are adapted to each other, and by which this earth itself is adapted to the well-being of its inhabitants—of the flora which deck, and the fauna which enliven its surface.

69. Let us therefore consider the influence of the Gulf Stream upon the meteorology of the ocean.

To use a sailor expression, the Gulf Stream is the great "weather breeder" of the North Atlantic Ocean. The most furious gales of wind sweep along with it; and the fogs of Newfoundland, which so much endanger navigation in winter, doubtless owe their existence to the presence, in that cold sea, of immense volumes of warm water brought by the Gulf Stream. Sir Philip Brooke found the air on each side of it at the freezing point, while that of its waters was 80°. "The heavy, warm, damp air over the current produced great irregularities in his chronometers." The excess of heat daily brought into such a region by the waters of the Gulf Stream would, if suddenly stricken from them, be sufficient to make the column of superincumbent atmosphere hotter than melted iron.

With such an element of atmospherical disturbance in its bosom, we might expect storms of the most violent kind to accompany it in its course. Accordingly, the most terrific that rage on the ocean have been known to spend their fury in and near its borders.

Our nautical works tell us of a storm which forced this stream back to its sources, and piled up the water in the Gulf to the height of thirty feet. The Ledbury Snow attempted to ride it out. When it abated, she found herself high up on the dry land, and discovered that she had let go her anchor among the tree tops on Elliott's Key. The Florida Keys were inundated many feet, and, it is said, the scene presented in the Gulf Stream was never surpassed in awful sublimity on the ocean. The water thus dammed up is said to have rushed out with wonderful velocity against the fury of the gale, producing a sea that beggared description.

The "great hurricane" of 1780 commenced at Barbadoes. In it, the bark was blown from the trees, and the fruits of the earth destroyed; the very bottom and depths of the sea were uprooted, and the waves rose to such a height that forts and castles were washed away, and their great guns carried about in the air; houses were blown down, ships were wrecked, and the bodies of men and beasts lifted up above the earth and dashed to pieces in the storm. At the different islands, not less than twenty thousand persons lost their lives on shore, while farther to the north, the "Sterling Castle" and the "Dover Castle," men-of-war, were wrecked at sea, and fifty sail driven on shore at the Bermudas.

Several years ago, the British Admiralty set on foot inquiries as to the cause of the storms in certain parts of the Atlantic, which so often rage with disastrous effects to navigation. The result may be summed up in the conclusion to which the investigation led: that they are occasioned by the irregularity between the temperature of the Gulf Stream and of the neighboring regions, both in the air and water.

70. The habitual dampness of the climate of the British Islands, as well as the occasional dampness of that along the Atlantic coasts of the United States when easterly winds prevail, is attributable also to the Gulf Stream. They come to us loaded with vapors gathered from its warm and smoking waters.

It carries the temperature of summer, even in the dead of winter, as far north as the Grand Banks of Newfoundland.

71. One of the poles of maximum cold is, according to theory, situated in latitude 80° north, longitude 100° west. It is distant but little more than two thousand miles, in a northwestwardly direction, from the summer-heated waters of this stream. This proximity of extremes of greatest cold and summer heat, will, as observations are multiplied and discussed, be probably found to have much to do with the storms that rage with such fury on the left side of the Gulf Stream.

72. I am not prepared to maintain that the Gulf Stream is really the "Storm King" of the Atlantic, which has power to control the march of every gale that is raised there; but the course of many gales has been traced from the place of their origin directly to the Gulf Stream. Gales that take their rise on the coast of Africa, and even as far down on that side as the parallel of 10° or 15° north latitude, have, it has been shown by an examination of log-books, made straight for the Gulf Stream; joining it, they have then been known to turn about, and, traveling with this stream, to recross the Atlantic, and so reach the shores of Europe. In this way the tracks of storms have been traced out and followed for a week or ten days. Their path is marked by wreck and disaster. At the meeting of the American Association for the advancement of Science in 1854, Mr. Redfield mentioned one which he had traced out, and in which no less than seventy odd vessels had been wrecked, dismasted, or damaged.

Plate X. was prepared by Lieutenant B. S. Porter, from data furnished by the log-books at the Observatory. It represents one of these storms that commenced in August, 1848. It commenced more than a thousand miles from the Gulf Stream, made a straight course for it, and traveled with it for many days.

The dark shading shows the space covered by the gale, and

the white line in the middle shows the axis of the gale, or the line of minimum barometric pressure. There are many other instances of similar gales.

Now what should attract these terrific storms to the Gulf Stream? Sailors dread storms in the Gulf Stream more than they do in any other part of the ocean. It is not the fury of the storm alone that they dread, but it is the "ugly sea" which these storms raise. The current of the stream running in one direction, and the wind blowing in another, creates a sea that is often frightful.

In the month of December, 1853, the fine new steam-ship San Francisco sailed from New York with a regiment of United States troops on board, bound around Cape Horn for California. She was overtaken, while crossing the Gulf Stream, by a gale of wind, in which she was terribly crippled. Her decks were swept, and by one single blow of those terrible seas that the storms there raise, one hundred and seventy-nine souls, officers and soldiers, were washed overboard and drowned.

The day after this disaster she was seen by one vessel, and again the next day, December 26th, by another, but neither of them could render her any assistance.

When they arrived in the United States and reported what they had seen, the most painful apprehensions were entertained by friends for the safety of those on board. Vessels were sent out to search for and relieve her. But which way should these vessels go? where should they look?

An appeal was made to know what light the system of researches carried on at the National Observatory concerning winds and currents could throw upon the subject.

73. The materials that had been discussed were examined, and a chart was prepared to show the course of the Gulf Stream at that season of the year. (See the limits of the Gulf Stream for March, Plate VI.) Upon the supposition that the steamer had been completely disabled, the lines *a b* were drawn to define the limits of her drift. Between these two lines, it was said, the steamer, if she could neither steam nor sail after the gale, had drifted.

By request, I prepared instructions for two revenue cutters that were sent to search for her. One of them, being at New London, was told to go along the dotted track leading to *c*, expecting thereby to keep inside of the line along which the steamer had drifted, with the view of intercepting and speaking homeward-bound vessels that might have seen the wreck.

The cutter was to proceed to *c*, where she might expect to fall in with the line of drift taken by the steamer. The last that was seen of that ill-fated vessel was when she was at *o*. So, if the cutter had been in time, she had instructions that would have taken her in sight of the object of her search.

It is true that, before the cutter sailed, the Kilby, the Three Bells, and the Antarctic, unknown to anxious friends at home, had fallen in with and relieved the wreck; but that does not detract from the system of observations, of the results of which, and their practical application, it is the object of this work to treat.

A beautiful illustration of their usefulness is the fact that, though the bark Kilby lost sight of the wreck at night, and the next morning did not know which way to look for it, and could not find it, yet, by a system of philosophical deduction, we on shore could point out the whereabouts of the disabled steamer so closely, that vessels could be directed to look for her exactly where she was to be seen.

74. These storms, for which the Gulf Stream has such attraction, and over which it seems to exercise so much control, are said to be, for the most part, whirlwinds. All boys are familiar with miniature whirlwinds on shore. They are seen, especially in the autumn, sweeping along the roads and streets, raising columns of dust, leaves, &c., which rise up like inverted cones in the air, and gyrate about the centre or axis of the storm. Thus, while the axis, and the dust, and the leaves, and all those things which mark the course of the whirlwind, are traveling in one direction, it may be seen that the wind is blowing around this axis in all directions.

Just so with some of these Gulf Stream storms. That represented on Plate X. is such a one. It was a rotary storm. Mr. Piddington, an eminent meteorologist of Calcutta, calls them *Cycloins*.

75. Now, what should make these storms travel toward the Gulf Stream, and then, joining it, travel along with its current? It is the high temperature of its waters, say mariners. But why, or wherefore, should the spirits of the storm obey in this manner

the influence of these high temperatures, philosophers have not been able to explain.

76. *The influence of the Gulf Stream upon commerce and navigation.*

Formerly the Gulf Stream controlled commerce across the Atlantic by governing vessels in their routes through this ocean to a greater extent than it does now, and simply for the reason that ships are faster, instruments better, and navigators are more skillful now than formerly they were.

Up to the close of the last century, the navigator *guessed* as much as he *calculated* the place of his ship: vessels from Europe to Boston frequently made New York, and thought the land-fall by no means bad. Chronometers, now so accurate, were then an experiment. The Nautical Ephemeris itself was faulty, and gave tables which involved errors of thirty miles in the longitude. The instruments of navigation erred by *degrees* quite as much as they now do by *minutes;* for the rude "cross staff" and "back staff," the "sea-ring" and "mariner's bow," had not yet given place to the nicer sextant and circle of reflection of the present day. Instances are numerous of vessels navigating the Atlantic in those times being 6°, 8°, and even 10° of longitude out of their reckoning in as many days from port.

77. Though navigators had been in the habit of crossing and recrossing the Gulf Stream almost daily for three centuries, it never occurred to them to make use of it as a means of giving them their longitude, and of warning them of their approach to the shores of this continent.

Dr. Franklin was the first to suggest this use of it. The contrast afforded by the temperature of its waters and that of the sea between the Stream and the shores of America was striking. The dividing line between the warm and the cool waters was sharp (§ 2); and this dividing line, especially that on the western side of the stream, never changed its position as much in longitude as mariners erred in their reckoning.

78. When he was in London in 1770, he happened to be consulted as to a memorial which the Board of Customs at Boston sent to the Lords of the Treasury, stating that the Falmouth packets were generally a fortnight longer to Boston than common traders were from London to Providence, Rhode Island.

They therefore asked that the Falmouth packets might be sent to Providence instead of to Boston. This appeared strange to the doctor, for London was much farther than Falmouth, and from Falmouth the routes were the same, and the difference should have been the other way. He, however, consulted Captain Folger, a Nantucket whaler, who chanced to be in London also; the fisherman explained to him that the difference arose from the circumstance that the Rhode Island captains were acquainted with the Gulf Stream, while those of the English packets were not. The latter kept in it, and were set back sixty or seventy miles a day, while the former avoided it altogether. He had been made acquainted with it by the whales which were found on either side of it, but never in it (§ 65). At the request of the doctor, he then traced on a chart the course of this stream from the Straits of Florida. The doctor had it engraved at Tower Hill, and sent copies of it to the Falmouth captains, who paid no attention to it. The course of the Gulf Stream, as laid down by that fisherman from his general recollection of it, has been retained and quoted on the charts for navigation, we may say, until the present day.

But the investigations of which we are treating are beginning to throw more light upon this subject; they are giving us more correct knowledge in every respect with regard to it, and to many other new and striking features in the physical geography of the sea.

79. No part of the world affords a more difficult or dangerous navigation than the approaches of our northern coast in winter. Before the warmth of the Gulf Stream was known, a voyage at this season from Europe to New England, New York, and even to the Capes of the Delaware or Chesapeake, was many times more trying, difficult, and dangerous than it now is. In making this part of the coast, vessels are frequently met by snow-storms and gales which mock the seaman's strength and set at naught his skill. In a little while his bark becomes a mass of ice; with her crew frosted and helpless, she remains obedient only to her helm, and is kept away for the Gulf Stream. After a few hours' run, she reaches its edge, and almost at the next bound passes from the midst of winter into a sea at summer heat. Now the ice disappears from her apparel; the sailor bathes his stiffened limbs in tepid waters; feeling himself invigorated and refreshed with the

genial warmth about him, he realizes, out there at sea, the fable of Antæus and his mother Earth. He rises up and attempts to make his port again, and is again as rudely met and beat back from the northwest; but each time that he is driven off from the contest, he comes forth from this stream, like the ancient son of Neptune, stronger and stronger, until, after many days, his freshened strength prevails, and he at last triumphs and enters his haven in safety; though in this contest he sometimes falls to rise no more, for it is often terrible. Many ships annually founder in these gales; and I might name instances, for they are not uncommon, in which vessels bound to Norfolk or Baltimore, with their crews enervated in tropical climates, have encountered, as far down as the Capes of Virginia, snow-storms that have driven them back into the Gulf Stream time and again, and have kept them out for forty, fifty, and even for sixty days, trying to make an anchorage.

80. Nevertheless, the presence of the warm waters of the Gulf Stream, with their summer heat in mid-winter, off the shores of New England, is a great boon to navigation. At this season of the year especially, the number of wrecks and the loss of life along the Atlantic sea-front are frightful. The month's average of wrecks has been as high as three a day. How many escape by seeking refuge from the cold in the warm waters of the Gulf Stream is matter of conjecture. Suffice it to say, that before their temperature was known, vessels thus distressed knew of no place of refuge short of the West Indies; and the newspapers of that day—Franklin's Pennsylvania Gazette among them—inform us that it was no uncommon occurrence for vessels, bound for the Capes of the Delaware in winter, to be blown off and to go to the West Indies, and there wait for the return of spring before they would attempt another approach to this part of the coast.

81. Accordingly, Dr. Franklin's discovery with regard to the Gulf Stream temperature was looked upon as one of great importance, not only on account of its affording to the frosted mariner in winter a convenient refuge from the snow-storm, but because of its serving the navigator with an excellent land-mark or beacon for our coast in all weathers. And so viewing it, the doctor concealed his discovery, for we were then at war with England. It was then not uncommon for vessels to be as much as 10° out in

their reckoning. He himself was 5°. Therefore, in approaching the coast, the current of warm water in the Gulf Stream, and of cold water on this side of it, if tried with the thermometer, would enable the mariner to judge with great certainty, and in the worst of weather, as to his position. Jonathan Williams afterward, in speaking of the importance which the discovery of these warm and cold currents would prove to navigation, pertinently asked the question, "If these stripes of water had been distinguished by the colors of red, white, and blue, could they be more distinctly discovered than they are by the constant use of the thermometer?" And he might have added, could they have marked the position of the ship more clearly?

When his work on Thermometrical Navigation appeared, Commodore Truxton wrote to him: "Your publication will be of use to navigation by rendering sea voyages secure far beyond what even you yourself will immediately calculate, for I have proved the utility of the thermometer very often since we sailed together.

"It will be found a most valuable instrument in the hands of mariners, and particularly as to those who are unacquainted with astronomical observations; . . . . . these particularly stand in need of a simple method of ascertaining their approach to or distance from the coast, especially in the winter season; for it is then that passages are often prolonged, and ships blown off the coast by hard westerly winds, and vessels get into the Gulf Stream without its being known; on which account they are often hove to by the captains' supposing themselves near the coast when they are very far off (having been drifted by the currents). On the other hand, ships are often cast on the coast by sailing in the eddy of the Stream, which causes them to outrun their common reckoning. Every year produces new proofs of these facts, and of the calamities incident thereto."

82. Though Dr. Franklin's discovery was made in 1775, yet, for political reasons, it was not generally made known till 1790. Its immediate effect in navigation was to make the ports of the North as accessible in winter as in summer. What agency this circumstance had in the decline of the direct trade of the South, which followed this discovery, would be, at least to the political economist, a subject for much curious and interesting speculation. I have referred to the commercial tables of the time, and have com-

pared the trade of Charleston with that of the northern cities for several years, both before and after the discovery of Dr. Franklin became generally known to navigators. The comparison shows an immediate decline in the Southern trade and a wonderful increase in that of the North. But whether this discovery in navigation and this revolution in trade stand in the relation of cause and effect, or be merely a coincidence, let others judge.

83. In 1769, the commerce of the two Carolinas equaled that of all the New England States together; it was more than double that of New York, and exceeded that of Pennsylvania by one third.* In 1792, the exports from New York amounted in value to two millions and a half; from Pennsylvania, to $3,820,000; and from Charleston alone, to $3,834,000.

But in 1795, by which time the Gulf Stream began to be as well understood by navigators as it now is, and the average passages from Europe to the North were shortened nearly one half, while those to the South remained about the same, the customs at Philadelphia alone amounted to $2,941,000,† or more than one half of those collected in all the states together.

Nor did the effect of the doctor's discovery end here. Before

* *From M'Pherson's Annals of Commerce.—Exports and Imports in* 1769, *valued in Sterling Money.*

EXPORTS.

	To Gr. Britain.			Sou. of Europe.			West Indies.			Africa.			Total.		
	£	s.	d.	£	s.	d.	£	s.	d.	£	s.	d.	£	s.	d.
New England	142,775	12	9	81,173	16	2	308,427	9	6	17,713	0	9	550,089	19	2
New York	113,382	8	8	50,885	13	0	66,324	17	5	1,313	2	6	231,906	1	7
Pennsylvania	28,112	6	9	203,762	11	11	178,331	7	8	560	9	9	410,756	16	1
North and South Carolina	405,014	13	1	76,119	12	10	87,758	19	3	691	12	1	569,584	17	3
IMPORTS.															
New England	223,695	11	6	25,408	17	9	314,749	14	5	180	0	0	564,034	3	8
New York	75,930	19	7	14,927	7	8	97,420	4	0	697	10	0	188,976	1	3
Pennsylvania	204,979	17	4	14,249	8	4	180,591	12	4				399,830	18	0
North and South Carolina	327,084	8	6	7,099	5	10	76,269	17	11	137,620	10	0	535,714	2	3

† *Value of Exports in Dollars.*‡

	1791.	1792.	1793.	1794.	1795.	1796.
Massachusetts	2,519,651	2,888,104	3,755,347	5,292,441	7,117,907	9,949,345
New York	2,505,465	2,535,790	2,932,370	5,442,000	10,304,000	12,208,027
Pennsylvania	3,436,000	3,820,000	6,958,000	6,643,000	11,518,000	17,513,866
South Carolina	2,693,000	2,428,000	3,191,000	3,868,000	5,998,000	7,620,000

Duties on Imports in Dollars.

	1791.	1792.	1793.	1794.	1795.	1796.	1833.
Massachusetts	1,006,000	723,000	1,044,000	1,121,000	1,520,000	1,460,000	3,055,000
New York	1,334,000	1,173,000	1,204,000	1,878,000	2,028,000	2,187,000	10,713,000
Pennsylvania	1,466,000	1,100,000	1,823,000	1,498,000	2,300,000	2,050,000	2,207,000
South Carolina	523,000	359,000	360,000	661,000	722,000	66,000	389,000

‡ Doc. No. 330, H. R., 2d Session, 25th Congress. Some of its statements do not agree with those taken from M'Pherson, and previously quoted.

it was made, the Gulf Stream was altogether insidious in its effects. By it, vessels were often drifted many miles out of their course without knowing it; and in bad and cloudy weather, when many days would intervene from one observation to another, the set of the current, though really felt for but a few hours during the interval, could only be proportioned out equally among the whole number of days. Therefore navigators could have only very vague ideas either as to the strength or the actual limits of the Gulf Stream, until they were marked out to the Nantucket fishermen by the whales, or made known by Captain Folger to Dr. Franklin. The discovery, therefore, of its high temperature, assured the navigator of the presence of a current of surprising velocity, and which, now turned to certain account, would hasten, as it had retarded his voyage in a wonderful degree.

84. Such, at the present day, is the degree of perfection to which nautical tables and instruments have been brought, that the navigator may now detect, and with great certainty, every current that thwarts his way. He makes great use of them. Colonel Sabine, in his passage, a few years ago, from Sierra Leone to New York, was drifted one thousand six hundred miles of his way by the force of currents alone; and, since the application of the thermometer to the Gulf Stream, the average passage from England has been reduced from upward of eight weeks to a little more than four.

85. Some political economists of America have ascribed the great decline of Southern commerce which followed the adoption of the Constitution of the United States to the protection given by legislation to Northern interests. But I think these statements and figures show that this decline was in no small degree owing to the Gulf Stream and the water thermometer; for they changed the relations of Charleston—the great Southern emporium of the times—removing it from its position as a half-way house, and placing it in the category of an outside station.

86. The plan of our work takes us necessarily into the air, for the sea derives from the winds some of the most striking features in its physical geography. Without a knowledge of the winds, we can neither understand the navigation of the ocean, nor make ourselves intelligently acquainted with the great highways across it. As with the land, so with the sea; some parts of it are as un-

traveled and as unknown as the great Amazonian wilderness of Brazil, or the inland basins of Central Africa. To the south of a line extending from Cape Horn to the Cape of Good Hope (Plate VIII.) is an immense waste of waters. None of the commercial thoroughfares of the ocean lead through it; only the adventurous whaleman finds his way there now and then in pursuit of his game; but for all the purposes of science and navigation, it is a vast unknown region. Now, were the prevailing winds of the South Atlantic northerly or southerly, instead of easterly or westerly, this unplowed sea would be an oft-used thoroughfare.

87. Nay, more, the sea supplies the winds with food for the rain which these busy messengers convey away from the ocean to "the springs in the valleys which run among the hills." To the philosopher, the places which supply the vapors are as suggestive and as interesting for the instruction they afford, as the places are upon which the vapors are showered down. Therefore, as he who studies the physical geography of the land is expected to make himself acquainted with the regions of precipitation, so he who looks into the physical geography of the sea should search for the regions of evaporation, and for those springs in the ocean which supply the reservoirs among the mountains with water to feed the rivers; and, in order to conduct this search properly, he must consult the winds, and make himself acquainted with their "circuits." Hence, in a work on the Physical Geography of the Sea, we treat also of the ATMOSPHERE.

CHAPTER III.

THE ATMOSPHERE.

The Relation of the Winds to the Physical Geography of the Sea, § 88.—No Expression of Nature without Meaning, 93.—*The Circulation of the Atmosphere,* Plate I., 95.—Southeast Trade-wind Region the larger, 109.—How the Winds approach the Poles, 112.—The Offices of the Atmosphere, 114.—It is a powerful Machine, 118.—Whence come the Rains that feed the great Rivers? 120.—How Vapor passes from one Hemisphere to the other, 123.—Evaporation greatest about Latitude 17°–20°, 127.—Explanation, 128.—The Rainy Seasons: how caused, 129.—Why there is one Rainy Season in California, 130—One at Panama, 131—Two at Bogotá, 132.—Rainless Regions explained, 135.—Why Australia is a Dry Country, 136.—Why Mountains have a dry and a rainy Side, 137.—The immense Fall of Rain upon the Western Ghauts in India; how caused, 139.—Vapor for the Patagonia Rains comes from the North Pacific, 141.—The mean annual Fall of Rain, 144.—Evaporation from the Indian Ocean, 146.—Evidences of Design, 148.

88. A PHILOSOPHER of the East,* with a richness of imagery truly Oriental, describes the atmosphere as "a spherical shell which surrounds our planet to a depth which is unknown to us, by reason of its growing tenuity, as it is released from the pressure of its own superincumbent mass. Its upper surface can not be nearer to us than fifty, and can scarcely be more remote than five hundred miles. It surrounds us on all sides, yet we see it not; it presses on us with a load of fifteen pounds on every square inch of surface of our bodies, or from seventy to one hundred tons on us in all, yet we do not so much as feel its weight. Softer than the softest down—more impalpable than the finest gossamer—it leaves the cobweb undisturbed, and scarcely stirs the lightest flower that feeds on the dew it supplies; yet it bears the fleets of nations on its wings around the world, and crushes the most refractory substances with its weight. When in motion, its force is sufficient to level the most stately forests and stable buildings with the earth—to raise the waters of the ocean into ridges like mountains, and dash the strongest ships to pieces like toys. It warms and cools by turns the earth and the living creatures that inhabit it. It draws up vapors from the sea and land, retains

* Dr. Buist, of Bombay.

them dissolved in itself, or suspended in cisterns of clouds, and throws them down again as rain or dew when they are required. It bends the rays of the sun from their path, to give us the twilight of evening and of dawn; it disperses and refracts their various tints to beautify the approach and the retreat of the orb of day. But for the atmosphere, sunshine would burst on us and fail us at once, and at once remove us from midnight darkness to the blaze of noon. We should have no twilight to soften and beautify the landscape; no clouds to shade us from the scorching heat, but the bald earth, as it revolved on its axis, would turn its tanned and weakened front to the full and unmitigated rays of the lord of day. It affords the gas which vivifies and warms our frames, and receives into itself that which has been polluted by use, and is thrown off as noxious. It feeds the flame of life exactly as it does that of the fire—it is in both cases consumed, and affords the food of consumption—in both cases it becomes combined with charcoal, which requires it for combustion, and is removed by it when this is over."

"It is only the girdling encircling air," says another philosopher,* "that flows above and around all, that makes the whole world kin. The carbonic acid with which to-day our breathing fills the air, to-morrow seeks its way round the world. The date-trees that grow round the falls of the Nile will drink it in by their leaves; the cedars of Lebanon will take of it to add to their stature; the cocoa-nuts of Tahiti will grow rapidly upon it, and the palms and bananas of Japan will change it into flowers. The oxygen we are breathing was distilled for us some short time ago by the magnolias of the Susquehanna, and the great trees that skirt the Orinoco and the Amazon—the giant rhododendrons of the Himalayas contributed to it, and the roses and myrtles of Cashmere, the cinnamon-tree of Ceylon, and the forest older than the flood, buried deep in the heart of Africa, far behind the Mountains of the Moon. The rain we see descending was thawed for us out of the icebergs which have watched the polar star for ages, and the lotus lilies have soaked up from the Nile, and exhaled as vapor, snows that rested on the summits of the Alps."

89. "The atmosphere," continues Maun, "which forms the outer surface of the habitable world, is a vast reservoir, into which the

* *Vide* North British Review.

supply of food designed for living creatures is thrown; or, in one word, it is itself the food, in its simple form, of all living creatures. The animal grinds down the fibre and the tissue of the plant, or the nutritious store that has been laid up within its cells, and converts these into the substance of which its own organs are composed. The plant acquires the organs and nutritious store thus yielded up as food to the animal, from the invulnerable air surrounding it."

"But animals are furnished with the means of locomotion and of seizure—they can approach their food, and lay hold of and swallow it; plants must wait till their food comes to them. No solid particles find access to their frames; the restless ambient air which rushes past them loaded with the carbon, the hydrogen, the oxygen, the water—every thing they need in the shape of supplies is constantly at hand to minister to their wants, not only to afford them food in due season, but in the shape and fashion in which alone it can avail them."

90. There is no more worthy or suitable employment of the human mind than to trace the evidences of design and purpose in the Creator, which are visible in many parts of the creation. Hence, to the right-minded mariner, and to him who studies the physical relations of earth, sea, and air, the atmosphere is something more than a shoreless ocean, at the bottom of which his bark is wafted or driven along. It is an envelope or covering for the dispersion of light and heat over the surface of the earth; it is a sewer into which, with every breath we draw, we cast vast quantities of dead animal matter; it is a laboratory for purification, in which that matter is recompounded, and wrought again into wholesome and healthful shapes; it is a machine (§ 87) for pumping up all the rivers from the sea, and conveying the waters for their fountains on the ocean to their sources in the mountains.

91. Upon the proper working of this machine depends the well-being of every plant and animal that inhabits the earth; therefore the management of it, or its movement, or the performance of its offices, can not be left to chance. They are, we may rely upon it, guided by laws that make all parts, functions, and movements of the machinery as obedient to order as are the planets in their orbits.

92. An examination into the economy of the universe will be sufficient to satisfy the well-balanced minds of observant men that the laws which govern the atmosphere and the laws which govern the ocean (§ 67) are laws which were put in force by the Creator when the foundations of the earth were laid, and that, therefore, they are laws of order; else, why should the Gulf Stream, for instance, be always where it is, and running from the Gulf of Mexico, and not somewhere else, and sometimes running into it? Why should there be a perpetual drought in one part of the world, and continual showers in another? Or why should the winds and sea obey the voice of rebuke?

93. To one who looks abroad to contemplate the agents of nature, as he sees them at work upon our planet, no expression uttered nor act performed by them is without meaning. By such an one, the wind and rain, the vapor and the cloud, the tide, the current, the saltness, and depth, and warmth, and color of the sea, the shade of the sky, the temperature of the air, the tint and shape of the clouds, the height of the tree on the shore, the size of its leaves, the brilliancy of its flowers—each and all may be regarded as the exponent of certain physical combinations, and therefore as the expression in which Nature chooses to announce her own doings, or, if we please, as the language in which she writes down or chooses to make known her own laws. To understand that language and to interpret aright those laws is the object of the undertaking which we now have in hand. No fact gathered in such a field as the one before us can, therefore, come amiss to those who tread the walks of inductive philosophy; for, in the hand-book of nature, every such fact is a syllable; and it is by patiently collecting fact after fact, and by joining together syllable after syllable, that we may finally seek to read aright from the great volume which the mariner at sea and the philosopher on the mountain see spread out before them.

94. Of its Circulation.—We have seen (§ 31) that there are constant currents in the ocean; we shall now see that there are also regular currents in the atmosphere.

95. From the parallel of about 30° north and south, nearly to the equator, we have, extending entirely around the earth, two zones of perpetual winds, viz., the zone of northeast trades on this side, and of southeast on that. They blow perpetually, and are

as steady and as constant as the currents of the Mississippi River —always moving in the same direction (Plate I.). As these two

PLATE I.

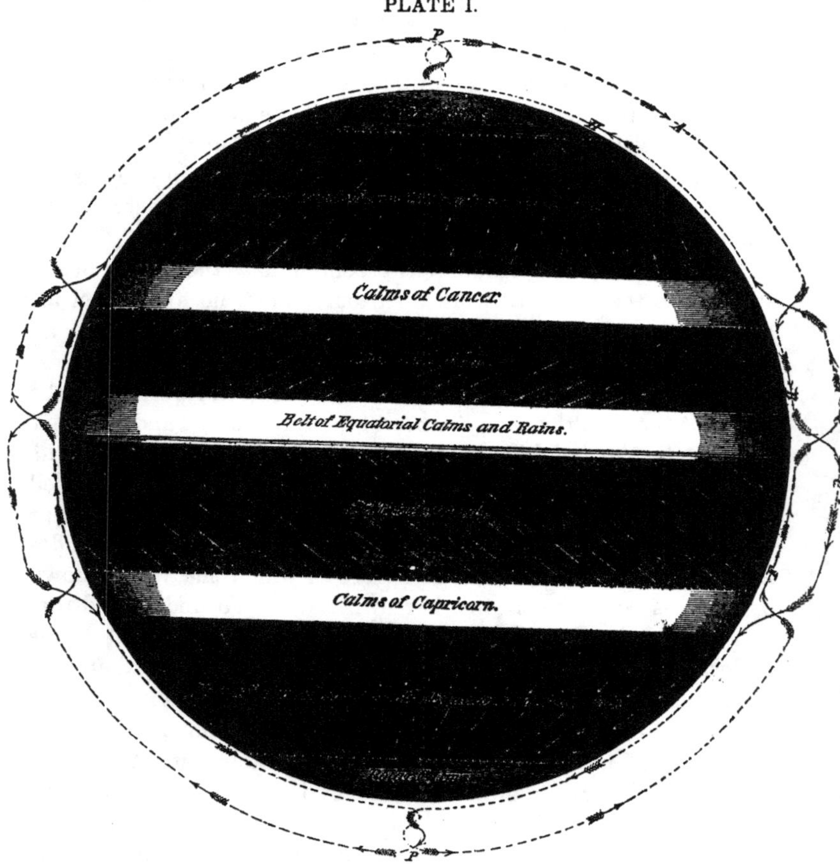

DIAGRAM OF THE WINDS.

currents of air are constantly flowing from the poles toward the equator, we are safe in assuming that the air which they keep in motion must return by some channel to the place near the poles whence it came in order to supply the trades. If this were not so, these winds would soon exhaust the polar regions of atmosphere, and pile it up about the equator, and then cease to blow for the want of air to make more wind of.

96. This return current, therefore, must be in the upper regions of the atmosphere, at least until it passes over those parallels between which the trade-winds are always blowing on the surface. The return current must also move in the direction opposite to that wind the place of which it is intended to supply. These direct and counter currents are also made to move in a sort of spiral or loxodromic curve, turning to the west as they go from the poles to the equator, and in the opposite direction as they move from the equator to the poles. This turning is caused by the rotation of the earth on its axis.

97. The earth, we know, moves from west to east. Now if we imagine a particle of atmosphere at the north pole, where it is at rest, to be put in motion in a straight line toward the equator, we can easily see how this particle of air, coming from the very axis of the pole, where it did not partake of the diurnal motion of the earth, would, in consequence of its *vis inertiæ*, find, as it travels south, the earth slipping from under it, as it were, and thus it would appear to be coming from the northeast and going toward the southwest; in other words, it would be a northeast wind.

The better to explain, let us take a common terrestrial globe for the illustration. Bring the island of Madeira, or any other place about the same parallel, under the brazen meridian; put a finger of the left hand on the place; then, moving the finger down along the meridian to the south, to represent the particle of air, turn the globe on its axis from west to east, to represent the diurnal rotation of the earth, and when the finger reaches the equator, stop. It will now be seen that the place on the globe under the finger is to the southward and westward of the place from which the finger started; in other words, the track of the finger over the surface of the globe, like the track of the particle of air upon the earth, has been from the northward and eastward.

98. On the other hand, we can perceive how a like particle of atmosphere that starts from the equator, to take the place of the other at the pole, would, as it travels north, in consequence of its *vis inertiæ*, be going toward the east faster than the earth. It would, therefore, appear to be blowing from the southwest, and going toward the northeast, and exactly in the opposite direction to the other. Writing south for north, the same takes place between the south pole and the equator.

Such is the process which is actually going on in nature; and if we take the motions of these two particles as the type of the motion of all, we shall have an illustration of the great currents in the air, the equator being near one of the nodes, and there being two systems of currents, an upper and an under, between it and each pole.

Halley, in his theory of the trade-winds, pointed out the key to the explanation so far, of the atmospherical circulation; but, were the explanation to rest here, a northeast trade-wind extending from the pole to the equator would satisfy it; and were this so, we should have, on the surface, no winds but the northeast trade-winds on this side, and none but southeast trade-winds on the other side, of the equator.

99. Let us return now to our northern particle (Plate I., p. 70), and follow it in a round from the north pole across the equator to the south pole, and back again. Setting off from the polar regions, this particle of air, for some reason which does not appear to have been very satisfactorily explained by philosophers, instead of traveling (§ 98) on the surface all the way from the pole to the equator, travels in the upper regions of the atmosphere until it gets near the parallel of 30°. Here it meets, also in the clouds, the hypothetical particle that is coming from the south, and going north to take its place.

100. About this parallel of 30° north, then, these two particles press against each other with the whole amount of their motive power, and produce a calm and an accumulation of atmosphere: this accumulation is sufficient to balance the pressure of the two winds from the north and south.

101. From under this bank of calms, which seamen call the "horse latitudes" (I have called them the calms of Cancer), two surface currents of wind are ejected; one toward the equator, as the northeast trades, the other toward the pole, as the southwest passage-winds.

These winds come out at the lower surface of the calm region, and consequently the place of the air borne away in this manner must be supplied, we may infer, by downward currents from the superincumbent air of the calm region. Like the case of a vessel of water which has two streams from opposite directions running in at the top, and two of equal capacity discharging in opposite directions at the bottom, the motion of the water would be downward, so is the motion of the air in this calm zone.

102. The barometer, in this calm region, is said to stand higher than it does either to the north or to the south of it; and this is another proof as to the banking up here of the atmosphere, and pressure from its downward motion.

103. Following our imaginary particle of air from the north across this calm belt, we now feel it moving on the surface of the earth as the northeast trade-wind; and as such it continues, till it arrives near the equator, where it meets a like hypothetical particle, which, starting from the south at the same time the other started from the north pole, has blown as the southeast trade-wind.

104. Here, at this equatorial place of meeting, there is another conflict of winds and another calm region, for a northeast and southeast wind can not blow at the same time in the same place. The two particles have been put in motion by the same power; they meet with equal force; and, therefore, at their place of meeting, are stopped in their course. Here, therefore, there is a calm belt.

105. Warmed now by the heat of the sun, and pressed on each side by the whole force of the northeast and southeast trades, these two hypothetical particles, taken as the type of the whole, cease to move onward and ascend. This operation is the reverse of that which took place at the meeting (§ 100) near the parallel of 30°.

106. This imaginary particle then, having ascended to the upper regions of the atmosphere again, travels there counter to the southeast trades, until it meets, near the calm belt of Capricorn, another particle from the south pole; here there is a descent as before (§ 101); it then (§ 98) flows on toward the south pole as a surface wind from the northwest.

Entering the polar regions obliquely, it is pressed upon by similar particles flowing in oblique currents across every meridian; and here again is a calm place or node; for, as our imaginary particle approaches the parallels near the polar calms more and more obliquely, it, with all the rest, is whirled about the pole in a continued circular gale; finally, reaching the vortex or the calm place, it is carried upward to the regions of atmosphere above, whence it commences again its circuit to the north as an upper current, as far as the calm belt of Capricorn; here it encounters (§ 106) its fellow from the north (§ 98); they stop, descend, and flow out as surface currents (§ 101), the one with which the imagination is traveling, to the equatorial calms as the southeast trade-wind; here (§ 104) it ascends, traveling thence to the calm belt of Cancer as an upper current counter to the northeast trades. Here (§ 100 and 99) it ceases to be an upper current, but, descending (§ 101), travels on with the southwest passage-winds toward the pole.

Now the course we have imagined an atom of air to take is this (Plate I.): an ascent at P, at the north pole; an efflux thence as an upper current (§ 99) until it meets G (also an upper current) over the calms of Cancer. Here (§ 100) there is supposed to be a descent, as shown by the arrows along the wavy lines which envelop the circle. This upper current from the pole (§ 97) now becomes the northeast trade-wind B (§ 103), on the surface, until it meets the southeast trades in the equatorial calms, when it ascends and travels as C with the upper current to the calms of Capricorn, then as D with the prevailing northwest surface current to the south pole, thence up with the arrow P, and around with the hands of a watch, and back, as indicated by the arrows along E, F, G, and H.

107. The Bible frequently makes allusions to the laws of nature, their operation and effects. But such allusions are often so wrapped in the folds of the peculiar and graceful drapery with which its language is occasionally clothed, that the meaning, though peeping out from its thin covering all the while, yet lies in some sense concealed, until the lights and revelations of science are thrown upon it; then it bursts out and strikes us with the more force and beauty.

As our knowledge of Nature and her laws has increased, so has our understanding of many passages in the Bible been improved. The Bible called the earth "the round world;" yet for ages it was the most damnable heresy for Christian men to say the world is round; and, finally, sailors circumnavigated the globe, proved the Bible to be right, and saved Christian men of science from the stake.

"Canst thou tell the sweet influences of the Pleiades?"

Astronomers of the present day, if they have not answered this question, have thrown so much light upon it as to show that, if ever it be answered by man, he must consult the science of astronomy. It has been recently all but proved, that the earth and sun, with their splendid retinue of comets, satellites, and planets, are all in motion around some point or centre of attraction inconceivably remote, and that that point is in the direction of the star Alcyon, one of the Pleiades! Who but the astronomer, then, could tell their "sweet influences?"

And as for the general system of atmospherical circulation which I have been so long endeavoring to describe, the Bible tells it all in a single sentence: "The wind goeth toward the south, and turneth about unto the north; it whirleth about continually, and the wind returneth again according to his circuits."—Eccl., i., 6.

108. Of course, as the surface winds H and D (Plate I.) approach the poles, there must be a sloughing off, if I may be allowed the expression, of air from the surface winds, in consequence of their approaching the poles. For as they near the poles, the parallels become smaller and smaller, and the surface current must either extend much higher up, and blow with greater rapidity as it approaches the poles, or else a part of it must be sloughed off above, and so turn back before reaching the poles. The latter is probably the case.

Our investigations show that the southeast trade-wind region is much larger than the northeast. I speak now of its extent over the Atlantic Ocean only; that the southeast trades are the fresher, and that they often push themselves up to 10° or 15° of north latitude; whereas the northeast trade-wind seldom gets south of the equator.

The peculiar clouds of the trade-winds are formed between the upper and lower currents of air. They are probably formed of vapor condensed from the upper current, and evaporated as it descends by the lower and dry current from the poles. It is the same phenomenon up there which is so often observed here below; when a cool and dry current of air meets a warm and wet one, an evolution of vapor or fog ensues.

We now see the general course of the "wind in his circuits," as we see the general course of the water in a river. There are many abrading surfaces, irregularities, &c., which produce a thousand eddies in the main stream; yet, nevertheless, the general direction of the whole is not disturbed nor affected by those counter currents; so with the atmosphere and the variable winds which we find here in this latitude.

Have I not, therefore, very good grounds for the opinion (§ 92) that the "wind in his circuits," though apparently to us never so wayward, is as obedient to law and as subservient to order as were the morning stars when they "sang together?"

109. There are at least two forces concerned in driving the wind through its circuits. We have seen (§ 97 and § 98) whence that force is derived which gives easting to the winds as they approach the equator, and westing as they approach the poles, and allusion, without explanation, has been made (§ 105) to the source whence they derive their northing and their southing. The trade-winds are caused, it is said, by the inter-tropical heat of the sun, which, expanding the air, causes it to rise up near the equator; it then flows off in the upper currents north and south, and there is a rush of air at the surface both from the north and the south to restore the equilibrium—hence the trade-winds. But to the north side of the trade-wind belt in the northern, and on the south side in the southern hemisphere, the prevailing direction of the winds is not toward the source of heat about the equator, but exactly in the opposite direction. In the extra-tropical region of each hemisphere the prevailing winds blow from the equator toward the poles. It therefore at first appears paradoxical to say that heat makes the easterly winds of the torrid zone blow toward the equator, and the westerly winds of the temperate zones to blow toward the poles. Let us illustrate:

110. The *primum mobile* of the extra-tropical winds toward the equator is, as just intimated, generally ascribed to heat, and in this wise, viz.: Suppose, for the moment, the earth to have no diurnal rotation; that it is at rest; that the rays of the sun have been cut off from it; that the atmosphere has assumed a mean uniformity of temperature, the thermometer at the equator and the thermometer at the poles giving the same reading; that the winds are still, and that the whole aerial ocean is in equilibrium and at rest. Now imagine the screen which is supposed to have shut off the influence of the sun to be removed, and the whole atmosphere to assume the various temperatures in the various parts

of the world that it actually has at this moment, what would take place, supposing the uniform temperature to be a mean between that at the equator and that at the poles? Why, this would take place: a swelling up of the atmosphere about the equator by the expansive force of inter-tropical heat, and a contraction of it about the poles in consequence of the cold. These two forces, considering them under their most obvious effects, would disturb the supposed atmospherical equilibrium by altering the level of the great aerial ocean; the expansive force of heat elevating it about the equator, and the contracting powers of cold depressing it about the poles. And forthwith two systems of winds would commence to blow, viz., one in the upper regions from the equator toward the poles, and as this warm and expanded air should flow toward either pole, seeking its level, a wind would blow on the surface from either pole to restore the air to the equator which the upper current had carried off.

These two winds would blow due north and south; the effects of heat at the equator, and cold at the poles, would cause them so to do. Now suppose the earth to commence its diurnal rotation; then, instead of having these winds north and south winds, they will, for reasons already explained (§ 97), approach the equator on both sides with *easting* in them, and each pole with westing.

111. The circumference of the earth measured on the parallel of 60° is only half what it is when measured on the equator. Therefore, supposing velocity to be the same, only half the volume of atmosphere (§ 109) that sets off from the equator as an upper current toward the poles can cross the parallel of 60° north or south. The other moiety has been gradually drawn in and carried back (§ 108) by the current which is moving in the opposite direction.

Such, and such only, would be the extent of the power of the sun to create a polar and equatorial flow of air, were its power confined simply to a change of level. But the atmosphere has been invested with another property which increases its mobility, and gives the heat of the sun still more power to put it in motion, and it is this: as heat changes the atmospherical level, it changes also the specific gravity of the air acted upon. If, therefore, the level of the great aerial ocean were undisturbed by the sun's rays, and if the air were adapted to a change of specific gravity alone, without any change in volume, this quality would also be the source of at least two systems of currents in the air, viz., an upper and a lower. The two agents combined, viz., that which changes level or volume, and that which changes specific gravity, give us the general currents under consideration. Hence we say that the *primum mobile* of the air is derived from change of specific gravity induced by the freezing temperature of the polar regions, as well as from change of specific gravity due the expanding force of the sun's rays within the tropics.

112. Therefore, fairly to appreciate the extent of the influence due the heat of the sun in causing the winds, it should be recollected that we may with as much reason ascribe to the intertropical heat of the sun the northwest winds, which are the prevailing winds of the extra-tropical regions of the southern hemisphere, or the southwest winds, which are the prevailing winds of the extra-tropical regions of the northern hemisphere, as we may the trade-winds, which blow in the opposite directions. Paradoxical, therefore, as it seems for us to say that the heat of the sun causes the winds between the parallels of 25° or 30° north and south to blow toward the equator, and that it also causes the prevailing winds on the polar sides of these same parallels to blow toward the poles, yet the paradox ceases when we come to recollect that by the process of equatorial heating and polar cooling which is going on in the atmosphere, the specific gravity of the air is changed as well as its level. Nevertheless, as Halley said, in his paper read before the Royal Society in London in 1686, and as we also have said (§ 99), "it is likewise very hard to conceive why the limits of the trade-wind should be fixed about the parallel of latitude 30° all around the globe, and that they should so seldom exceed or fall short of those bounds."

113. Operated upon by the equilibrating tendency of the atmosphere and by diurnal rotation, the wind approaches the north pole, for example, by a series of spirals from the southwest. If we draw a circle about this pole on a common terrestrial globe, and intersect it by spirals to represent the direction of the wind, we shall see that the wind enters all parts of this circle from the southwest, and, consequently, that a whirl ought to be created thereby, in which the ascending column of air revolves from right to left, or *against* the hands of a watch. At the south pole the

winds come from the northwest (§ 106), and consequently there they revolve about it *with* the hands of a watch.

That this should be so will be obvious to any one who will look at the arrows on the polar sides of the calms of Cancer and Capricorn (Plate I., p. 70). These arrows are intended to represent the prevailing direction of the wind at the surface of the earth on the polar side of these calms.

114. It is a singular coincidence between these two facts thus deduced, and other facts which have been observed, and which have been set forth by Redfield, Reid, Piddington, and others, viz., that all rotary storms in the northern hemisphere revolve as do the whirlwinds about the north pole, viz., from right to left, and that all circular gales in the southern hemisphere revolve in the opposite direction, as does the whirl about the south pole.

How can there be any connection between the rotary motion of the wind about the pole, and the rotary motion of it in a gale caused here by local agents?

That there is probably such a connection has been suggested by other facts and circumstances, and perhaps I shall be enabled to make myself clearer when we come to treat of these facts and circumstances, and to inquire farther, as at § 172, into the relations between magnetism and the circulation of the atmosphere; for, although the theory of heat satisfies many conditions of the problem, and though heat, doubtless, is one of the chief agents in keeping up the circulation of the atmosphere, yet it can be made to appear that it is not the *sole* agent.

115. Some of its Meteorological Agencies.—So far, we see how the atmosphere moves; but the atmosphere, like every other department in the economy of nature, has its offices to perform, and they are many. I have already alluded to some of them; but I only propose, at this time, to consider some of the meteorological agencies at sea, which, in the grand design of creation, have probably been assigned to this wonderful machine.

To distribute moisture over the surface of the earth, and to temper the climate of different latitudes, it would seem, are two great offices assigned by their Creator to the ocean and the air.

When the northeast and southeast trades meet and produce the equatorial calms (§ 104), the air, by this time, is heavily laden with moisture, for in each hemisphere it has traveled obliquely over a large space of the ocean. It has no room for escape but in the upward direction (§ 105). It expands as it ascends, and becomes cooler; a portion of its vapor is thus condensed, and comes down in the shape of rain. Therefore it is that, under these calms, we have a region of constant precipitation. Old sailors tell us of such dead calms of long continuance here, of such heavy and constant rains, that they have scooped up fresh water from the surface of the sea.

116. The conditions to which this air is exposed here under the equator are probably not such as to cause it to precipitate all the moisture that it has taken up in its long sweep across the waters. Let us see what becomes of the rest; for Nature, in her economy, permits nothing to be taken away from the earth which is not to be restored to it again in some form, and at some time or other.

Consider the great rivers—the Amazon and the Mississippi, for example. We see them day after day, and year after year, discharging an immense volume of water into the ocean.

"All the rivers run into the sea, yet the sea is not full."—Ecc., i., 7. Where do the waters so discharged go, and where do they come from? They come from their sources, you will say. But whence are their sources supplied? for, unless what the fountain sends forth be returned to it again, it will fail and be dry.

117. We see simply, in the waters that are discharged by these rivers, the amount by which the precipitation exceeds the evaporation throughout the whole extent of valley drained by them; and by precipitation I mean the total amount of water that falls from, or is deposited by the atmosphere, whether as dew, rain, hail, or snow.

The springs of these rivers (§ 87) are supplied from the rains of heaven, and these rains are formed of vapors which are taken up from the sea, that "it be not full," and carried up to the mountains through the air.

"Note the place whence the rivers come, thither they return again."

118. Behold now the waters of the Amazon, of the Mississippi, the St. Lawrence, and all the great rivers of America, Europe, and Asia, lifted up by the atmosphere, and flowing in invisible streams back through the air to their sources among the hills (§ 87), and that through channels so regular, certain, and well de-

fined, that the quantity thus conveyed one year with the other is nearly the same: for that is the quantity which we see running down to the ocean through these rivers; and the quantity discharged annually by each river is, as far as we can judge, nearly constant.

We now begin to conceive what a powerful machine the atmosphere must be; and, though it is apparently so capricious and wayward in its movements, here is evidence of order and arrangement which we must admit, and proof which we can not deny, that it performs this mighty office with regularity and certainty, and is therefore as obedient to law as is the steam-engine to the will of its builder. (See Appendix A.)

119. It, too, is an engine. The South Seas themselves, in all their vast inter-tropical extent, are the boiler for it, and the northern hemisphere is its condenser.

120. *Where does the vapor that makes the rains which feed the rivers of the northern hemisphere come from?*

The proportion between the land and water in the northern hemisphere is very different from the proportion between them in the southern. In the northern hemisphere, the land and water are nearly equally divided. In the southern, there is several times more water than land. All the great rivers in the world are in the northern hemisphere, where there is less ocean to supply them. Whence, then, are their sources replenished? Those of the Amazon are supplied with rains from the equatorial calms and trade-winds of the Atlantic. That river runs east, its branches come from the north and south; it is always the rainy season on one side or the other of it; consequently, it is a river without periodic stages of a very marked character. It is always near its high-water mark. For one half of the year its northern tributaries are flooded, and its southern for the other half. It discharges under the line, and as its tributaries come from both hemispheres, it can not be said to belong exclusively to either. It is supplied with water from the Atlantic Ocean. Taking the Amazon, therefore, out of the count, the Rio de la Plata is the only great river of the southern hemisphere.

There is no large river in New Holland. The South Sea Islands give rise to none, nor is there one in South Africa that we know of.

121. The great rivers of North America and North Africa, and all the rivers of Europe and Asia, lie wholly within the northern hemisphere. How is it, then, considering that the evaporating surface lies mainly in the southern hemisphere—how is it, I say, that we should have the evaporation to take place in one hemisphere and the condensation in the other? The total amount of rain which falls in the northern hemisphere is much greater, meteorologists tell us, than that which falls in the southern. The annual amount of rain in the north temperate zone is half as much again as that of the south temperate.

122. How is it, then, that this vapor gets, as stated § 119, from the southern into the northern hemisphere, and comes with such regularity that our rivers never go dry and our springs fail not? It is because of the beautiful operations and the exquisite *compensation* of this grand machine, the atmosphere. It is exquisitely and wonderfully counterpoised. Late in the autumn of the north, throughout its winter, and in early spring, the sun is pouring his rays with the greatest intensity down upon the seas of the southern hemisphere, and this powerful engine which we are contemplating is pumping up the water there (§ 119) for our rivers with the greatest activity. At this time, the mean temperature of the entire southern hemisphere is said to be about 10° higher than the northern.

123. The heat which this heavy evaporation absorbs becomes latent, and, with the moisture, is carried through the upper regions of the atmosphere until it reaches our climates. Here the vapor is formed into clouds, condensed, and precipitated. The heat which held this water in the state of vapor is set free, it becomes sensible heat, and it is that which contributes so much to temper our winter climate. It clouds up in winter, turns warm, and we say we are going to have falling weather. That is because the process of condensation has already commenced, though no rain or snow may have fallen: thus we feel this southern heat, that has been collected from the rays of the sun by the sea, been bottled away by the winds in the clouds of a southern summer, and set free in the process of condensation in our northern winter.

124. If the Plate at page 70 fairly represent the course of the winds, the southeast trade-winds would enter the northern hemisphere, and, as an upper current, bear into it all their moisture,

except that which is precipitated in the region of equatorial calms.

The South Seas, then, according to § 119, should supply mainly the water for this engine, while the northern hemisphere condenses it; we should, therefore, have more rain in the northern hemisphere. The rivers tell us that we have—at least on the land: for the great water-courses of the globe, and half the fresh water in the world, are found on our side of the equator. This fact alone is strongly corroborative of this hypothesis.

The rain gauge tells us also the same story. The yearly average of rain in the north temperate zone is, according to Johnston, thirty-seven inches. He gives but twenty-six in the south temperate.

125. Moisture is never extracted from the air by subjecting it from a low to a higher temperature, but the reverse. Thus, all the air which comes loaded with moisture from the other hemisphere, and is borne into this with the southeast trade-winds, travels in the upper regions of the atmosphere (§ 100) until it reaches the calms of Cancer; here it becomes the surface wind that prevails from the southward and westward. As it goes north it grows cooler, and the process of condensation commences.

We may now liken it to the wet sponge, and the decrease of temperature to the hand that squeezes that sponge. Finally reaching the cold latitudes, all the moisture that a dew-point of zero, and even far below, can extract, is wrung from it; and this air then commences "to return according to his circuits" as dry atmosphere. And here we can quote Scripture again: "The north wind driveth away rain." This is a meteorological fact of high authority and great importance in the study of the circulation of the atmosphere.

126. By reasoning in this manner, we are led to the conclusion that our rivers are supplied with their waters principally from the trade-wind regions—the extra-tropical northern rivers from the southern trades, and the extra-tropioal southern rivers from the northern trade-winds, for the trade-winds are the evaporating winds.

Taking for our guide such faint glimmerings of light as we can catch from these facts, and supposing these views to be correct, then the saltest portion of the sea should be in the trade-wind regions, where the water for all the rivers is evaporated ; and there the saltest portions are found.

127. Dr. Ruschenberger, of the Navy, on his late voyage to India, was kind enough to conduct a series of observations on the specific gravity of sea water. In about the parallel of 17° north and south—midway of the trade-wind regions—he found the heaviest water. Though so warm, the water there was heavier than the cold water to the south of the Cape of Good Hope. Lieutenant D. D. Porter, in the steam-ship Golden Age, found the heaviest water about the parallels of 20° north and 17° south.

In summing up the evidence in favor of this view of the general system of atmospherical circulation, it remains to be shown how it is, if the view be correct, there should be smaller rivers and less rain in the southern hemisphere.

128. *The Explanation.*—The winds that are to blow as the northeast trade-winds, returning from the polar regions, where the moisture (§ 125) has been compressed out of them, remain, as we have seen, dry winds until they cross the calm zone of Cancer, and are felt on the surface as the northeast trades. About two thirds of them only can then blow over the ocean; the rest blow over the land, over Asia, Africa, and North America, where there is but comparatively a small portion of evaporating surface exposed to their action.

The zone of the northeast trades extends, on an average, from about 29° north to 7° north. Now, if we examine the globe, to see how much of this zone is land and how much water, we shall find, commencing with China and coming over Asia, the broad part of Africa, and so on, across the continent of America to the Pacific, land enough to fill up, as nearly as may be, just one third of it. This land, if thrown into one body between these parallels, would make a belt equal to 120° of longitude by 22° of latitude.

According to the hypothesis, illustrated by Plate I., p. 70, as to the circulation of the atmosphere, it is these northeast trade-winds that take up and carry over, after they rise up in the belt of equatorial calms, the vapors which make the rains that feed the rivers in the extra-tropical regions of the southern hemisphere.

Upon this supposition, then, two thirds only of the northeast trade-winds are fully charged with moisture, and only two thirds of the amount of rain that falls in the northern hemisphere should fall in the southern, and this is just about the proportion (§ 124) that observation gives.

In like manner, the southeast trade-winds take up the vapors which make our rivers, and as they prevail to a much greater extent at sea, and have exposed to their action about three times as much ocean as the northeast trade-winds have, we might expect, according to this hypothesis, more rains in the northern—and, consequently, more and larger rivers—than in the southern hemisphere. A glance at Plate VIII. will show how very much larger that part of the ocean over which the southeast trades prevail is than that where the northeast trade-winds blow.

This estimate as to the quantity of rain in the two hemispheres is one which is not capable of verification by any more than the rudest approximations; for the greater extent of southeast trades on one side, and of high mountains on the other, must each of necessity, and independent of other agents, have their effects. Nevertheless, this estimate gives as close an approximation as we can make out from any other data.

129. *The rainy seasons, how caused.*—The calm and trade-wind regions or belts move up and down the earth, annually, in latitude nearly a thousand miles. In July and August the zone of equatorial calms is found between 7° north and 12° north; sometimes higher; in March and April, between latitude 5° south and 2° north.

With this fact and these points of view before us, it is easy to perceive why it is that we have a rainy season in Oregon, a rainy and dry season in California, another at Panama, two at Bogotá, none in Peru, and one in Chili.

In Oregon it rains every month, but more in the winter months. The winter there is the summer of the southern hemisphere, when this steam-engine is working with the greatest pressure. The vapor that is taken up by the southeast trades is borne along over the region of northeast trades to latitude 35° or 40° north (§ 124), where it descends and appears on the surface with the southwest winds of those latitudes. Driving upon the highlands of the continent, this vapor is condensed and precipitated, during this part of the year, almost in constant showers.

130. In the winter, the calm belt of Cancer approaches the equator. This whole system of zones, viz., of trades, calms, and westerly winds, follows the sun; and they of our hemisphere are

nearer the equator in the winter and spring months than at any other season.

The southwest winds commence at this season to prevail as far down as the lower part of California. In winter and spring, the land in California is cooler than the sea air, and is quite cold enough to extract moisture from it. But in summer and autumn the land is the warmer, and can not condense the vapors of water held by the air. So the same cause which made it rain in Oregon now makes it rain in California. As the sun returns to the north, he brings the calm belt of Cancer and the northeast trades along with him; and now, at places where, six months before, the southwest winds were the prevailing winds, the northeast trades are found to blow. This is the case in the latitude of California. The prevailing winds, then, instead of going from a warmer to a cooler climate, as before, are going the opposite way. Consequently, they can not, if they have the moisture in them to make rains of, precipitate it under such circumstances.

131. Panama is in the region of equatorial calms. This belt of calms travels during the year, back and forth, over about 17° of latitude, coming farther north in the summer, where it tarries for several months, and then returns so as to reach its extreme southern latitude some time in March or April. Where these calms are it is always raining, and the chart shows that they hang over the latitude of Panama from June to November; consequently, from June to November is the rainy season at Panama. The rest of the year that place is in the region of the northeast trades, which, before they arrive there, have to cross the mountains of the isthmus, on the cool tops of which they deposit their moisture, and leave Panama rainless and pleasant until the sun returns north with the belt of equatorial calms after him. They then push the belt of northeast trades farther to the north, occupy a part of the winter zone, and refresh that part of the earth with summer rains. This belt of calms moves over more than double of its breadth, and nearly the entire motion from south to north is accomplished generally in two months, May and June.

132. Take the parallel of 4° north as an illustration: during these two months the entire belt of calms crosses this parallel, and then leaves it in the region of the southeast trades. During these two months it was pouring down rain on that parallel. After the

calm belt passes it the rains cease, and the people in that latitude have no more wet weather till the fall, when the belt of calms recrosses this parallel on its way to the south. By examining the "Trade-wind Chart," it may be seen what the latitudes are that have two rainy seasons, and that Bogotá is within the bi-rainy latitudes.

133. *The Rainless Regions.*—The coast of Peru is within the region of perpetual southeast trade-winds. Though the Peruvian shores are on the verge of the great South Sea boiler, yet it never rains there. The reason is plain.

The southeast trade-winds in the Atlantic Ocean first strike the water on the coast of Africa. Traveling to the northwest, they blow obliquely across the ocean until they reach the coast of Brazil. By this time they are heavily laden with vapor, which they continue to bear along across the continent, depositing it as they go, and supplying with it the sources of the Rio de la Plata and the southern tributaries of the Amazon.

Finally they reach the snow-capped Andes, and here is wrung from them the last particle of moisture that that very low temperature can extract.

Reaching the summit of that range, they now tumble down as cool and dry winds on the Pacific slopes beyond. Meeting with no evaporating surface, and with no temperature *colder* than that to which they were subjected on the mountain-tops, they reach the ocean before they become charged with fresh vapor, and before, therefore, they have any which the Peruvian climate can extract. Thus we see how the top of the Andes becomes the reservoir from which are supplied the rivers of Chili and Peru.

134. The other rainless or almost rainless regions are the western coasts of Mexico, the deserts of Africa, Asia, North America, and Australia. Now study the geographical features of the country surrounding those regions; see how the mountain ranges run; then turn to Plate VIII. to see how the winds blow, and where the sources are (§ 87) which supply them with vapors. This plate shows the prevailing direction of the wind only at sea; but knowing it there, we may infer what it is on the land. Supposing it to prevail on the land as it generally does in corresponding latitudes at sea, then the Plate will suggest readily enough how the winds that blow over these deserts came to be robbed of their moisture,

or, rather, to have so much of it taken from them as to reduce their dew-point below the Desert temperature; for *the air can never deposit its moisture when its temperature is higher than its dew-point.*

135. We have a rainless region about the Red Sea, because the Red Sea, for the most part, lies within the northeast trade-wind region, and these winds, when they reach that region, are dry winds, for they have as yet, in their course, crossed no wide sheets of water from which they could take up a supply of vapor.

136. Most of New Holland lies within the southeast trade-wind region; so does most of inter-tropical South America. But inter-tropical South America is the land of showers. The largest rivers and most copiously watered country in the world are to be found there, whereas almost exactly the reverse is the case in Australia. Whence this difference? Examine the direction of the winds with regard to the shore-line of these two regions, and the explanation will at once be suggested. In Australia—east coast—the shore-line is stretched out in the direction of the trades; in South America—east coast—it is perpendicular to their direction. In Australia, they fringe this shore only with their vapor, and so stint that thirsty land with showers that the trees can not afford to spread their leaves out to the sun, for it evaporates all the moisture from them; their instincts, therefore, teach them to turn their edges to his rays. In America, they blow perpendicularly upon the shore, penetrating the very heart of the country with their moisture. Here the leaves—as the plantain, &c.—turn their broad sides up to the sun, and court his rays.

137. *Why there is more rain on one side of a mountain than on the other.*

We may now, from what has been said, see why the Andes and all other mountains which run north and south have a dry and a rainy side, and how the prevailing winds of the latitude determine which is the rainy and which the dry side.

Thus, let us take the southern coast of Chili for illustration. In our summer time, when the sun comes north, and drags after him his belts of perpetual winds and calms, that coast is left within the regions of the northwest winds—the winds that are counter to the southeast trades—which, cooled by the winter temperature of the highlands of Chili, deposit their moisture copiously. During the rest of the year, the most of Chili is in the region of the southeast trades, and the same causes which operate in California to prevent rain there, operate in Chili; only the dry season in one place is the rainy season of the other.

Hence we see that the weather side of all such mountains as the Andes is the wet side, and the lee side the dry.

138. The same phenomenon, from a like cause, is repeated in inter-tropical India, only in that country each side of the mountain is made alternately the wet and the dry side by a change in the prevailing direction of the wind. Plate VIII. shows India to be in one of the monsoon regions: it is the most famous of them all. From October to April the northeast trades prevail. They evaporate from the Bay of Bengal water enough to feed with rains, during this season, the western shores of this bay and the Ghauts range of mountains. This range holds the relation to these winds that the Andes of Peru (§ 133) hold to the southeast trades; it first cools and then relieves them of their moisture, and they tumble down on the western slopes of the Ghauts, Peruvian-like (§ 137), cool, rainless, and dry; wherefore that narrow strip of country between the Ghauts and the Arabian Sea would, like that in Peru between the Andes and the Pacific, remain without rain forever, were it not for other agents which are at work about India and not about Peru. The work of the agents to which I allude is felt in the monsoons, and these prevail in India and not in Peru.

139. After the northeast trades have blown out their season, which in India ends in April (§ 138), the great arid plains of Central Asia, of Tartary, Thibet, and Mongolia, become heated up, react upon these northeast trades, turn them back, and convert them, during the summer and early autumn, into southwest monsoons. These then come from the Indian Ocean and Sea of Arabia loaded with moisture, and striking with it perpendicularly upon the Ghauts, precipitate upon that narrow strip of land between this range and the Arabian Sea an amount of water that is truly astonishing. Here, then, are not only the conditions for causing more rain, now on the west, now on the east side of this mountain range, but the conditions also for the most copious precipitation. Accordingly, when we come to consult rain gauges, and to ask meteorological observers in India about the fall of rain, they tell us that on the western slopes of the Ghauts it some-

times reaches the enormous depth of twelve or fifteen inches in one day.*

140. These winds then continue their course to the Himalaya range as dry winds. In crossing this range, they are subjected to a lower temperature than that to which they were exposed in crossing the Ghauts. Here they drop more of their moisture in the shape of snow and rain, and then pass over into the thirsty lands beyond with scarcely enough vapor in them to make even a cloud. Thence they ascend into the upper air, there to become counter-currents in the general system of atmospherical circulation. By studying Plate VIII., where the rainless regions and inland basins, as well as the course of the prevailing winds, are shown, these facts will become obvious.

141. *The Regions of Greatest Precipitation.*—We shall now be enabled to determine, if the views which I have been endeavoring to present be correct, what parts of the earth are subject to the greatest fall of rain. They should be on the slopes of those mountains which the trade-winds first strike, after having blown across the greatest tract of ocean. The more abrupt the elevation, and the shorter the distance between the mountain top and the ocean, the greater the amount of precipitation.

If, therefore, we commence at the parallel of about 30° north in the Pacific, where the northeast trade-winds first strike that ocean, and trace them through their circuits till they first strike high mountains, we ought to find such a place of heavy rains.

Commencing at this parallel of 30°, therefore, in the North Pacific, and tracing thence the course of the northeast trade-winds, we shall find that they blow thence, and reach the region of equatorial calms near the Caroline Islands. Here they rise up; but, instead of pursuing the same course in the upper stratum of winds through the southern hemisphere, they, in consequence of the rotation of the earth (§ 98), are made to take a southeast course. They keep in this upper stratum until they reach the calms of Capricorn, between the parallels of 30° and 40°; after which they become the prevailing northwest winds of the southern hemisphere, which correspond to the southwest of the northern. Continuing on to the southeast, they are now the surface winds; they are going from warmer to cooler latitudes; they become as the

* Keith Johnston.

wet sponge (§ 125), and are abruptly intercepted by the Andes of Patagonia, whose cold summit compresses them, and with its low dew-point squeezes the water out of them. Captain King found the astonishing fall of water here of nearly thirteen feet (one hundred and fifty-one inches) in forty-one days; and Mr. Darwin reports that the sea water along this part of the South American coast is sometimes quite fresh, from the vast quantity of rain that falls.

142. We ought to expect a corresponding rainy region to be found to the north of Oregon; but there the mountains are not so high, the obstruction to the southwest winds is not so abrupt, the highlands are farther from the coast, and the air which these winds carry in their circulation to that part of the coast, though it be as heavily charged with moisture as at Patagonia, has a greater extent of country over which to deposit its rain, and consequently the fall to the square inch will not be as great.*

143. In like manner, we should be enabled to say in what part of the world the most equable climates are to be found. They are to be found in the equatorial calms, where the northeast and southeast trades meet fresh from the ocean, and keep the temperature uniform under a canopy of perpetual clouds.

144. *Amount of Evaporation.*—The mean annual fall of rain on the entire surface of the earth is estimated at about five feet.

145. To evaporate water enough annually from the ocean to cover the earth, on the average, five feet deep with rain; to transport it from one zone to another; and to precipitate it in the right places, at suitable times, and in the proportions due, is one of the offices of the grand atmospherical machine. This water is evaporated principally from the torrid zone. Supposing it all to come thence, we shall have, encircling the earth, a belt of ocean three thousand miles in breadth, from which this atmosphere evaporates a layer of water annually sixteen feet in depth. And to hoist up as high as the clouds, and lower down again all the water in a lake sixteen feet deep, and three thousand miles broad, and

* I have since, through the kindness of A. Holbrook, Esq., United States Attorney for Oregon, received the *Oregon Spectator* of February 13, 1851, containing the Rev. G. H. Atkinson's Meteorological Journal, kept in Oregon City during the month of January, 1851. The quantity of rain and snow for that month is 13.63 inches, or about one third the average quantity that falls at Washington during the year.

twenty-four thousand long, is the yearly business of this invisible machinery. What a powerful engine is the atmosphere! and how nicely adjusted must be all the cogs, and wheels, and springs, and pinions of this exquisite piece of machinery, that it never wears out nor breaks down, nor fails to do its work at the right time and in the right way!

146. In his annual report to the Society (*Transactions of the Bombay Geographical Society* from May, 1849, to August, 1850, vol. ix.), Dr. Buist, the secretary, states, on the authority of Mr. Laidly, the evaporation at Calcutta to be "about fifteen feet annually; that between the Cape and Calcutta it averages, in October and November, nearly three fourths of an inch daily; between 10° and 20° in the Bay of Bengal, it was found to exceed an inch daily. Supposing this to be double the average throughout the year, we should," continues the doctor, "have eighteen feet of evaporation annually."

147. If, in considering the direct observations upon the daily rate of evaporation in India, it be remembered that the seasons there are divided into wet and dry; that in the dry season, evaporation in the Indian Ocean, because of its high temperature, and also of the high temperature and dry state of the wind, probably goes on as rapidly as it does any where else in the world; if, moreover, we remember that the regular trade-wind regions proper are, for the most part, rainless regions at sea; that evaporation is going on from them all the year round, we shall have reason to consider the estimate of sixteen feet annually for the trade-wind surface of the ocean not too high.

148. We see the light beginning to break upon us, for we now begin to perceive why it is that the proportions between the land and water were made as we find them in nature. If there had been more water and less land, we should have had more rain, and *vice versa;* and then climates would have been different from what they now are, and the inhabitants, animal or vegetable, would not have been as they are. And as they are, that wise Being who, in his kind providence, so watches over and regards the things of this world that he takes notice of the sparrow's fall, and numbers the very hairs of our head, doubtless designed them to be.

The mind is delighted, and the imagination charmed, by contemplating the physical arrangements of the earth from such points of view as this is which we now have before us; from it the sea, and the air, and the land, appear each as a part of that grand machinery upon which the well-being of all the inhabitants of earth, sea, and air depends; and which, in the beautiful adaptations that we are pointing out, affords new and striking evidence that they all have their origin in ONE omniscient idea, just as the different parts of a watch may be considered to have been constructed and arranged according to *one* human design.

149. In some parts of the earth the precipitation is greater than the evaporation; thus the amount of water borne down by every river that runs into the sea may be considered as the excess of the precipitation over the evaporation that takes place in the valley drained by that river.

150. This excess comes from the sea; the winds convey it to the interior; and the forces of gravity, dashing it along in mountain torrents or gentle streams, hurry it back to the sea again.

151. In other parts of the earth the evaporation and precipitation are exactly equal, as in those inland basins such as that in which the city of Mexico, Lake Titicaca, the Caspian Sea, &c., &c., are situated, which basins have no ocean drainage.

152. If more rain fell in the valley of the Caspian Sea than is evaporated from it, that sea would finally get full and overflow the whole of that great basin. If less fell than is evaporated from it again, then that sea, in the course of time, would dry up, and plants and animals there would all perish for the want of water.

153. In the sheets of water which we find distributed over that and every other inhabitable inland basin, we see reservoirs or evaporating surfaces just sufficient for the supply of that degree of moisture which is best adapted to the well-being of the plants and animals that people such basins.

In other parts of the earth still, we find places, as the Desert of Sahara, in which neither evaporation nor precipitation takes place, and in which we find neither plant nor animal.

154. ADAPTATIONS.—In contemplating the system of terrestrial adaptations, these researches teach one to regard the mountain ranges and the great deserts of the earth as the astronomer does the counterpoises to his telescope—though they be mere dead weights, they are, nevertheless, necessary to make the balance

complete, the adjustments of this machine perfect. These counterpoises give ease to the motions, stability to the performance, and accuracy to the workings of the instrument. They are *compensations.*

155. Whenever I turn to contemplate the works of nature, I am struck with the admirable system of compensation, with the beauty and nicety with which every department is poised by the others; things and principles are meted out in directions the most opposite, but in proportions so exactly balanced and nicely adjusted, that results the most harmonious are produced.

It is by the action of opposite and compensating forces that the earth is kept in its orbit, and the stars are held suspended in the azure vault of heaven; and these forces are so exquisitely adjusted, that, at the end of a thousand years, the earth, the sun, and moon, and every star in the firmament, is found to come to its proper place at the proper moment.

Nay, philosophy teaches us, when the little snow-drop, which in our garden walks we see raising its beautiful head to remind us that spring is at hand, was created, that the whole mass of the earth, from pole to pole, and from circumference to centre, must have been taken into account and weighed, in order that the proper degree of strength might be given to the fibres of even this little plant.

Botanists tell us that the constitution of this plant is such as to require that, at a certain stage of its growth, the stalk should bend, and the flower should bow its head, that an operation may take place which is necessary in order that the herb should produce seed after its kind; and that, after this, its vegetable health requires that it should lift its head again and stand erect. Now, if the mass of the earth had been greater or less, the force of gravity would have been different; in that case, the strength of fibre in the snow-drop, as it is, would have been too much or too little; the plant could not bow or raise its head at the right time, fecundation could not take place, and its family would have become extinct with the first individual that was planted, because its "seed" would not have been "in itself," and therefore it could not reproduce itself.

Now, if we see such perfect adaptation, such exquisite adjustment, in the case of one of the smallest flowers of the field, how much more may we not expect "compensation" in the atmosphere and the ocean, upon the right adjustment and due performance of which depends not only the life of that plant, but the well-being of every individual that is found in the entire vegetable and animal kingdoms of the world?

When the east winds blow along the Atlantic coast for a little while, they bring us air saturated with moisture from the Gulf Stream, and we complain of the sultry, oppressive, heavy atmosphere; the invalid grows worse, and the well man feels ill, because, when he takes this atmosphere into his lungs, it is already so charged with moisture that it can not take up and carry off that which encumbers his lungs, and which nature has caused his blood to bring and leave there, that respiration may take up and carry off. At other times the air is dry and hot; he feels that it is conveying off matter from the lungs too fast; he realizes the idea that it is consuming him, and he calls the sensation parching.

156. Therefore, in considering the general laws which govern the physical agents of the universe, and regulate them in the due performance of their offices, I have felt myself constrained to set out with the assumption that, if the atmosphere had had a greater or less capacity for moisture, or if the proportion of land and water had been different—if the earth, air, and water had not been in exact counterpoise—the whole arrangement of the animal and vegetable kingdoms would have varied from their present state. But God chose to make those kingdoms what they are; for this purpose it was necessary, in his judgment, to establish the proportions between the land and water, and the desert, just as they are, and to make the capacity of the air to circulate heat and moisture just what it is, and to have it to do all its work in obedience to law and in subservience to order. If it were not so, why was power given to the winds to lift up and transport moisture, or the property given to the sea by which its waters may become first vapor, and then fruitful showers or gentle dews? If the proportions and properties of land, sea, and air were not adjusted according to the reciprocal capacities of all to perform the functions required by each, why should we be told that he "measured the waters in the hollow of his hand, and comprehended the dust in a measure, and weighed the mountains in scales, and the hills in a balance?" Why did he span the heavens, but that he might mete out the atmosphere in exact proportion to all the rest,

and impart to it those properties and powers which it was necessary for it to have, in order that it might perform all those offices and duties for which he designed it?

Harmonious in their action, the air and sea are obedient to law and subject to order in all their movements; when we consult them in the performance of their offices, they teach us lessons concerning the wonders of the deep, the mysteries of the sky, the greatness, and the wisdom, and goodness of the Creator. The investigations into the broad-spreading circle of phenomena connected with the winds of heaven and the waves of the sea are second to none for the good which they do and the lessons which they teach. The astronomer is said to see the hand of God in the sky; but does not the right-minded mariner, who looks aloft as he ponders over these things, hear his voice in every wave of the sea that "claps its hands," and feel his presence in every breeze that blows?

CHAPTER IV.

RED FOGS AND SEA DUST.

157. SEAMEN tell us of "red fogs" which they sometimes encounter, especially in the vicinity of the Cape de Verd Islands. In other parts of the sea also they meet showers of dust. What these showers precipitate in the Mediterranean is called "sirocco dust," and in other parts "African dust," because the winds which accompany them are supposed to come from the Sirocco desert, or some other parched land of the continent of Africa. It is of a brick-red or cinnamon color, and it sometimes comes down in such quantities as to cover the sails and rigging, though the vessel may be hundreds of miles from the land.

Now the patient reader, who has had the heart to follow me in the preceding chapters around with "the wind in his circuits," will perceive that proof is yet wanting to establish it as a fact that the northeast and southeast trades, after meeting and rising up in the equatorial calms, do cross over and take the tracks represented by C and G, Plate I.

Statements, and reasons, and arguments enough have already been made and adduced to make it highly probable, according to human reasoning, that such is the case; and though the theoretical deductions showing such to be the case be never so good, positive proof that they are true can not fail to be received with delight and satisfaction.

Were it possible to take a portion of this air, as it travels down the southeast trades, representing the general course of atmospherical circulation, and to put a tally on it by which we could always recognize it again, then we might hope actually to prove, by evidence the most positive, the channels through which the air of the trade-winds, after ascending at the equator, returns whence it came.

But the air is invisible; and it is not easily perceived how either marks or tallies may be put upon it, that it may be traced in its paths through the clouds.

The skeptic, therefore, who finds it hard to believe that the general circulation is such as Plate I. represents it to be, might consider himself safe in his unbelief were he to declare his willingness to give it up the moment any one should put tallies on the wings of the wind, which would enable him to recognize that air again, and those tallies, when found at other parts of the earth's surface.

As difficult as this seems to be, it has actually been done. Ehrenberg, with his microscope, has established, almost beyond a doubt, that the air which the southeast trade-winds bring to the equator does rise up there and pass over into the northern hemisphere.

158. The Sirocco, or African dust, which he has been observing so closely, has turned out to be tallies put upon the wind in the other hemisphere; and this beautiful instrument of his enables us to detect the marks on these little tallies as plainly as though those marks had been written upon labels of wood and tied to the wings of the wind.

This dust, when subjected to microscopic examination, is found to consist of infusoria and organisms whose *habitat* is not Africa, but South America, and in the southeast trade-wind region of South America. Professor Ehrenberg has examined specimens of sea dust from the Cape de Verds and the regions thereabout, from Malta, Genoa, Lyons, and the Tyrol; and he has found a similarity among them as striking as it would have been had these specimens been all taken from the same pile. South American forms he recognizes in all of them; indeed, they are the prevailing forms in every specimen he has examined.

It may, I think, be now regarded as an established fact, that there is a perpetual upper current of air from South America to North Africa; and that the volume of air which flows to the northward in these upper currents is nearly equal to the volume which flows to the southward with the northeast trade-winds, there can be no doubt.

The "rain dust" has been observed most frequently to fall in spring and autumn; that is, the fall has occurred after the equinoxes, but at intervals from them varying from thirty to sixty days, more or less. To account for this sort of periodical occurrence of the falls of this dust, Ehrenberg thinks it "necessary to suppose *a dust-cloud to be held constantly swimming in the atmosphere by continuous currents of air, and lying in the region of the trade-winds, but suffering partial and periodical deviations.*"

It has already been shown (§ 128) that the rain or calm belt between the trades travels up and down the earth from north to south, making the rainy season wherever it goes. The reason of this will be explained in another place.

159. This dust is probably taken up in the dry, and not in the wet season; instead, therefore, of its being "held in clouds suffering partial and periodical deviations," as Ehrenberg suggests, it more probably comes from one place about the vernal, and from another about the autumnal equinox; for places which have their rainy season at one equinox have their dry season at the other.

160. At the time of the vernal equinox, the valley of the Lower Oronoco is then in its dry season—every thing is parched up with the drought; the pools are dry, and the marshes and plains arid wastes. All vegetation has ceased; the great serpents and reptiles have buried themselves for hibernation;* the hum of insect life is hushed, and the stillness of death reigns through the valley.

Under these circumstances, the light breeze, raising dust from lakes that are dried up, and lifting motes from the brown savannas, will bear them away like clouds in the air.

This is the period of the year when the surface of the earth in this region, strewed with impalpable and feather-light remains of animal and vegetable organisms, is swept over by whirlwinds, gales, and tornadoes of terrific force; this is the period for the general atmospheric disturbances which have made characteristic the equinoxes. Do not these conditions appear sufficient to afford the "rain dust" for the spring showers?

161. At the period of the autumnal equinox, another portion of the Amazonian basin is parched with drought, and liable to winds that fill the air with dust, and with the remains of dead animal and vegetable matter; these impalpable organisms, which each rainy season calls into being, to perish the succeeding season of drought, are perhaps distended and made even lighter by the gases of decomposition which has been going on in the period of drought.

* Humboldt.

162. May not, therefore, the whirlwinds which accompany the vernal equinox, and sweep over the lifeless plains of the Lower Oronoco, take up the "rain dust" which descends in the northern hemisphere in April and May? and may it not be the atmospherical disturbances which accompany the autumnal equinox that take up the microscopic organisms from the Upper Oronoco and the great Amazonian basin for the showers of October?

163. The Baron von Humboldt, in his *Aspects of Nature*, thus contrasts the wet and the dry seasons there:

"When, under the vertical rays of the never-clouded sun, the carbonized turfy covering falls into dust, the indurated soil cracks asunder as if from the shock of an earthquake. If at such times two opposing currents of air, whose conflict produces a rotary motion, come in contact with the soil, the plain assumes a strange and singular aspect. Like conical-shaped clouds, the points of which descend to the earth, the sand rises through the rarefied air on the electrically-charged centre of the whirling current, resembling the loud water-spout, dreaded by the experienced mariner. The lowering sky sheds a dim, almost straw-colored light on the desolate plain. The horizon draws suddenly nearer, the steppe seems to contract, and with it the heart of the wanderer. The hot, dusty particles which fill the air increase its suffocating heat, and the east wind, blowing over the long-heated soil, brings with it no refreshment, but rather a still more burning glow. The pools which the yellow, fading branches of the fan-palm had protected from evaporation, now gradually disappear. As in the icy north the animals become torpid with cold, so here, under the influence of the parching drought, the crocodile and the boa become motionless and fall asleep, deeply buried in the dry mud. . . . . .

"The distant palm-bush, apparently raised by the influence of the contact of unequally heated and therefore unequally dense strata of air, hovers above the ground, from which it is separated by a narrow intervening margin. Half concealed by the dense clouds of dust, restless with the pain of thirst and hunger, the horses and cattle roam around, the cattle lowing dismally, and the horses stretching out their long necks and snuffing the wind, if haply a moister current may betray the neighborhood of a not wholly dried-up pool. . . . . .

"At length, after the long drought, the welcome season of the rain arrives; and then how suddenly is the scene changed! . . . . .

"Hardly has the surface of the earth received the refreshing moisture, when the previously barren steppe begins to exhale sweet odors, and to clothe itself with killingias, the many panicles of the paspulum, and a variety of grasses. The herbaceous mimosas, with renewed sensibility to the influence of light, unfold their drooping, slumbering leaves to greet the rising sun; and the early song of birds and the opening blossoms of the water plants join to salute the morning."

164. The color of the "rain dust," when collected in parcels and sent to Ehrenberg, is "brick-red," or "yellow ochre;" when seen by Humboldt in the air, it was less deeply shaded, and is described *by him* as imparting a "straw color" to the atmosphere. In the search of spider lines for the diaphragm of my telescopes, I procured the finest and best threads from a cocoon of a mud-red color; but the threads of this cocoon, as seen singly in the diaphragm, were of a golden color; there would seem, therefore, no difficulty in reconciling the difference between the colors of the rain dust, when viewed in little piles by the microscopist, and when seen attenuated and floating in the wind by the great traveler.

It appears, therefore, that we here have placed in our hands a clew, which, attenuated and gossamer-like though it at first appears, is nevertheless palpable and strong enough to guide us along the "circuits of the wind" till we enter "the chambers of the south."

165. The frequency of the fall of "rain dust" between the parallels of 17° and 25° north, and in the vicinity of the Cape Verd Islands, is remarked upon with emphasis by the microscopist. It is worthy of remark, because, in connection with the investigations at the Observatory, it is significant.

166. The latitudinal limits of the northern edge of the northeast trade-winds are variable. In the spring they are nearest to the equator, extending sometimes at this season not farther from the equator than the parallel of 15° north.

167. The breadth of the calms of Cancer is also variable; so also are their limits. The extreme vibration of this zone is between the parallels of 17° and 38° north, according to the season of the year.

According to the hypothesis (§ 42) suggested by my researches, this is the zone in which the upper currents of atmosphere that ascended in the equatorial calms, and flowed off to the northward and eastward, are supposed to descend. This, therefore, is the zone in which the atmosphere that bears the "rain dust," or "African sand," descends to the surface; and this, therefore, is the zone, it might be supposed, which would be the most liable to showers of this "dust." This is the zone in which the Cape Verd Islands are situated; they are in the direction which theory gives to the upper current of air from the Oronoco and Amazon with its "rain dust," and they are in the region of the most frequent showers of "rain dust," all of which are in striking conformity with this theory as to the circulation of the atmosphere.

It is true that, in the present state of our information, we can not tell why this "rain dust" should not be gradually precipitated from this upper current, and descend into the stratum of trade-winds, as it passes from the equator to higher northern latitudes; neither can we tell why the vapor which the same winds carry along should not, in like manner, be precipitated on the way; nor why we should have a thunder-storm, a gale of wind, or the display of any other atmospherical phenomenon to-morrow, and not to-day: all that we can say is, that the conditions of to-day are not such as the phenomenon requires for its own development.

168. Therefore, though we can not tell why the sea dust should not fall always in the same place, we may nevertheless suppose that it is not always in the atmosphere, for the storms that take it up occur only occasionally, and that when up, and in passing the same parallels, it does not always meet with the conditions—electrical and others—favorable to its descent, and that these conditions might occur now in this place, now in that. But that the fall does occur always in the same atmospherical vein or general direction, my investigations would suggest, and Ehrenberg's researches prove.

169. Judging by the fall of sea or rain dust, we may suppose that the currents in the upper regions of the atmosphere are remarkable for their general regularity, as well as for their general direction and sharpness of limits, so to speak.

We may imagine that certain electrical conditions are necessary to a shower of "sea dust" as well as to a thunder-storm; and that the interval between the time of the equinoctial disturbances in the atmosphere and the occurrence of these showers, though it does not enable us to determine the true rate of motion in the general system of atmospherical circulation, yet it assures us that it is not less on the average than a certain rate.

I do not offer these remarks as an explanation with which we ought to rest satisfied, provided other proof can be obtained; I rather offer them in the true philosophical spirit of the distinguished microscopist himself, simply as affording, as far as they are entitled to be called an explanation, that explanation which is most in conformity with the facts before us, and which is suggested by the results of a novel and beautiful system of philosophical research.

170. Thus, though we have tallied the air, and put labels on the wind, to "tell whence it cometh and whither it goeth," yet there evidently is an agent concerned in the circulation of the atmosphere whose functions are manifest, but whose presence has never yet been clearly recognized.

171. When the air which the northeast trade-winds bring down meets in the equatorial calms that which the southeast trade-winds convey, and the two rise up together, what is it that makes them cross? where is the power that guides that from the north over to the south, and that from the south up to the north?

The conjectures in the next chapter as to "the relation between magnetism and the circulation of the atmosphere" may perhaps throw some light upon the answer to this question.

CHAPTER V.

ON THE PROBABLE RELATION BETWEEN MAGNETISM AND THE CIRCULATION OF THE ATMOSPHERE.

Reasons for supposing that the Air of the Northeast and of the Southeast Trades cross at the calm Belts, § 174.—What Observations have shown, 184.—Physical Agencies not left to Chance, 188.—Conjectures, 192.—Reasons for supposing that there is a crossing of Trade-wind Air at the Equator, 194.—Why the extra-tropical Regions of the Northern Hemisphere are likened to the Condenser of a Steam-boiler in the South, 199.—Illustration, 200.—A Coincidence, 202.—Proof, 203.—Nature affords nothing in contradiction to the supposed System of Circulation, 204. Objections answered, 205.—Why the Air brought to the Equator by the Northeast Trades will not readily mix with that brought by the Southeast, 207.—Additional Evidence, 209.—Rains for the Mississippi River are not supplied from the Atlantic, 210.—Traced to the South Pacific, 213.—Anticipation of Light from the Polar Regions, 216.—Received from the Microscope of Ehrenberg, 217, and the Experiments of Faraday, 219.—More Light, 221.—Why there should be a calm Place near each Pole, 222.—Why the Whirlwinds of the North should revolve against the Sun, 223.—Why certain Countries should have scanty Rains, 228.—Magnetism the Agent that causes the Atmospherical Crossings at the calm Places, 231.

172. Oxygen, philosophers say, comprises one fifth part of the atmosphere, and Faraday has discovered that it is magnetic.

This discovery presents itself to the mind as a great physical fact, which is perhaps to serve as the keystone for some of the grand and beautiful structures which philosophy is building up for monuments to the genius of the age.

173. Certain facts and deductions elicited in the course of these investigations had directed my mind to the workings in the atmosphere of some agent, as to whose character and nature I was ignorant. Heat, and the diurnal rotation of the earth on its axis, were not, it appeared to me, sufficient to account for all the currents of both sea and air which investigation was bringing to light.

174. For instance, there was reason to suppose that there is a crossing of winds at the three calm belts; that is, that the southeast trade-winds, when they arrive at the belt of equatorial calms and ascend, cross over and continue their course as an upper current to the calms of Cancer, while the air that the northeast trade-

winds discharge into the equatorial calm belt continues to go south, as an upper current bound for the calms of Capricorn. But what should cause this wind to cross over? Why should there not be a general mingling in this calm belt of the air brought by the two trade-winds, and why should not that which the southeast winds convey there be left, after its ascent, to flow off either to the north or to the south, as chance directs?

175. In the first place, it was at variance with my belief in the grand design; for I could not bring myself to believe that the operations of such an important machine as the atmosphere should be left to chance, even for a moment. Yet I knew of no agent which should guide the wind across these calm belts, and lead it out always on the side opposite to that on which it entered; nevertheless, certain circumstances seemed to indicate that such a crossing does take place.

176. Evidence in favor of it seemed to be afforded by this circumstance, viz., our researches enabled us to trace from the belt of calms, near the tropic of Cancer, which extends entirely across the seas, an efflux of air both to the north and to the south; from the south side of this belt the air flows in a never-ceasing breeze, called the northeast trade-winds, toward the equator. (Plate I.)

On the north side of it, the prevailing winds come from it also, but they go toward the northeast. They are the well-known southwesterly winds which prevail along the route from this country to England, in the ratio of two to one. But why should we suppose a crossing to take place here?

177. We suppose so, because these last-named winds are going from a warmer to a colder climate; and therefore it may be inferred that nature exacts from them what we know she exacts from the air under similar circumstances, but on a smaller scale, before our eyes, viz., more precipitation than evaporation.

178. But where, it may be asked, does the vapor which these winds carry along, for the replenishing of the whole extra-tropical regions of the north, come from? They did not get it as they came along in the upper regions, a counter-current to the northeast trades. They did not get it from the surface of the sea in the calm belt of Cancer, for they did not tarry long enough there to become saturated with moisture. Thus circumstances again pointed to the southeast trade-wind regions as the place of supply.

179. Moreover, these researches afforded grounds for the supposition that the air of which the northeast trade-winds are composed, and which comes out of the same zone of calms as do these southwesterly winds, so far from being saturated with vapor at its exodus, is dry; for near their polar edge, the northeast trade-winds are, for the most part, dry winds. Reason suggests, and philosophy teaches, that, going from a lower to a higher temperature, the evaporating powers of these winds are increased; that they have to travel, in their oblique course toward the equator, a distance of nearly three thousand miles; that, as a general rule, they evaporate all the time, and all the way, and precipitate little or none on their route; investigations have proved that they are not saturated with moisture until they have arrived fully up to the regions of equatorial calms, a zone of constant precipitation.

This calm zone of Cancer borders also, it was perceived, upon a rainy region.

180. Where does the vapor which here, on the northern edge of this zone of Cancer, is condensed into rains, come from?—and where, also—was the oft-repeated question—does the vapor which is condensed into rains for the extra-tropical regions of the north generally come from? By what agency is it conveyed across this calm belt from its birth-place between the tropics?

181. I know of no law of nature or rule of philosophy which would forbid the supposition that the air which has been brought along as the northeast trade-winds to the equatorial calms does, after ascending there, return by the counter and upper currents to the calm zone of Cancer, here descend and reappear on the surface as the northeast trade-winds again. I know of no agent in nature which would *prevent* it from taking this circuit, nor do I know of any which would compel it to take this circuit; but while I know of no agent in nature that would prevent it from taking this circuit, I know, on the other hand, of circumstances which rendered it probable that such, in general, is not the course of atmospherical circulation—that it does not take this circuit. I speak of the rule, not of the exceptions; these are infinite, and, for the most part, are caused by the land.

182. And I moreover knew of facts which go to strengthen the supposition that the winds which have come in the upper

regions of the atmosphere from the equator, do not, after arriving at the calms of Cancer, and descending, return to the equator on the surface, but that they continue on the surface toward the pole. But why should they? What agent in nature is there that can compel these, rather than any other winds, to take such a circuit?

183. The following are some of the facts and circumstances which give strength to the supposition that these winds do continue from the calm belt of Cancer toward the pole as the prevailing southwesterly winds of the extra-tropical north:

We have seen (Plate I.) that, on the north side of this calm zone of Cancer, the prevailing winds on the surface are from this zone toward the pole, and that these winds return as A through the upper regions from the pole; that, arriving at the calms of Cancer, this upper current A meets another upper current G from the equator, where they neutralize each other, produce a calm, descend, and come out as surface winds, viz., A as B, or the trade-winds; and G as H, or the variable winds.

184. Now observations have shown that the winds represented by H are rain winds; those represented by B, dry winds; and it is evident that A could not bring any vapors to these calms to serve for H to make rains of; for the winds represented by A have already performed the circuit of surface winds as far as the pole, during which journey they parted with all their moisture, and, returning through the upper regions of the air to the calm belt of Cancer, they arrived there as dry winds. The winds represented by B are dry winds; therefore it was supposed that these are but a continuation of the winds A.

185. On the other hand, if the winds A, after descending, do turn about and become the surface winds H, they would first have to remain a long time in contact with the sea, in order to be supplied with vapor enough to feed the great rivers, and supply the rains for the whole earth between us and the north pole.

In this case, we should have an evaporating region on the north as well as on the south side of this zone of Cancer; but investigation shows no such region; I speak exclusively of the ocean.

186. Hence it was inferred that A and G do come out on the surface as represented by Plate I. But what is the agent that should lead them out by such opposite paths?

187. According to this mode of reasoning, the vapors which

supply the rains for H would be taken up in the southeast trade-wind region by F, and conveyed thence by G, and delivered to H. And if this mode of reasoning be admitted as plausible—if it be true that G have the vapor which, by condensation, is to water with showers the extra-tropical regions of the northern hemisphere, Nature, we may be sure, has provided a guide for conducting G across this belt of calms, and for sending it on in the right way. Here it was, then, at this crossing of the winds, that I thought I first saw the foot-prints of an agent whose character I could not comprehend. Could it be the magnetism that resides in the oxygen of the air?

188. Heat and cold, the early and the latter rain, clouds and sunshine, are not, we may rely upon it, distributed over the earth by chance; they are distributed in obedience to laws that are as certain and as sure in their operations as the seasons in their rounds. If it depended upon chance whether the dry air should come out on this side or on that of this calm belt, or whether the moist air should return or not whence it came—if such were the case in nature, we perceive that, so far from any regularity as to seasons, we should have, or might have, years of droughts the most excessive, and then again seasons of rains the most destructive; but, so far from this, we find for each place a mean annual proportion of both, and that so regulated withal, that year after year the quantity is preserved with remarkable regularity.

189. Having thus shown that there is no reason for supposing that the upper currents of air, when they meet over the calms of Cancer and Capricorn, are turned back to the equator, but having shown that there is reason for supposing that the air of each current, after descending, continues on in the direction toward which it was traveling before it descended, we may go farther, and, by a similar train of circumstantial evidence, afforded by these researches and other sources of information, show that the air, kept in motion on the surface by the two systems of trade-winds, when it arrives at the belt of equatorial calms, and ascends, continues on thence, each current toward the pole which it was approaching while on the surface.

190. In a problem like this, demonstration in the positive way is difficult, if not impossible. We must rely for our proof upon philosophical deduction, guided by the lights of reason; and in all

cases in which positive proof can not be adduced, it is permitted to bring in circumstantial evidence.

I am endeavoring, let it be borne in mind, to show cause for the conjecture that the magnetism of the oxygen of the atmosphere is concerned in conducting the air which has blown as the southeast trade-winds, and after it has arrived at the belt of equatorial calms and risen up, over into the northern hemisphere, and so on through its channels of circulation, as traced on Plate I.

But, in order to show reasonable grounds for this conjecture, I want to establish, by circumstantial evidence and such indirect proof as my investigations afford, that such is the course of the "wind in his circuits," and that the winds represented by F, Plate I., *do* become those represented by G, H, A, B, and C successively.

191. In the first place, F represents the southeast trade-winds—*i. e.*, all the winds of the southern hemisphere as they approach the equator; and is there any reason for supposing that the atmosphere does not pass freely from one hemisphere to another? On the contrary, many reasons present themselves for supposing that it does.

192. If it did not, the proportion of land and water, and consequently of plants and warm-blooded animals, being so different in the two hemispheres, we might imagine that the constituents of the atmosphere in them would, in the course of ages, probably become different, and that consequently, in such a case, man could not safely pass from one hemisphere to the other.

193. Consider the manifold beauties in the whole system of terrestrial adaptations; remember what a perfect and wonderful machine (§ 118) is this atmosphere; how exquisitely balanced and beautifully compensated it is in all its parts. We know that it is perfect; that in the performance of its various offices it is never left to the guidance of chance—no, not for a moment. Therefore I was led to ask myself why the air of the southeast trades, when arrived at the zone of equatorial calms, should not, after ascending, rather return to the south than go on to the north. Where and what is the agency by which its course is decided?

194. Here I found circumstances which again induced me to suppose it probable that it neither turned back to the south nor mingled with the air which came from the regions of the north-

east trades, ascended, and then flowed indiscriminately to the north or the south.

But I saw reasons for supposing that what came to the equatorial calms as the southeast trade-winds continued to the north as an upper current, and that what had come to the same zone as northeast trade-winds ascended and continued over into the southern hemisphere as an upper current, bound for the calm zone of Capricorn.

And these are the principal reasons and conjectures upon which these suppositions were based:

195. At the seasons of the year when the sun is evaporating most rapidly in the southern hemisphere, the most rain is falling in the northern. Therefore it is fair to suppose that much of the vapor which is taken up on that side of the equator is precipitated on this.

The evaporating surface in the southern hemisphere is greater, much greater, than it is in the northern; still, all the great rivers are in the northern hemisphere, the Amazon being regarded as common to both; and this fact, as far as it goes, tends to corroborate the suggestion as to the crossing of the trade-winds at the equatorial calms.

196. Independently of other sources of information, my investigations also taught me to believe that the mean temperature of the tropical regions was higher in the northern than in the southern hemisphere, for they show that the difference is such as to draw the equatorial edge of the southeast trades far over on this side of the equator, and to give them force enough to keep the northeast trade-winds out of the southern hemisphere almost entirely.

197. Consequently, as before stated, the southeast trade-winds being in contact with a more extended evaporating surface, and continuing in contact with it for a longer time or through a greater distance, they would probably arrive at the trade-wind place of meeting more heavily laden with moisture than the others.

198. Taking the laws and rates of evaporation into consideration, I could find no part of the ocean of the northern hemisphere from which the sources of the Mississippi, the St. Lawrence, and the other great rivers of our hemisphere could be supplied.

Hence, by this process of reasoning, I was induced to regard the extra-tropical regions of the northern hemisphere as standing in the relation of a condenser to a grand steam machine (§ 120), the boiler of which is in the region of the southeast trade-winds, and to consider the trade-winds of this hemisphere as performing the like office for the regions beyond Capricorn.

199. The calm zone of Capricorn is the duplicate of that of Cancer, and the winds flow from it as they do from that, both north and south; but with this difference: that on the polar side of the Capricorn belt they prevail from the northwest instead of the southwest, and on the equatorial side from the southeast instead of the northeast.

Now if it be true that the vapor of the northeast trade-winds is condensed in the extra-tropical regions of the southern hemisphere, the following path, on account of the effect of diurnal rotation of the earth upon the course of the winds, would represent the mean circuit of a portion of the atmosphere moving according to the general system of its circulation over the Pacific Ocean, viz., coming down from the north as an upper current, and appearing on the surface of the earth in about longitude 120° west, and near the tropic of Cancer, it would here commence to blow the northeast trade-winds of that region.

200. To make this clear, see Plate VII., on which I have marked the course of such vapor-bearing winds; A being a breadth or *swath* of winds in the northeast trades; B, the same wind as the upper and counter-current to the southeast trades; and C, the same wind after it has descended in the calm belt of Capricorn, and come out on the polar side thereof, as the rain winds and prevailing northwest winds of the extra-tropical regions of the southern hemisphere.

This, as the northeast trades, is the evaporating wind. As the northeast trade-wind, it sweeps over a great waste of waters lying between the tropic of Cancer and the equator.

201. Meeting no land in this long oblique track over the tepid waters of a tropical sea, it would, if such were its route, arrive somewhere about the meridian of 140° or 150° west, at the belt of equatorial calms, which always divides the northeast from the southeast trade-winds. Here, depositing a portion of its vapor as it ascends, it would, with the residuum, take, on account of diurnal rotation, a course in the upper region of the atmosphere to the southeast, as far as the calms of Capricorn. Here it descends

and continues on toward the coast of South America, in the same direction, appearing now as the prevailing northwest wind of the extra-tropical regions of the southern hemisphere. Traveling on the surface from warmer to colder regions, it must, in this part of its circuit, precipitate more than it evaporates.

202. Now it is a coincidence, at *least*, that this is the route by which, on account of the land in the northern hemisphere, the northeast trade-winds have the fairest sweep over that ocean. This is the route by which they are longest in contact with an evaporating surface; the route by which all circumstances are most favorable to complete saturation; and this is the route by which they can pass over into the southern hemisphere most heavily laden with vapors for the extra-tropical regions of that half of the globe; and this is the supposed route which the northeast trade-winds of the Pacific take to reach the equator and to pass from it.

203. Accordingly, if this process of reasoning be good, that portion of South America between the calms of Capricorn and Cape Horn, upon the mountain ranges of which this part of the atmosphere, whose circuit I am considering as a type, first impinges, ought to be a region of copious precipitation.

Now let us turn to the works on Physical Geography, and see what we can find upon this subject. In Berghaus and Johnston —department Hyetography—it is stated, on the authority of Captain King, R. N., that upward of twelve feet (one hundred and fifty-three inches) of rain fell in forty-one days on that part of the coast of Patagonia which lies within the sweep of the winds just described. So much rain falls there, navigators say, that they sometimes find the water on the top of the sea fresh and sweet.

After impinging upon the cold hill-tops of the Patagonian coast, and passing the snow-clad summits of the Andes, this same wind tumbles down upon the eastern slopes of the range as a dry wind; as such, it traverses the almost rainless and barren regions of Cis-Andean Patagonia and South Buenos Ayres.

204. These conditions, the direction of the prevailing winds, and the amount of precipitation, may be regarded as evidence afforded by nature, if not in favor of, certainly not against, the conjecture that such may have been the voyage of this vapor through

the air. At any rate, here is proof of the immense quantity of vapor which these winds of the extra-tropical regions carry along with them toward the poles; and I can imagine no other place than that suggested, whence these winds could get so much vapor.

I am not unaware of the theory, or of the weight attached to it, which requires precipitation to take place in the upper regions of the atmosphere on account of the cold there, irrespective of proximity to mountain tops and snow-clad hills.

But the facts and conditions developed by this system of research upon the high seas are in many respects irreconcilable with that theory. With a new system of facts before me, I have, independent of all preconceived notions and opinions, set about to seek among them for explanations and reconciliations.

These may not in all cases be satisfactory to every one; indeed, notwithstanding the amount of circumstantial evidence that has already been brought to show that the air which the northeast and the southeast trade-winds discharge into the belts of equatorial calms, does, in ascending, cross—that from the southern passing over into the northern, and that from the northern passing over into the southern hemisphere (see F and G, B and C, Plate I.)—yet some have implied doubt by asking the question, "How are two such currents of air to pass each other?" And, for the want of light upon this point, the correctness of reasoning, facts, inferences, and deductions have been questioned.

205. In the first place, it may be said in reply, the belt of equatorial calms is often several hundred miles across, seldom less than sixty; whereas the depth of the volume of air that the trade-winds pour into it is only about three miles, for that is supposed to be about the height to which the trade-winds extend.

Thus we have the air passing into these calms by an opening on the north side for the northeast trades, and another on the south for the southeast trades, having a cross section of three miles vertically to each opening. It then escapes by an opening upward, the cross section of which is sixty or one hundred, or even three hundred miles. A very slow motion upward there will carry off the air in that direction as fast as the two systems of trade-winds, with their motion of twenty miles an hour, can pour it in; and that *curds* or columns of air can readily cross each other and pass in different directions without interfering the one with the other, or at least to that degree which obstructs or prevents, we all know.

206. For example, open the window of a warm room in winter, and immediately there are two currents of air ready at once to set through it; viz., a current of warm air flowing out at the top, and one of cold coming in below.

But the brown fields in summer afford evidence on a larger scale, and in a still more striking manner, of the fact that, in nature, columns, or streamlets, or curdles of air do readily move among each other without obstruction. That tremulous motion which we so often observe above stubble-fields, barren wastes, or above any heated surface, is caused by the ascent and descent, at one and the same time, of columns of air at different temperatures, the cool coming down, the warm going up. They do not readily commingle, for the astronomer, long after nightfall, when he turns his telescope upon the heavens, perceives and laments the unsteadiness they produce in the sky.

207. If the air brought down by the northeast trade-winds differ in temperature (and why not?) from that brought by the southeast trades, we have the authority of nature for saying that the two currents would not readily commingle. Proof is daily afforded that they would not, and there is reason to believe that the air of each current, in streaks, or patches, or *curdles*, does thread its way through the air of the other without difficulty. Now, if the air of these two currents differs as to magnetism, might not that be an additional reason for their not mixing, and for their taking the direction of opposite poles after ascending?

208. Therefore we may assume it as a postulate which nature concedes, that there is no difficulty as to the two currents of air, which come into those calm belts from different directions, crossing over, each in its proper direction, without mingling.

209. Thus, having shown that there is nothing to *prevent* the crossing of the air in these calm belts, I return to the process of reasoning by induction, and offer additional circumstantial evidence to prove that such a crossing does take place. Let us therefore catechise, on this head, the waters which the Mississippi pours into the sea, inquiring of them as to the channels among the clouds through which they were brought from the ocean to the fountains of that mighty river.

It rains more in the valley drained by that river than is evaporated from it again. The difference for a year is the volume of water annually discharged by that river into the sea (§ 117).

At the time and place that the vapor which supplies this immense volume of water was lifted by the atmosphere up from the sea, the thermometer, we may infer, stood higher than it did at the time and place where this vapor was condensed and fell down as rain in the Mississippi Valley.

210. I looked to the south for the springs in the Atlantic which supply the fountains of this river with rain. But I could not find spare evaporating surface enough for it, in the first place; and if the vapor, I could not find the winds which would convey it to the right place.

The prevailing winds in the Caribbean Sea and southern parts of the Gulf of Mexico are the northeast trade-winds. They have their offices to perform in the river basins of tropical America, and the rains which they may discharge into the Mississippi Valley now and then are exceptions, not the rule.

211. The winds from the north can not bring vapors from the great lakes to make rains for the Mississippi, for two reasons: 1st. The basin of the great lakes receives from the atmosphere more water in the shape of rain than they give back in the shape of vapor. The St. Lawrence River carries off the excess. 2d. The mean climate of the lake country is colder than that of the Mississippi Valley, and therefore, as a general rule, the temperature of the Mississippi Valley is unfavorable for condensing vapor from that quarter.

212. It can not come from the Atlantic, because the greater part of the Mississippi Valley is to the windward of the Atlantic. The winds that blow across this ocean go to Europe with their vapors; and in the Pacific, from the parallels of California down to the equator, the direction of the wind at the surface is from, not toward the basin of the Mississippi. Therefore it seemed to be established with some degree of probability, or, if that expression be too strong, with something like apparent plausibility, that the rain winds of the Mississippi Valley do not, as a general rule, get their vapors from the North Atlantic Ocean, nor from the Gulf of Mexico, nor from the great lakes, nor from that part of the Pacific Ocean over which the northeast trade-winds prevail.

The same process of reasoning which conducted us (§ 203) into the trade-wind region of the northern hemisphere for the sources of the Patagonian rains, now invites us into the trade-wind regions of the South Pacific Ocean to look for the vapor springs of the Mississippi.

213. If the rain winds of the Mississippi Valley come from the east, then we should have reason to suppose that their vapors were taken up from the Atlantic Ocean and Gulf Stream; if the rain winds come from the south, then the vapor springs might, perhaps, be in the Gulf of Mexico; if the rain winds come from the north, then the great lakes might be supposed to feed the air with moisture for the fountains of that river; but if the rains come from the west, where, short of the great Pacific Ocean, should we look for the place of evaporation?

Wondering where, I addressed a circular letter to farmers and planters of the Mississippi Valley, requesting to be informed as to the direction of their rain winds.

214. I received replies from Virginia, Mississippi, Tennessee, Missouri, Indiana, and Ohio; and they all, with the exception of one person in Missouri, said, "The southwest winds bring us our rains."

215. These winds certainly can not get their vapors from the Rocky Mountains, nor from the Salt Lake, for they rain quite as much upon that basin as they evaporate from it again; if they did not, they would, in the process of time, have evaporated all the water there, and the lake would now be dry.

These winds, that feed the sources of the Mississippi with rain, like those between the same parallels upon the ocean, are going from a higher to a lower temperature; and these winds in the Mississippi Valley, not being in contact with the ocean, or with any other evaporating surface to supply them with moisture, must bring with them from some sea or another that which they deposit.

Therefore, though it may be urged, inasmuch as the winds which brought the rains to Patagonia came direct from the sea, that they therefore took up their vapors as they came along, yet it can not be so urged in this case; and if these winds could pass with their vapors from the equatorial calms through the upper regions of the atmosphere to the calms of Cancer, and then as surface winds into the Mississippi Valley, it was not perceived why the Patagonian rain winds should not bring their moisture by a similar route. These last are from the northwest, from warmer to colder latitudes; therefore, being once charged with vapors, they must precipitate as they go, and take up less moisture than they deposit.

216. This was circumstantial evidence. No fact had yet been elicited to prove that the course of atmospherical circulation suggested by my investigations is the actual course in nature. It is a case in which I could yet hope for nothing more direct than such conclusions as might legitimately flow from circumstances.

My friend Lieutenant De Haven was about to sail in command of the American Arctic Expedition in search of Sir John Franklin. Infusoria are sometimes found in sea-dust, rain-drops, hailstones, or snow-flakes; and if by any chance it should so turn out that the *locus* of any of the microscopic infusoria which might be found descending with the precipitation of the Arctic regions should be identified as belonging to the regions of the southeast trade-winds, we should thus add somewhat to the strength of the many clews by which we have been seeking to enter into the chambers of the wind, and to "tell whence it cometh and whither it goeth."

It is not for man to follow the "wind in his circuits;" and all that could be hoped was, after a close examination of all the facts and circumstances which these researches upon the sea have placed within my reach, to point out that course which seemed to be most in accordance with them; and then, having established a probability, or even a possibility, as to the true course of the atmospheric circulation, to make it known, and leave it for future investigations to confirm or set aside.

217. It was at this stage of the matter that my friend Baron von Gerolt, the Prussian minister, had the kindness to place in my hand Ehrenberg's work, "Passat-Staub und Blut-Regen."

Here I found the clew which I hoped, almost against hope, De Haven would place in my hands (§ 216).

That celebrated microscopist reports that he found South American infusoria in the blood-rains and sea-dust of the Cape Verd Islands—Lyons, Genoa, and other places (§ 158).

Thus confirming, as far as such evidence can, the indications of our observations, and increasing the probability that the general course of atmospherical circulation is in conformity with the suggestions of the facts gathered from the sea as I had interpreted them, viz., that the trade-winds of the southern hemisphere, after arriving at the belt of equatorial calms, ascend and continue in their course toward the calms of Cancer as an upper current from the southwest, and that, after passing this zone of calms, they are felt on the surface as the prevailing southwest winds of the extra-tropical parts of our hemisphere; and that, for the most part, they bring their moisture with them from the trade-wind regions of the opposite hemisphere.

218. I have marked on Plate VII. the supposed track of the "Passat-Staub," showing where it was taken up in South America, as at P, P, and where it was found, as at S, S; the part of the line in dots denoting where it was in the upper current, and the unbroken line where it was wafted by a surface current; also on the same plate is designated the part of the South Pacific in which the vapor-springs for the Mississippi rains are supposed to be. The hands (☞) point out the direction of the wind. Where the shading is light, the vapor is supposed to be carried by an upper current.

Such is the character of the circumstantial evidence which induced me to suspect that some agent, whose office in the grand system of atmospherical circulation is neither understood nor recognized, was at work in these calm belts.

219. Dr. Faraday has shown that, as the temperature of oxygen is raised, its paramagnetic force diminishes, being resumed as the temperature falls again.

"These properties it carries into the atmosphere, so that the latter is, in reality, a magnetic medium, ever varying, from the influence of natural circumstances, in its magnetic power. If a mass of air be cooled, it becomes more paramagnetic; if heated, it becomes less paramagnetic (or diamagnetic), as compared with the air in a mean or normal condition."*

220. Now, is it not more than probable that here we have, in the magnetism of the atmosphere, that agent which guides the air from the south (§ 217) through the calms of Capricorn, of the equator, and of Cancer, and conducts it into the north; that agent which causes the atmosphere, with its vapors and infusoria, to flow

* Philosophical Magazine and Journal of Science, 4th series, No. 1, January, 1851, page 73.

above the clouds from one hemisphere into the other, and whose footprints had become so palpable?

221. Taking up the theory of Ampère with regard to the magnetic polarity induced by an electrical current, according as it passes through wire coiled *with* or coiled *against* the sun, and expanding it in conformity with the discoveries of Faraday and the experiments of a Prussian philosopher,* we perceive a series of facts and principles which, being applied to the circulation of the atmosphere, make the conclusions to which I have been led touching these crossings in the air, and the continual "whirl" of the wind in the Arctic regions *against*, and in the Antarctic *with the hands of a watch*, very significant.

In this view of the subject, we see light springing up from various sources, by which the shadows of approaching confirmation are clearly perceived. One such source of light comes from the observations of my excellent friend Quetelet, at Brussels, which show that the great electrical reservoir of the atmosphere is in the upper regions of the air. It is filled with positive electricity, which increases as the temperature diminishes.

222. May we not look, therefore, to find about the north and south magnetic poles these atmospherical nodes or calm regions which I have theoretically pointed out there? In other words, are not the magnetic poles of the earth in those atmospherical nodes, the two standing in the relation of cause and effect, the one to the other?

This question was first asked several years ago,† and I was then moved to propound it by the inductions of theoretical reasoning.

Observers, perhaps, will never reach those inhospitable regions with their instruments to shed light upon this subject; but Parry and Barrow have found reasons to believe in the existence of a perpetual calm about the north pole. Professor J. H. Coffin, in an elaborate and valuable paper‡ on the "WINDS OF THE NORTHERN HEMISPHERE," arrives at a like conclusion. In that paper he has discussed the records at no less than five hundred and seventy-nine meteorological stations, embracing a totality of observa-

* Professor Von Feilitzsch, of the University of Greifswald. Philosophical Magazine, January, 1851.

† Maury's Sailing Directions.

‡ Smithsonian Contributions to Knowledge, vol. vi., 1854.

tions for two thousand eight hundred and twenty-nine years. He places his "meteorological pole"—pole of the winds—near latitude 84° north, longitude 105° west. The pole of maximum cold, by another school of philosophers, Sir David Brewster among them, has been placed in latitude 80° north, longitude 100° west; and the magnetic pole, by still another school,* in latitude 73° 35′ north, longitude 95° 39′ west.

223. Neither of these poles is a point susceptible of definite and exact position. The polar calms are no more a point than the equatorial calms are a line; and, considering that these poles are areas, not points, is it not a little curious that philosophers in different parts of the world, using different data, and following up investigation each through a separate and independent system of research, and each aiming at the solution of different problems, should nevertheless agree in assigning very nearly the same position to them all? Are these three poles grouped together by chance, or by some physical cause? By the latter, undoubtedly. Here, then, we have another of those gossamer-like clews, that sometimes seem almost palpable enough for the mind, in its happiest mood, to lay hold of, and follow up to the very portals of knowledge, where pausing to knock, we may boldly demand that the chambers of hidden things be thrown wide open, that we may see and understand the mysteries of the winds, the frost, and the trembling needle.

224. In the polar calms there is (§ 113) an ascent of air; if an ascent, a diminution of pressure and an expansion; and if expansion, a decrease of temperature. Therefore we have palpably enough a connecting link here between the polar calms and the polar place of maximum cold. Thus we establish a relation between the pole of the winds and the pole of cold, with evident indications that there is also a physical connection between these and the magnetic pole. Here the outcroppings of the relation between magnetism and the circulation of the atmosphere again appear.

May we not find in such evidence as this, threads, attenuated and almost air drawn though they be when taken singly and alone, yet nevertheless proving, when brought together, to have a consistency sufficient, with the lights of reason, to guide us as we seek to trace the wind in his circuits? The winds (§ 106) approach

* Gauss.

these polar calms by a circular or spiral motion, traveling in the northern hemisphere *against*, and in the southern *with* the hands of a watch. The circular gales of the northern hemisphere are said also to revolve in like manner against the hands of a watch, while those in the southern hemisphere travel the other way. Now, should not this discovery of these three poles, this coincidence of revolving winds, with the other circumstances that have been brought to light, encourage us to look to the magnetism of the air for the key to these mysterious but striking coincidences?

Indeed, so wide for speculation is the field presented by these discoveries, that we may in some respects regard this great globe itself, with its "cups" and spiral wires of air, earth, and water, as an immense "pile" and helix, which, being excited by the natural batteries in the sea and atmosphere of the tropics, excites in turn its oxygen, and imparts to atmospherical matter the properties of magnetism.

225. With the lights which these discoveries cast, we see (Plate I.) why air, which has completed its circuit to the whirl* about the Antarctic regions, should then, according to the laws of magnetism, be repelled from the south, and attracted by the opposite pole toward the north.

And when the southeast and the northeast trade-winds meet in the equatorial calms of the Pacific, would not these magnetic forces be sufficient to determine the course of each current, bringing the former, with its vapors of the southern hemisphere, over into this, by the courses already suggested?

226. This force and the heat of the sun would propel it to the north. The diurnal rotation of the earth propels it to the east; consequently, its course, first through the upper regions of the atmosphere, and then on the surface of the earth, after being conducted by this newly-discovered agent across the calms of Cancer, would be *from* the southward and westward to the northward and eastward.

These are the winds (§ 122) which, on their way to the north from the South Pacific, would pass over the Mississippi Valley, and they appear (§ 214) to be the rain winds there. Whence, then, if not from the trade-wind regions of the South Pacific, can the vapors for those rains come?

* "It whirleth about continually."—*Bible.*

227. According to this view, and not taking into account any of the exceptions produced by the land and other circumstances upon the general circulation of the atmosphere over the ocean, the southeast trade-winds, which reach the shores of Brazil near the parallel of Rio, and which blow thence for the most part over the land, should be the winds which, in the general course of circulation, would be carried, after crossing the Andes and rising up in the belt of equatorial calms, toward Northern Africa, Spain, and the South of Europe.

They might carry with them the infusoria of Ehrenberg (§ 158), but, according to this theory, they would be wanting in moisture. Now, are not those portions of the Old World, for the most part dry countries, receiving but a small amount of precipitation?

228. Hence the general rule: those countries to the north of the calms of Cancer, which have large bodies of land situated to the southward and westward of them, in the southeast trade-wind region of the earth, should have a scanty supply of rain, and *vice versa*.

229. Let us try this rule: The extra-tropical part of New Holland comprises a portion of land thus situated in the southern hemisphere. Tropical India is to the northward and westward of it; and tropical India is in the northeast trade-wind region, and should give extra-tropical New Holland a slender supply of rain. But what modifications the monsoons of the Indian Ocean may make to this rule, or what effect they may have upon the rains in New Holland, my investigations in that part of the ocean have not been carried far enough for final decision; though New Holland is a dry country. Referring back to p. 79 for what has been already said concerning the "Meteorological Agencies" (§ 115) of the atmosphere, it will be observed that cases are there brought forward which afford trials for this rule, every one of which holds good.

230. Thus, though it be not proved as a mathematical truth that magnetism is the power which guides the storm from right to left and from left to right, which conducts the moist and the dry air each in its appointed paths, and which regulates the "wind in his circuits," yet that it is such a power is rendered very probable; for, under the supposition that there is such a crossing of the air at the five calm places, as Plate, p. 70, represents (§ 106), we

can reconcile a greater number of known facts and phenomena than we can under the supposition that there is no such crossing. The rules of scientific investigation always require us, when we enter the domains of conjecture, to adopt that hypothesis by which the greatest number of known facts and phenomena may be reconciled; and therefore we are entitled to assume that this crossing does take place, and to hold fast to the theory so maintaining until it is shown not to be sound.

231. That the magnetism of the atmosphere is the agent which guides the air across the calm belts, and prevents that which enters them from escaping on the side upon which it entered, we can not, of our own knowledge, positively affirm. Suffice it to say, that we recognize in this property of the oxygen of air an agent that, for aught we as yet know to the contrary, may serve as such a guide; and we do not know of the existence of any other agent in the atmosphere that can perform the offices which the hypothesis requires. Hence the suspicion that magnetism and electricity are among the forces concerned in the circulation of the atmosphere.

CHAPTER VI.

CURRENTS OF THE SEA.

232. LET us, in this chapter, set out with the postulate that the sea, as well as the air, has its system of circulation, and that this system, whatever it be, and wherever its channels lie, whether in the waters at or below the surface, is in obedience to physical laws. The sea, by the circulation of its waters, has its offices to perform in the terrestrial economy; and when we see the currents in the ocean running hither and thither, we feel that they were not put in motion without a cause. On the contrary, reason assures us that they move in obedience to some law of Nature, be it recorded down in the depths below, never so far beyond the reach

of human ken; and being a law of Nature, we know who gave it, and that neither chance nor accident had any thing to do with its enactment.

Nature grants us all that this postulate demands, repeating it to us in many forms of expression; she utters it in the blade of green grass which she causes to grow in climates and soils made kind and genial by warmth and moisture, that some current of the sea or air has conveyed far away from under a tropical sun. She murmurs it out in the cooling current of the north; the whales of the sea tell of it (§ 65), and all its inhabitants proclaim it.

233. The fauna and the flora of the sea are as much the creatures of climate (§ 66), and are as dependent for their well-being upon temperature as are the fauna and the flora of the dry land. Were it not so, we should find the fish and the algæ, the marine insect and the coral, distributed equally and alike in all parts of the ocean. The polar whale would delight in the torrid zone, and the habitat of the pearl oyster would be also under the iceberg, or in frigid waters colder than the melting ice.

234. Now water, while its capacities for heat are scarcely exceeded by those of any other substance, is one of the most complete of non-conductors. Heat does not permeate water as it does iron, for instance, or other good conductors. Heat the top of an iron plate, and the bottom becomes warm; but heat the top of a sheet of water, as in a pool or basin, and that at the bottom remains cool. The heat passes through iron by conduction, but to get through water it requires to be conveyed by a motion, which in fluids we call currents.

235. Therefore the study of the climates of the sea involves a knowledge of its currents, both cold and warm. They are the channels through which the waters circulate, and by means of which the harmonies of old ocean are preserved.

236. Hence, in studying the system of oceanic circulation, we set out with the very simple assumption, viz., that from whatever part of the ocean a current is found to run, to the same part a current of equal volume is obliged to return; for upon this principle is based the whole system of currents and counter-currents of the air as well as of the water. (See Appendix B.)

237. It is not necessary to associate with oceanic currents the idea that they must of necessity, as on land, run from a higher to

a lower level. So far from this being the case, some currents of the sea actually run up hill, while others run on a level.

The Gulf Stream is of the first class (§ 10).

238. The currents which run from the Atlantic into the Mediterranean, and from the Indian Ocean into the Red Sea, are the reverse of this. Here the bottom of the current is probably a water-level, and the top an inclined plane, running *down hill.* Take the Red Sea current as an illustration. That sea lies, for the most part, within a rainless and riverless district. It may be compared to a long and narrow trough. Being in a rainless district, the evaporation from it is immense; none of the water thus taken up is returned to it either by rivers or rains. It is about one thousand miles long; it lies nearly north and south, and extends from latitude 13° to the parallel of 30° north.

239. From May to October, the water in the upper part of this sea is said to be two feet lower than it is near the mouth.* This change or difference of level is ascribed to the effect of the wind, which, prevailing from the north at that season, is supposed to blow the water out.

But from May to October is also the hot season; it is the season when evaporation is going on most rapidly; and when we consider how dry and how hot the winds are which blow upon this sea at this season of the year, we may suppose the daily evaporation to be immense; not less, certainly, than half an inch, and probably twice that amount. We know that the waste from canals by evaporation, in the summer time, is an element which the engineer, when taking the capacity of his feeders into calculation, has to consider. With him it is an important element; how much more so must the waste by evaporation from this sea be, when we consider the physical conditions under which it is placed. Its feeder, the Arabian Sea, is a thousand miles from its head; its shores are burning sands; the evaporation is *ceaseless;* and none of the vapors, which the scorching winds that blow over it carry away, are returned to it again in the shape of rains.

240. The Red Sea vapors are carried off and precipitated elsewhere. The depression in the level of its head waters in the summer time, therefore, it appears, is owing quite as much to the effect of evaporation as to that of the wind blowing the waters back.

* Johnston's Physical Atlas.

241. The evaporation in certain parts of the Indian Ocean (§ 33) is from three fourths of an inch to an inch daily. Suppose it for the Red Sea in the summer time to average only half an inch a day.

Now, if we suppose the velocity of the current which runs into that sea to average, from mouth to head, twenty miles a day, it would take the water fifty days to reach the head of it. If it lose half an inch from its surface by evaporation daily, it would, by the time it reaches the Isthmus of Suez, lose twenty-five inches from its surface.

242. Thus the waters of the Red Sea ought to be lower at the Isthmus of Suez than they are at the Straits of Babelmandeb. Independently of the waters forced out by the wind, they ought to be lower from two other causes, viz., evaporation and temperature, for the temperature of that sea is necessarily lower at Suez, in latitude 30°, than it is at Babelmandeb, in latitude 13°.

243. To make it quite clear that the surface of the Red Sea is not a sea level, but is an inclined plane, suppose the channel of the Red Sea to have a perfectly smooth and level floor, with no water in it, and a wave ten feet high to enter the Straits of Babelmandeb, and to flow up the channel at the rate of twenty miles a day for fifty days, losing daily, by evaporation, half an inch; it is easy to perceive that, at the end of the fiftieth day, this wave would not be so high, by two feet (twenty-five inches), as it was the first day it commenced to flow.

244. The top of that sea, therefore, may be regarded as an inclined plane, made so by evaporation.

245. But the salt water, which has lost so much of its freshness by evaporation, becomes salter, and therefore heavier. The lighter water at the Straits can not balance the heavier water at the Isthmus, and the colder and salter, and therefore heavier water, must either run out as an under current, or it must deposit its surplus salt in the shape of crystals, and thus gradually make the bottom of the Red Sea a salt-bed, or it must abstract all the salt from the ocean to make the Red Sea brine—and we know that neither the one process nor the other is going on. Hence we infer that there is from the Red Sea an under or outer current, as there is from the Mediterranean through the Straits of Gibraltar,

and that the surface waters near Suez are salter than those near the mouth of the Red Sea.

246. And, to show why there should be an outer and under current from each of these two seas, let us suppose the case of a long trough, opening into a vat of oil, with a partition to keep the oil from running into the trough. Now suppose the trough to be filled up with wine on one side of the partition to the level of the oil on the other. The oil is introduced to represent the lighter water as it enters either of these seas from the ocean, and the wine the same water after it has lost some of its freshness by evaporation, and therefore has become salter and heavier. Now suppose the partition to be raised, what would take place? Why, the oil would run in as an upper current, overflowing the wine, and the wine would run out as an under current.

247. The rivers which discharge in the Mediterranean are not sufficient to supply the waste of evaporation, and it is by a process similar to this that the salt which is carried in from the ocean is returned to the ocean again; were it not so, the bed of that sea would be a mass of solid salt. The equilibrium of the seas is preserved, beyond a doubt, by a system of compensation as exquisitely adjusted as are those by which the "music of the spheres" is maintained. (See Appendix C.)

248. The above about under currents is theory: Now let us see the results of actual observation upon the density of water in the Red Sea and the Mediterranean, and upon the under currents that run out from these seas.

Four or five years ago, Mr. Morris, chief engineer of the Oriental Company's steam-ship Ajdaha, collected specimens of Red Sea water all the way from Suez to the Straits of Babelmandeb, which were afterward examined by Dr. Giraud, who reported the following results:*

		Latitude. °	Longitude. °	Spec. Grav.	Saline Cont. 1000 parts.
No. 1.	Sea at Suez	—	—	1027	41.0
No. 2.	Gulf of Suez	27.49	33.44	1026	40.0
No. 3.	Red Sea	24.29	36.	1024	39.2
No. 4.	do.	20.55	38.18	1026	40.5
No. 5.	do.	20.43	40.03	1024	39.8
No. 6.	do.	14.34	42.43	1024	39.9
No. 7.	do.	12.39	44.45	1023	39.2

* Transact. of the Bombay Geograph. Soc., vol. ix., May, 1849, to August, 1850.

249. These observations agree with the theoretical deductions just announced, and show that the surface waters at the head are heavier and salter than the surface waters at the mouth of the Red Sea.

250. In the same paper, the temperature of the air between Suez and Aden often rises, it is said, to 90°, "and probably averages little less than 75° day and night all the year round. The surface of the sea varies in heat from 65° to 85°, and the difference between the wet and dry bulb thermometers often amounts to 25°—in the kamsin, or desert winds, to from 30° to 40°; the average evaporation at Aden is about eight feet for the year." "Now assuming," says Dr. Buist, "the evaporation of the Red Sea to be no greater than that of Aden, a sheet of water eight feet thick, equal in area to the whole expanse of the sea, will be carried off annually in vapor; or, assuming the Red Sea to be eight hundred feet in depth at an average—and this, most assuredly, is more than double the fact—the whole of it would be dried up, were no water to enter from the ocean, in one hundred years. The waters of the Red Sea, throughout, contain some four per cent. of salt by weight—or, as salt is a half heavier than water, some 2.7 per cent. in bulk—or, in round numbers, say three per cent. In the course of three thousand years, on the assumptions just made, the Red Sea ought to have been one mass of solid salt, if there were no current running out."

251. Now we know the Red Sea is more than three thousand years old, and that it is not filled with salt; and the reason is, that as fast as the upper currents bring the salt in at the top, the under currents carry it out at the bottom.

252. Mediterranean Currents.—With regard to an under current from the Mediterranean, we may begin by remarking that we know that there is a current always setting in at the surface from the Atlantic, and that this is a salt-water current, which carries an immense amount of salt into that sea. We know, moreover, that that sea is not salting up; and therefore, independently of the postulate (§ 236) and of observations (§ 253), we might infer the existence of an under current, through which this salt finds its way out into the broad ocean again.*

* Dr. Smith appears to have been the first to *conjecture* this explanation, which he did in 1683 (*vide* Philosophical Transactions). This continual indraught into the

With regard to this outer and under current, we have observations telling of its existence as long ago as 1712.

"In the year 1712," says Dr. Hudson, in a paper communicated to the Philosophical Society in 1724, "Monsieur du L'Aigle, that fortunate and generous commander of the privateer called the Phœnix, of Marseilles, giving chase near Ceuta Point to a Dutch ship bound to Holland, came up with her in the middle of the Gut between Tariffa and Tangier, and there gave her one broadside, which directly sunk her, all her men being saved by Monsieur du L'Aigle; and a few days after, the Dutch ship, with her cargo of brandy and oil, arose on the shore near Tangier, which is at least four leagues to the westward of the place where she sunk, and directly against the strength of the current, which has persuaded many men that there is a recurrency in the deep water in the middle of the Gut that sets outward to the grand ocean, which this accident very much demonstrates; and, possibly, a great part of the water which runs into the Straits returns that way, and along the two coasts before mentioned; otherwise, this ship must, of course, have been driven toward Ceuta, and so upward. The water in the Gut must be very deep; several of the commanders of our ships of war having attempted to sound it with the longest lines they could contrive, but could never find any bottom."

In 1828, Dr. Wollaston, in a paper before the Philosophical Society, stated that he found the specific gravity of a specimen of sea water, from a depth of six hundred and seventy fathoms, fifty miles within the Straits, to have a "density exceeding that of dis-

Mediterranean appears to have been a vexed question among the navigators and philosophers even of those times. Dr. Smith alludes to several hypotheses which had been invented to solve these phenomena, such as subterraneous vents, cavities, exhalation by the sun's beams, &c., and then offers his *conjecture*, which, in his own words, is, "that there is an under current, by which as great a quantity of water is carried out as comes flowing in. To confirm which, besides what I have said above about the difference of tides in the offing and at the shore in the Downs, which necessarily supposes an under current, I shall present you with an instance of the like nature in the Baltic Sound, as I received it from an able seaman, who was at the making of the trial. He told me that, being there in one of the king's frigates, they went with their pinnace into the mid stream, and were carried violently by the current; that, soon after this, they sunk a bucket with a heavy cannon ball to a certain depth of water, which gave a check to the boat's motion; and, sinking it still lower and lower, the boat was driven ahead to the windward against the upper current: the current aloft, as he added, not being over four or five fathoms deep, and that the lower the bucket was let fall, they found the under current the stronger."

tilled water by more than four times the usual excess, and accordingly leaves, upon evaporation, more than four times the usual quantity of saline residuum. Hence it is clear that an under current outward of such denser water, if of equal breadth and depth with the current inward near the surface, would carry out as much salt below as is brought in above, although it moved with less than one fourth part of the velocity, and would thus prevent a perpetual increase of saltness in the Mediterranean Sea beyond that existing in the Atlantic."

The doctor obtained this specimen of sea water from Captain, now Admiral Smyth, of the English navy, who had collected it for Dr. Marcet. Dr. Marcet died before receiving it, and it had remained in the admiral's hands some time before it came into those of Wollaston.

It may, therefore, have lost something by evaporation; for it is difficult to conceive that all the river water, and three fourths of the sea water which runs into the Mediterranean, is evaporated from it, leaving a brine for the under current having four times as much salt as the water at the surface of the sea usually contains. Very recently, M. Coupvent des Bois is said to have shown, by actual observation, the existence of an outer and under current from the Mediterranean.

However that may be, these facts, and the statements of the Secretary of the Geographical Society of Bombay (§ 250), seem to leave no room to doubt as to the existence of an under current both from the Red Sea and Mediterranean, and as to the cause of the surface current which flows into them. I think it a matter of demonstration. It is accounted for (§ 245) by the salts of the sea.

253. Writers whose opinions are entitled to great respect differ with me as to the proof of this demonstration. Among these writers are Admiral Smyth, of the British Navy, and Sir Charles Lyell, who also differ with each other. In 1820, Dr. Marcet, being then engaged in studying the chemical composition of sea water, the admiral, with his usual alacrity for doing "a kind turn," undertook to collect for the doctor specimens of Mediterranean water from various depths, especially in and about the Straits of Gibraltar. Among these was the one (§ 252) taken fifty miles within the Straits from the depth of six hundred and seventy

fathoms (four thousand and twenty feet), which, being four times salter than common sea water, left, as we have just seen (§ 252), no doubt in the mind of Dr. Wollaston as to the existence of this under current of brine.

But the indefatigable admiral, in the course of his celebrated survey of the Mediterranean, discovered that, while inside of the Straits the depth was upward of nine hundred fathoms, yet in the Straits themselves the depth across the shoalest section is not more than one hundred and sixty* fathoms.

"Such being the case, we can now prove," exclaims Sir Charles Lyell, "that the vast amount of salt brought into the Mediterranean *does not* pass out again by the Straits; for it appears by Captain Smyth's soundings, which Dr. Wollaston had not seen, that between the Capes of Trafalgar and Spartel, which are twenty-two miles apart, and where the Straits are shallowest, the deepest part, which is on the side of Cape Spartel, is only two hundred and twenty fathoms.† It is therefore evident, that if water sinks in certain parts of the Mediterranean, in consequence of the increase of its specific gravity, to greater depths than two hundred and twenty fathoms, it can never flow out again into the Atlantic, since it must be stopped by the submarine barrier which crosses the shallowest part of the Straits of Gibraltar."‡

254. According to this reasoning, all the cavities, the hollows and the valleys at the bottom of the sea, especially in the trade-wind region, where evaporation is so constant and great, ought to be salting up or filling up with brine. Is it probable that such a process is actually going on? No.

According to this reasoning, the water at the bottom of the great American lakes ought to be salt, for the rivers and the rains, it is admitted, bring the salts from the land and empty them into the sea. It is also admitted that the great lakes would, from this cause, be salt, if they had no sea drainage. The Niagara River passes these river salts from the upper lakes into Ontario, and the St. Lawrence conveys them thence to the sea. Now the basins or bottoms of all these upper lakes are far below the *top* of the rock over which the Niagara pitches its flood. And, were the position assumed by this writer correct, viz., that if the water in

* "The Mediterranean." † One hundred and sixty, Smyth.

‡ Lyell's Principles of Geology, p. 334–5, ninth edition. London, 1853.

any of these lakes should, in consequence of its specific gravity, once sink below the level of the shoals in the rivers and straits which connect them, it never could flow out again, and consequently must remain there forever*—were this principle physically correct, would not the water at the bottom of the lakes gradually have received salt sufficient, during the countless ages that they have been sending it off to the sea, to make this everlastingly pent-up water briny, or at least quite different in its constituents from that of the surface? We may presume that the water at the bottom of every extensive and quiet sheet of water, whether salt or fresh, is at the bottom by reason of specific gravity; but that it does not remain there forever we have abundant proof. If so, the Niagara River would be fed by Lake Erie only from that layer of water which is above the level of the top of the rock at the Falls. Consequently, wherever the breadth of that river is no greater than it is at the Falls, we should have a current as rapid as it is at the moment of passing the top of the rock to make the leap. To see that such is not the way of Nature, we have but to look at any common mill-pond when the water is running over the dam. The current in the pond that feeds the overflow is scarcely perceptible, for "still water runs deep." Moreover, we know it is not such a skimming current as the geologist would make, which runs from one lake to another; for wherever above the Niagara Falls the water is deep, there we are sure to find the current sluggish, in comparison with the rate it assumes as it approaches the Falls; and it is sluggish in deep places, rapid in shallow ones, because it is fed from below. The common "wastes" in our canals teach us this fact.

The reasoning of this celebrated geologist appears to be founded upon the assumption that when water, in consequence of its specific gravity, once sinks below the bottom of a current where it is shallowest, there is no force of traction in fluids, nor any other power, which can draw this heavy water up again. If such were the case, we could not have deep water immediately inside of the bars which obstruct the passage of the great rivers into the sea. Thus the bar at the mouth of the Mississippi, with only fifteen feet of water on it, is estimated to travel out to sea at rates varying from one hundred to twenty yards a year.

* See paragraph quoted (§ 253) from "Lyell's Principles of Geology."

In the place where that bar was when it was one thousand yards nearer to New Orleans than it now is, whether it were fifteen years ago or a century ago, with only fifteen or sixteen feet of water on it, we have now four or five times that depth. As new bars were successively formed seaward from the old, what dug up the sediment which formed the old, and lifted it up from where specific gravity had placed it, and carried it out to sea over a barrier not more than a few feet from the surface? Indeed, Sir Charles himself makes this majestic stream to tear up its own bottom to depths far below the top of the bar at its mouth. He describes the Mississippi as a river having nearly a uniform breadth to the distance of two thousand miles from the sea.* He makes it cut a bed for itself out of the soil, which is heavier than Admiral Smyth's deep sea water, to the depth of more than two hundred feet† below the top of the bar which obstructs its entrance into the sea. Could not the same power which scoops out this solid matter draw the brine up from the pool in the Mediterranean, and pass it out across the barrier in the Straits?

The *traction* of locomotives on rail-roads and the force of that traction are well understood. Now have not currents in the deep sea power derived from some such force? Suppose this under current from the Mediterranean to extend one hundred and sixty fathoms down, so as to chafe the barrier across the Straits. Upon the bottom of this current, then, there is a pressure of more than fifty atmospheres. Have we not here a source of power that would be capable of drawing up, by almost an insensibly slow motion, water from almost any depth? At any rate, it appears that the effect of currents by *traction*, or friction, or whatever force, does extend far below the level of their beds in shallow places. Were it not so—were the brine not drawn out again—it would be easy to prove that this indraught into the Mediterranean has taken, even during the period assigned by Sir Charles to the formation of the Delta of the Mississippi—one of the newest formations—salt enough to fill up the whole basin of the Mediterranean with

* "From near its mouth at the Balize, a steam-boat may ascend for two thousand miles with scarcely any perceptible difference in the width of the river."—*Lyell*, p. 263.

† "The Mississippi is continually shifting its course in the great alluvial plain, cutting frequently to the depth of one hundred, and even sometimes to the depth of two hundred and fifty feet."—*Lyell*, p. 273.

crystals. Admiral Smyth brought up bottom with his briny sample of deep sea water (six hundred and seventy fathoms), but no salt crystals.

The gallant admiral—appearing to withhold his assent both from Dr. Wollaston in his conclusions as to this under current, and from the geologist in his inferences as to the effect of the barrier in the Straits—suggests the probability that, in sounding for the heavy specimen of sea water, he struck a brine spring. But the specimen, according to analysis, was of sea water, and how did a brine spring of sea water get under the sea but through the process of evaporation on the surface, or by parting with a portion of its fresh water in some other way?

If we admit the principle assumed by Sir Charles Lyell, that water from the great pools and basins of the sea can never ascend to cross the ridges which form these pools and basins, then the harmonies of the sea are gone, and we are forced to conclude they never existed. Every particle of water that sinks below a submarine ridge is, *ipso facto*, by his reasoning, stricken from the channels of circulation, to become thenceforward forever motionless matter. The consequence would be "cold obstruction" in the depths of the sea, and a system of circulation between different seas of the waters only that float above the shoalest reefs and barriers. I do not believe in the existence of any such imperfect terrestrial mechanism, or in any such failures of design. To my mind, the proofs—the theoretical proofs—the proofs derived exclusively from reason and analogy—are as clear in favor of this under current from the Mediterranean as they were in favor of the existence of Leverrier's planet before it was seen through the telescope at Berlin.

Now suppose, as Sir Charles Lyell maintains, that none of these vast quantities of salt which this surface current takes into the Mediterranean find their way out again. It would not be difficult to show, even to the satisfaction of that eminent geologist, that this indraught conveys salt away from the Atlantic faster than all the *fresh*-water rivers empty fresh supplies of salt into the ocean. Now, besides this drain, vast quantities of salts are extracted from sea water for madrepores, coral reefs, shell banks, and marl beds; and by such reasoning as this, which is perfectly sound and good, we establish the existence of this under current, or else we are forced to the very unphilosophical conclusion that the sea must be losing its salts, and becoming less and less briny.

255. The Currents of the Indian Ocean.—By carefully examining the physical features of this sea (Plates VIII. and IX.), and studying its conditions, we are led to look for warm currents that have their genesis in this ocean, and that carry from it volumes of overheated water, probably exceeding in quantity many times that which is discharged by the Gulf Stream from its fountains (Plate VI.).

The Atlantic Ocean is open at the north, but tropical countries bound the Indian Ocean in that direction. The waters of this ocean are hotter than those of the Caribbean Sea, and the evaporating force there (§ 146) is much greater. That it is greater we might, without observation, infer from the fact of a higher temperature and a greater amount of precipitation on the neighboring shores (§ 139). These two facts, taken together, tend, it would seem, to show that large currents of warm water have their genesis in the Indian Ocean. One of them is the well-known Mozambique current, called at the Cape of Good Hope the Lagullas current.

256. Another of these currents makes its escape through the Straits of Malacca, and, being joined by other warm streams from the Java and China Seas, flows out into the Pacific, like another Gulf Stream, between the Philippines and the shores of Asia. Thence it attempts the great circle route (§ 69) for the Aleutian Islands, tempering climates, and losing itself in the sea on its route toward the northwest coast of America.

257. Between the physical features of this current and the Gulf Stream of the Atlantic there are several points of resemblance. Sumatra and Malacca correspond to Florida and Cuba; Borneo to the Bahamas, with the Old Providence Channel to the south, and the Florida Pass to the west. The coasts of China answer to those of the United States, the Philippines to the Bermudas, the Japan Islands to Newfoundland. As with the Gulf Stream, so also here with this China current, there is a counter-current of cold water between it and the shore. The climates of the Asiatic coast correspond with those of America along the Atlantic, and those of Columbia, Washington, and Vancouver are duplicates of those of Western Europe and the British Islands;

the climate of California (State) resembling that of Spain; the sandy plains and rainless regions of Lower California reminding one of Africa, with its deserts between the same parallels, &c.

Moreover, the North Pacific, like the North Atlantic, is enveloped, where these warm waters go, with mists and fogs, and streaked with *lightning*. The Aleutian Islands are as renowned for fogs and mists as are the Grand Banks of Newfoundland.

258. A surface current flows north through Behring's Strait into the Arctic Sea; but in the Atlantic the current is from, not into the Arctic Sea: it flows south on the surface, north below; Behring's Strait being too shallow to admit of mighty under currents, or to permit the introduction from the polar basin of any large icebergs into the Pacific.

259. Behring's Strait, in geographical position, answers to Davis's Strait in the Atlantic; and Alaska, with its Aleutian chain of islands, to Greenland. But instead of there being to the east of Alaska, as there is to the east of Greenland, an escape into the polar basin for these warm waters, the Pacific shore-line intervenes, and turns them down through a sort of North Sea along the western coast of the continent toward Mexico.

260. These contrasts show the principal points of resemblance and of difference between the currents and aqueous circulation in the two oceans. The ice-bearing currents of the North Atlantic are not repeated as to degree in the North Pacific, for there is no nursery for icebergs like the frozen ocean and its arms. The seas of Okotsk and Kamtschatka alone, and not the frozen seas of the Arctic, cradle the icebergs for the North Pacific.

There is, at times at least, another current of warm water from the Indian Ocean. It finds its way south midway between Africa and Australia. The whales (Plate IX.) give indications of it. Nor need we be surprised at such a vast flow of warm water as these three currents indicate from the Indian Ocean, when we recollect that this ocean (§ 255) is land-locked on the north, and that the temperature of its waters is frequently as high as 90° Fahr.

261. There must, therefore, be immense volumes of water flowing into the Indian Ocean to supply the waste created by these warm currents, and the fifteen or twenty feet of water that observations (§ 33) tell us are yearly carried off from this ocean by evaporation.

On either side of this warm current that escapes from the inter-tropical parts of the Indian Ocean (§ 260), midway between Africa and Australia, an ice-bearing current (Plate IX.) is found wending its way from the Antarctic regions with supplies of cold water to modify climates, and restore the aqueous equilibrium in that part of the world. These cold currents sometimes get as far north with their icebergs as 40° south. The Gulf Stream seldom permits them to get so near the equator as that in the North Atlantic, but I have known the ice-bearing current which passes east of Cape Horn into the South Atlantic to convey its bergs as far as the parallel of 37° south latitude. This is the nearest approach of icebergs to the equator.

262. These currents which run out from the inter-tropical basin of that immense sea—Indian Ocean—are active currents. They convey along immense volumes of water containing vast quantities of salt, and we know that sea water enough to convey back equal quantities of salt, and salt to keep up supplies for the out-going currents, must flow into or return to the inter-tropical regions of the same sea; therefore, if observations were silent upon the subject, reason would teach us to look for currents here that keep in motion immense volumes of water.

263. The Currents of the Pacific.—The contrast has been drawn (§ 257) between the China or " Gulf Stream" of the North Pacific, and the Gulf Stream of the North Atlantic. The course of the China Stream has never been traced out. There is (Plate IX.), along the coast of California and Mexico, a southwardly movement of waters, as there is along the west coast of Africa toward the Cape de Verd Islands.

264. In the open space west of this southwardly set along the African coast, there is the famous Sargasso Sea (Plate IX.), which is the general receptacle of the drift-wood and sea-weed of the Atlantic. So, in like manner, to the west from California of this other southwardly set, lies the pool into which the drift-wood and sea-weed of the North Pacific are generally gathered.

265. The natives of the Aleutian Islands, where no trees grow, depend upon the drift-wood cast ashore there for all the timber used in the construction of their boats, fishing-tackle, and household gear. Among this timber, the camphor-tree, and other woods of China and Japan, are said to be often recognized. In this fact

we have additional evidence touching this China Stream, as to which (§ 263) but little, at best, is known.

266. THE COLD ASIATIC CURRENT.—Inshore of, but counter to the China current, along the eastern shores of Asia, is found (§ 257) a streak, or layer, or current of cold water answering to that between the Gulf Stream and the American coast. This current, like its fellow in the Atlantic, is not strong enough at all times sensibly to affect the course of navigation; but, like that in the Atlantic, it is the nursery (§ 65) of most valuable fisheries. The fisheries of Japan are quite as extensive as those of Newfoundland, and the people of each country are indebted for their valuable supplies of excellent fish to the cold waters which the currents of the sea bring down to their shores.

267. HUMBOLDT'S CURRENT.—The currents of the Pacific are but little understood. Among those about which most is thought to be known is the Humboldt Current of Peru, which the great and good man whose name it bears was the first to discover. It has been traced on Plate IX. according to the best information —defective at best—upon the subject. This current is felt as far as the equator. (See Appendix D.)

268. I have, I believe, discovered the existence of a warm current in the inter-tropical regions of the Pacific, midway between the American coast and the shore-lines of Australia.

269. This region affords an immense surface for evaporation. No rivers empty into it; the annual fall of rain, except in the "Equatorial Doldrums," is small, and the evaporation is all that both the northeast and the southeast trade-winds can take up and carry off. I have marked on Plate IX. the direction of the supposed warm water current which conducts these overheated and briny waters from the tropics in mid ocean to the extra-tropical regions where precipitation is in excess. Here being cooled, and agitated, and mixed up with waters that are less salt, these overheated and over-salted waters from the tropics may be replenished and restored to their rounds in the wonderful system of oceanic circulation.

270. There are also about the equator in this ocean some curious currents which I do not understand, and as to which observations are not sufficient yet to afford the proper explanation or description. There are many of them, some of which, at times,

run with great force. On a voyage from the Society to the Sandwich Islands, I encountered one running at the rate of ninety-six miles a day.

And what else should we expect in this ocean but a system of currents and counter-currents apparently the most uncertain and complicated? The Pacific Ocean and the Indian Ocean may, in the view we are about to take, be considered as one sheet of water. This sheet of water covers an area quite equal in extent to one half of that embraced by the whole surface of the earth; and, according to Professor Alexander Keith Johnston, who so states it in the new edition of his splendid Physical Atlas, the total annual fall of rain on the earth's surface is one hundred and eighty-six thousand, two hundred and forty cubic imperial miles. Not less than three fourths of the vapor which makes this rain comes from this waste of waters; but supposing that only half of this quantity, *i. e.*, ninety-three thousand, one hundred and twenty cubic miles of rain falls upon this sea, and that that much, at least, is taken up from it again as vapor, this would give two hundred and fifty-five cubic miles as the quantity of water which is daily lifted up and poured back again into this expanse. It is taken up at one place and rained down at another, and in this process, therefore, we have agencies for multitudes of partial and conflicting currents, all, in their set and strength, apparently as uncertain as the winds.

The better to appreciate the operation of such agencies in producing currents in the sea, now here, now there, first this way, and then that, let us, by way of illustration, imagine a district of two hundred and fifty-five square miles in extent to be set apart, in the midst of the Pacific Ocean, as the scene of operations for one day. We must now conceive a machine capable of pumping up, in the twenty-four hours, all the water to the depth of one mile in this district. The machine must not only pump up and bear off this immense quantity of water, but it must discharge it again into the sea on the same day, but at some other place. Now here is a force for creating currents that is equivalent in its results to the effects that would be produced by bailing up, in twenty-four hours, two hundred and fifty-five cubic miles of water from one part of the Pacific Ocean, and emptying it out again upon another part. The currents that would be created by such an-operation would overwhelm navigation and desolate the sea; and, happily for the human race, the great atmospherical machine (§ 90), which actually does perform every day, on the average, all this lifting up, transporting, and letting down of water upon the face of the grand ocean, does not confine itself to an area of two hundred and fifty-five square miles, but to an area three hundred thousand times as great; yet, nevertheless, the same quantity of water is kept in motion, and the currents, in the aggregate, transport as much water to restore the equilibrium as they would have to do were all the disturbance to take place upon our hypothetical area of one mile deep over the space of two hundred and fifty-five square miles. Now when we come to recollect that evaporation is lifting up, that the winds are transporting, and that the clouds do let down every day actually such a body of water, but that it is done by little and little at a place, and by hair's breadths at a time, not by parallelopipedons one mile thick—that the evaporation is most rapid and the rains most copious, not always at the same place, but now here, now there, we shall see actually existing in nature a force sufficient to give rise to just such a system of currents as that which mariners find in the Pacific—currents which appear to rise in mid ocean, run at unequal rates, sometimes east, sometimes west, but which always lose themselves where they rise, viz., in mid ocean.

271. Under Currents.—Lieutenant J. C. Walsh, in the United States schooner "Taney," and Lieutenant S. P. Lee, in the United States brig "Dolphin," both, while they were carrying on a system of observations in connection with the Wind and Current Charts, had their attention directed to the subject of submarine currents.

They made some interesting experiments upon the subject. A block of wood was loaded to sinking, and, by means of a fishing-line or a bit of twine, let down to the depth of one hundred or five hundred fathoms (six hundred or three thousand feet). A small float, just sufficient to keep the block from sinking farther, was then tied to the line, and the whole let go from the boat.

To use their own expressions, "It was wonderful, indeed, to see this *barrega* move off, against wind, and sea, and surface current, at the rate of over one knot an hour, as was generally the case, and on one occasion as much as 1¾ knots. The men in the boat could not repress exclamations of surprise, for it really appeared as if some monster of the deep had hold of the weight below, and was walking off with it."* Both officers and men were amazed at the sight.

272. The experiments in deep-sea soundings have also thrown much light upon the subject of under currents. There is reason to believe that they exist in all, or almost all parts of the deep sea, for never in any instance yet has the deep-sea line ceased to run out, even after the plummet had reached the bottom.

If the line be held fast in the boat, it invariably parts, showing, when two or three miles of it are out, that the under-currents are sweeping against the bight of it with what seamen call a *swigging force*, that no sounding twine has yet proved strong enough to withstand.

Lieutenant J. P. Parker, of the United States frigate Congress, attempted, in 1852, a deep-sea sounding off the coast of South America. He was engaged with the experiment eight or nine hours, during which time a line nearly ten miles long was paid out. Night coming on, he had to part the line (which he did simply by attempting to haul it in) and return on board. Examination proved that the ocean there, instead of being over ten miles in depth, was not over three, and that the line was swept out by the force of one or more under currents. But in what direction these currents were running is not known.

273. It may, therefore, without doing any violence to the rules of philosophical investigation, be conjectured, that the equilibrium of all the seas is preserved, to a greater or less extent, by this system of currents and counter-currents at and below the surface.

If we except the tides, and the partial currents of the sea, such as those that may be created by the wind, we may lay it down as a rule (§ 34) that all the currents of the ocean owe their origin to difference of specific gravity between sea water at one place and sea water at another; for wherever there is such a difference, whether it be owing to difference of temperature or to difference of saltness, &c., it is a difference that disturbs equilibrium, and currents are the consequence. The heavier water goes toward the lighter, and the lighter whence the heavier comes; for two fluids differing in specific gravity (§ 36), and standing at the same

* Lieutenant Walsh.

level, can not balance each other. It is immaterial, as before stated, whether this difference of specific gravity be caused by temperature, by the matter held in solution, or by any other thing; the effect is the same, namely, a current.

274. That the sea, in all parts, holds in solution the same kind of solid matter; that its waters in this place, where it never rains, are not salter than the strongest brine; and that in another place, where the rain is incessant, they are not entirely without salt, may be taken as evidence in proof of a system of currents or of circulation in the sea, by which its waters are shaken up and kept mixed together as though they were in a phial. Moreover, we may lay it down as a law in the system of oceanic circulation, that every current in the sea has its counter current; in other words, that the currents of the sea are, like the nerves of the human system, arranged in pairs; for wherever one current is found carrying off water from this or that part of the sea, to the same part must some other current convey an equal volume of water, or else the first would, in the course of time, cease for the want of water to supply it.

275. Currents of the Atlantic.—The principal currents of the Atlantic have been described in the chapter on the Gulf Stream. Besides this, its eddies and its offsets, are the equatorial current (Plate VI.), and the St. Roque or Brazil Current. Their fountain-head is the same. It is in the warm waters about the equator, between Africa and America. The former, receiving the Amazon and the Oronoco as tributaries by the way, flows into the Caribbean Sea, and becomes, with the waters (§ 35) in which the vapors of the trade-winds leave their salts, the feeder of the Gulf Stream. The Brazil Current, coming from the same fountain, is supposed to be divided by Cape St. Roque, one branch going to the south under this name (Plate IX.), the other to the westward. This last has been a great bugbear to navigators, principally on account of the difficulties which a few dull vessels falling to leeward of St. Roque have found in beating up against it. It was said to have caused the loss of some English transports in the last century, which fell to leeward of the Cape on a voyage to the other hemisphere; and navigators, accordingly, were advised to shun it as a danger.

276. This current has been an object of special investigation

during my researches connected with the wind and current charts, and the result has satisfied me that it is neither a dangerous nor a constant current, notwithstanding older writers. Horsburgh, in his East India Directory, cautions navigators against it; and Keith Johnston, in his grand Physical Atlas, published in 1848, thus speaks of it:

"This current greatly impedes the progress of those vessels which cross the equator west of 23° west longitude, impelling them beyond Cape St. Roque, when they are drawn toward the northern coast of Brazil, and can not regain their course till after weeks or months of delay and exertion."

So far from this being the case, my researches abundantly prove that vessels which cross the equator five hundred miles to the west of longitude 23° west have no difficulty on account of this current in clearing that cape. I receive almost daily the abstract logs of vessels that cross the equator west of 30° west, and in three days from that crossing they are generally clear of that cape. A few of them report the current in their favor; most of them experience no current at all; but, now and then, some do find a current setting to the northward and westward, and operating against them at the rate of twenty miles a day. The inter-tropical regions of the Atlantic, like those of the other oceans (§ 270), abound with conflicting currents, which no researches yet have enabled the mariner to unravel so that he may at all times know where they are and tell how they run, in order that the navigator may be certain of their help when favorable, or sure of avoiding them if adverse.

277. I may here remark, that there seems to be a larger flow of polar waters into the Atlantic than of other waters from it, and I can not account for the preservation of the equilibrium of this ocean by any other hypothesis than that which calls in the aid of under currents. They, I have no doubt, bear an important part in the system of oceanic circulation.

Admiral Sir Francis Beaufort, the venerable hydrographer of England, made, when in command of her Britannic majesty's frigate *Frederiksteen*, in the Mediterranean, some interesting experiments upon under currents, which I should be glad to see repeated in other parts of the sea, especially between the tropics, in the Atlantic, Pacific, and Indian Oceans, and wherever the water is remarkably transparent. That officer says:

"The counter currents, or those which return beneath the surface of the water, are also very remarkable; in some parts of the Archipelago they are at times so strong as to prevent the steering of the ship; and, in one instance, on sinking the lead, when the sea was calm and clear, with shreds of bunting of various colors attached to every yard of the line, they pointed in different directions all round the compass."

These shreds of bunting probably "tailed out" straight from the line, not in consequence of currents, but by reason of their specific gravity, and their tendency to lie straight out from, rather than to coil around, the line. At any rate, it is an interesting experiment, and I hope some of those noble-hearted mariners who are co-operating with me in collecting facts concerning the physical laws of the sea will avail themselves of calms to repeat the experiment. A submarine kite—that is, a contrivance upon the principle of a boy's kite in the air—let down at various depths in the sea, would indicate both the direction and force of the under currents.

CHAPTER VII.

THE OPEN SEA IN THE ARCTIC OCEAN.

How Whales struck on the east Side of the Continent have been taken on the west Side, § 278.—Right Whales can not cross the Equator, 279.—How the Existence of a northwest Passage was proved by the Whales, 280.—Other Evidence in Favor of it, 281.—An under Current sets into the Arctic Ocean, 282.—Evidences of a milder Climate near the Pole, 284.—The Water Sky of Lieutenant De Haven, 285. —This open Sea not permanently in one Place, 286.

278. It is the custom among whalers to have their harpoons marked with date and the name of the ship; and Dr. Scoresby, in his work on Arctic voyages, mentions several instances of whales that have been taken near the Behring's Strait side with harpoons in them bearing the stamp of ships that were known to cruise on the Baffin's Bay side of the American continent; and as, in one or two instances, a very short time had elapsed between the date of capture in the Pacific and the date when the fish must have been struck on the Atlantic side, it was argued therefore that there was a northwest passage by which the whales passed from one side to the other, since the stricken animal could not have had the harpoon in him long enough to admit of a passage around either Cape Horn or the Cape of Good Hope.

The whale-fishing is, among the industrial pursuits of the sea, one of no little importance; and when the system of investigation out of which the "wind and current charts" have grown was commenced, the haunts of this animal did not escape attention or examination. The log-books of whalers were collected in great numbers, and patiently examined, co-ordinated, and discussed, in order to find out what parts of the ocean are frequented by this kind of whale, what parts by that, and what parts by neither. (See Plate IX.)

279. Log-books containing the records by different ships for hundreds of thousands of days were examined, and the observations in them co-ordinated for this chart. And this investigation,

as Plate IX. shows, led to the discovery that the tropical regions of the ocean are to the right whale as a sea of fire, through which he can not pass, and into which he never enters. The fact was also brought out that the same kind of whale that is found off the shores of Greenland, in Baffin's Bay, &c., is found also in the North Pacific, and about Behring's Strait, and that the right whale of the northern hemisphere is a different animal from that of the southern.

280. Thus the fact was established that the harpooned whales did not pass around Cape Horn or the Cape of Good Hope, for they were of the class that could not cross the equator. In this way we were furnished with circumstantial evidence affording the most irrefragable proof that there is, at times at least, open water communication through the Arctic Sea from one side of the continent to the other, for it is known that the whales can not travel under the ice for such a great distance as is that from one side of this continent to the other.

But this did not prove the existence of an open sea there; it only established the existence—the occasional existence, if you please—of a channel through which whales had passed. Therefore we felt bound to introduce other evidence before we could expect the reader to admit our proof, and to believe with us in the existence of an open sea in the Arctic Ocean.

281. There is an under current setting from the Atlantic through Davis's Strait into the Arctic Ocean, and there is a surface current setting out. Observations have pointed out the existence of this under current there, for navigators tell of immense icebergs which they have seen drifting rapidly to the north, and against a strong surface current. These icebergs were high above the water, and their depth below was seven times greater than their height above. No doubt they were drifted by a powerful under current.

282. Now this under current comes from the south, where it is warm, and the temperature of its waters is perhaps not below 32°; at any rate, they are comparatively warm. There must be a place somewhere in the Arctic seas where this under current ceases to flow north, and begins to flow south as a surface current; for the surface current, though its waters are mixed with the fresh waters of the rivers and of precipitation in the polar

basin, nevertheless bears out vast quantities of salt, which is furnished neither by the rivers nor the rains.

283. These salts are supplied by the under current; for as much salt as one current brings in, other currents (§ 252) must take out, else the polar basin would become a basin of salt; and where the under current transfers its waters to the surface, there is, it is supposed, a basin in which the waters, as they rise to the surface, are at 30°, or whatever be the temperature of the under current, which we know must be above the freezing point, for the current is of water in a fluid, not in a solid state.

An arrangement in nature, by which a basin of considerable area in the frozen ocean could be supplied by water coming in at the bottom and rising up at the top, with a temperature not below 30°, or even 28°—the freezing point of sea water—would go far to mitigate the climate in the regions round about.

284. And that there is a warmer climate somewhere in that inhospitable sea, the observations of many of the explorers who have visited it indicate. Its existence may be inferred also from the well-known fact that the birds and animals are found at certain seasons migrating to the north, evidently in search of milder climates. The instincts of these dumb creatures are unerring, and we can imagine no mitigation of the climate in that direction, unless it arise from the proximity or the presence there of a large body of open water. It is another furnace (§ 60) in the beautiful economy of Nature for tempering climates there.

285. Relying upon a process of reasoning like this, and the deductions flowing therefrom, Lieutenant De Haven, when he went in command of the American expedition in search of Sir John Franklin and his companions, was told, in his letter of instructions, to look, when he should get well up into Wellington Channel, for an open sea to the northward and westward. He looked, and saw in that direction a "water sky." Captain Penny afterward went there, found open water, and sailed upon it.

286. The open sea in the Arctic Ocean is probably not always in the same place, as the Gulf Stream (§ 54) is not always in one place. It probably is always where the waters of the under current are brought to the surface; and this, we may imagine, would depend upon the freedom of ingress for the under current. Its course may, perhaps, be modified more or less by the ice on the

surface, by changes, from whatever cause, in the course or velocity of the surface current, for obviously the under current could not bring more water into the frozen ocean than the surface current would carry out again, either as ice or water.

287. Every winter, an example of how very close warm water in the sea and a very severe climate on the land or the ice may be to each other, is afforded to us in the case of the Gulf Stream, and the Labrador-like climate of New England, Nova Scotia, and Newfoundland. In these countries, in winter, the thermometer frequently sinks far below zero, notwithstanding that the tepid waters of the Gulf Stream may be found with their summer temperature within one good day's sail of these very, very cold places.

CHAPTER VIII.

THE SALTS OF THE SEA.

288. In order to comprehend aright the currents of the sea, and to study with advantage its physical adaptations, it is necessary to understand the effects produced by the salts of the sea upon the equilibrium of its waters; for wherever equilibrium be destroyed, whether in the air or water (§ 276), it is restored by motion, and motion among fluid particles gives rise to currents, which, in turn, constitute circulation.

This chapter is therefore added as a sort of supplement, which will assist us in elucidating what has been advanced concerning the currents of the sea.

289. The question is often asked, "Why is the sea salt?" I think it can be shown that the circulation of the ocean depends, in a great measure, upon the salts of sea water; certainly its influences upon climate are greatly extended by reason of its saltness.

As a general rule, the sea is nearly of a uniform degree of saltness, and the constituents of sea water are as constant in their proportions as are the components of the atmosphere. It is true that we sometimes come across arms of the sea, or places in the ocean, where we find the water more salt or less salt than sea water is generally; but this circumstance is due to local causes of easy explanation. For instance: when we come to an arm of the sea, as the Red Sea (§ 238), upon which it never rains, and from which the atmosphere is continually abstracting, by evaporation, fresh water from the salt, we may naturally expect to find a greater proportion of salt in the sea water that remains than we do near the mouth of some great river, as the Amazon, or in the regions of constant precipitation, or other parts where it rains more than it evaporates. Therefore we do not find sea water from all parts of the ocean actually of the same degree of saltness, yet we do find, as in the case of the Red Sea, sea water that is continually giving off to evaporation fresh water in large quantities; nevertheless, for such water there is a degree, and a very moderate degree, of saltness which is a maximum; and we moreover find that, though the constituents of sea water, like those of the atmosphere, are not for every place invariably the same as to their proportions, yet they are the same, or nearly the same, as to their character.

290. When, therefore, we take into consideration the fact that, as a general rule, sea water is, with the exceptions above stated, every where and always the same, and that it can only be made so by being well shaken together, we find grounds on which to base the conjecture that the ocean has its system of circulation, which is probably as complete and not less wonderful than is the circulation of blood through the human system.

In order to investigate the currents of the sea, and to catch a glimpse of the laws by which the circulation of its waters is governed, hypothesis, in the present meagre state of absolute knowledge with regard to the subject, seems to be as necessary to progress as is a corner-stone to a building. To make progress with such investigations, we want something to build upon. In the absence of facts, we are sometimes permitted to suppose them; only, in supposing them, we should take not only the possible, but the probable; and in making the selection of the various hypotheses which are suggested, we are bound to prefer that one by which the greatest number of phenomena can be reconciled. When we have found, tried, and offered such an one, we are entitled to claim for it a respectful consideration at least, until we discover it leading us into some palpable absurdity, or until some other hypothesis be suggested which will account equally as well, but for a greater number of phenomena. Then, as honest searchers after truth, we should be ready to give up the former, adopt the latter, and to try it until some other better than either of the two be offered.

291. With this understanding, I venture to offer an hypothesis with regard to the agency of the salts or solid matter of the sea in imparting dynamical force to the waters of the ocean, and to suggest that one of the purposes which, in the grand design, it was probably intended to accomplish by having the sea salt, and not fresh, was to impart to its waters the forces and powers necessary to make their circulation complete.

In the first place, we do but conjecture when we say that there is a set of currents in the sea by which its waters are conveyed from place to place with regularity, certainty, and order. But this conjecture appears to be founded on reason; for if we take a sample of water which shall fairly represent, in the proportion of its constituents, the average water of the Pacific Ocean, and analyze it, and if we do the same by a similar sample from the Atlantic, we shall find the analysis of the one to resemble that of the other as closely as though the two samples had been taken from the same bottle after having been well shaken. How, then, shall we account for this, unless upon the supposition that sea water from one part of the world is, in the process of time, brought into contact and mixed up with sea water from all other parts of the world? Agents, therefore, it would seem, are at work, which shake up the waters of the sea as though they were in a bottle, and which, in the course of time, mingle those that are in one part of the ocean with those that are in another as thoroughly and completely as it is possible for man to do in a vessel of his own construction.

292. This fact, as to uniformity of components, appears to call for the hypothesis that sea water which to-day is in one part of the ocean, will, in the process of time, be found in another part the most remote. It must, therefore, be carried about by currents; and as these currents have their offices to perform in the terrestrial economy, they probably do not flow by chance, but in obedience to physical laws; they no doubt, therefore, maintain the order and preserve the harmony which characterize every de-

partment of God's handiwork, upon the threshold of which man has as yet been permitted to stand, to observe, and to comprehend.

293. Nay, having reached this threshold, and taken a survey of the surrounding ocean, we are ready to assert, with all the confidence of knowledge, that the sea has a system of circulation for its waters. We rest this assertion upon our faith in the physical adaptations with which the sea is invested. Take, for example, the coral islands, reefs, beds, and atolls with which the Pacific Ocean is studded and garnished. They were built up of materials which a certain kind of insect quarried from the sea water. The currents of the sea ministered to this little insect—they were its *hod carriers;* when fresh supplies of solid matter were wanted for the coral rock upon which the foundations of the Polynesian Islands were laid, they brought them; the obedient currents stood ready with fresh supplies in unfailing streams of sea water from which the solid ingredients had not been secreted. Now, unless the currents of the sea had been employed to carry off from this insect the waters that had been emptied by it of their lime, and to bring to it others charged with more, it is evident the little creature would have perished for want of food long before its task was half completed. But for currents, it would have been impaled in a nook of the very drop of water in which it was spawned; for it would have soon secreted the lime contained in this drop of water, and then, without the ministering aid of currents to bring it more, it would have perished for the want of food for itself and materials for its edifice; and thus, but for the benign currents which took this exhausted water away, there we perceive this emptied drop would have remained, not only as the grave of the little architect, but as a monument in attestation of the shocking monstrosity that there had been a failure in the sublime system of terrestrial adaptations—that the sea had not been adapted by its Creator to the well-being of all its inhabitants. Now we do know that its adaptations are suited to all the wants of every one of its inhabitants—to the wants of the coral insect as well as to those of the whale. Hence we say *we know* that the sea has its system of circulation, for it transports materials for the coral rock from one part of the world to another; its currents receive them from the rivers, and hand them over to the little mason for the struct-

ure of the most stupendous works of solid masonry that man has ever seen—the coral islands of the sea.

294. And thus, by a process of reasoning which is perfectly philosophical, we are irresistibly led to conjecture that there are regular and certain, if not appointed channels, through which the water travels from one part of the ocean to another, and that those channels belong to an arrangement which may make, and, for aught we know to the contrary, which does make the system of oceanic circulation as complete, as perfect, and as harmonious as is that of the atmosphere or the blood. Every drop of water in the sea is as obedient to law and order as are the members of the heavenly host in the remotest regions of space. For when the morning stars sang together in the almighty anthem, "the waves also lifted up their voice;" and doubtless, therefore, the harmony in the depths of the ocean is in tune with that which comes from the spheres above. We can not doubt it; for, were it not so, were there no channels of circulation from one ocean to another, and if, accordingly, the waters of the Atlantic were confined to the Atlantic, or if the waters of the arms and seas of the Atlantic were confined to those arms and seas, and had no channels of circulation by which they could pass out into the ocean, and traverse different latitudes and climates—if this were so, then the machinery of the ocean would be as incomplete as that of a watch without a balance-wheel; for the waters of these arms and seas would, as to their constituents, become, in the process of time, very different from the sea waters in other parts of the world, and their inhabitants would perish for the want of brine of the right strength or of water of the right temperature.

295. For instance, take the Red Sea and the Mediterranean by way of illustration. Upon the Red Sea there is no precipitation; it is a rainless region; not a river runs down to it, not a brook empties into it; therefore there is no process by which the salts and washings of the earth, which are taken up and held in solution by rain or river water, can be brought down into the Red Sea. Its salts come from the ocean, and the air takes up from it, in the process of evaporation, fresh water, leaving behind all the solid matter which this sea holds in solution (§ 239).

296. On the other hand, numerous rivers discharge into the Mediterranean, some of which are filtered through soils and among

minerals which yield one kind of salts or soluble matter, another river runs through a limestone or volcanic region of country, and brings down in solution solid matter—it may be common salt, sulphate or carbonate of lime, magnesia, soda, potash, or iron—either or all may be in its waters. Still, the constituents of sea water from the Mediterranean and of sea water from the Red Sea are quite the same. But the waters of the Dead Sea have no connection with those of the ocean; they are cut off from its channels of circulation, and are therefore quite different, as to their components, from any arm, frith, or gulf of the broad ocean. Its inhabitants are also different from those of the high seas.

297. "The solid constituents of sea water amount to about 3½ per cent. of its weight, or nearly half an ounce to the pound. Its saltness may be considered as a necessary result of the present order of things. Rivers which are constantly flowing into the ocean contain salts, varying from ten to fifty, and even one hundred grains per gallon. They are chiefly common salt, sulphate and carbonate of lime, magnesia,* soda, potash, and iron; and these are found to constitute the distinguishing characteristics of sea water. The water which evaporates from the sea is nearly pure, containing but very minute traces of salts. Falling as rain upon the land, it washes the soil, percolates through the rocky layers, and becomes charged with saline substances, which are borne seaward by the returning currents. The ocean, therefore, is the great depository of every thing that water can dissolve and carry down from the surface of the continents; and, as there is no channel for their escape, they of course consequently accumulate."†

298. "The case of the sea," says Fowner, "is but a magnified representation of what occurs in every lake into which rivers flow, but from which there is no outlet except by evaporation. Such a lake is invariably a salt lake. It is impossible that it can be otherwise; and it is curious to observe that this condition disappears when an artificial outlet is produced for the waters."

299. How, therefore, shall we account for this sameness of compound, this structure of coral (§ 293), this stability as to animal life in the sea, but upon the supposition of a general system of circulation in the ocean, by which, in process of time, water from one part is conveyed to another part the most remote, and

* See Appendix E. † Youmans's Chemistry.

by which a general interchange and commingling of the waters take place? In like manner, the constituents of the atmosphere, whether it be analyzed at the equator or the poles, are the same. By cutting off and shutting up from the general channels of circulation any portion of sea water, as in the Dead Sea, or of atmospheric air, as in mines or wells, we can easily fill either with gases or other matter that shall very much affect its character, or alter the proportion of its ingredients, and affect the health of its inhabitants.

300. The principal agents that are supposed to be concerned in giving circulation to the atmosphere, and in preserving the ratio among its components, are light, heat, electricity, and magnetism (§ 231). But with regard to the sea, it is not known what office is performed by electricity and magnetism, in giving dynamical force to its waters in their system of circulation. The chief motive power from which marine currents derive their velocity has been ascribed to heat; but a close study of the agents concerned has suggested that an important—nay, a powerful and active agency in the system of oceanic circulation is derived from the salts of the sea water, through the instrumentality of the winds, of marine plants, and animals. These give the ocean great dynamical force.

301. Let us, for the sake of illustrating and explaining this force, suppose the sea in all its parts—in its depths and at the surface, at the equator and about the poles—to be of one uniform temperature, and to be all of fresh water; and, moreover, that there be neither wind to disturb its surface, nor tides nor rains to raise the level in this part, or to depress it in that. In this case, there would be nothing of heat to disturb its equilibrium, and there would be no motive power (§ 288) to beget currents, or to set the water in motion by reason of the difference of level or of specific gravity due to water at different densities and temperatures.

302. Now let us suppose the winds, for the first time since the creation, to commence to blow upon this quiescent sea, and to ruffle its surface; they, by their force, would create partial surface currents, and thus agitating the waters to a certain depth, would give rise to a feeble and partial aqueous circulation in the supposed sea of fresh water.

303. This, then, is one of the sources whence power is given to the system of oceanic circulation; but, though a feeble one, it

is one which exists in reality, and, therefore, need not be regarded as hypothetical.

304. Let us next call in evaporation and precipitation, with heat and cold—more powerful agents. Suppose the evaporation to commence from this imaginary fresh-water ocean, and to go on as it does from the seas as they are. In those regions, as in the trade-wind regions, where evaporation is in excess of precipitation (§ 126), the general level of this supposed sea would be altered, and, immediately, as much water as is carried off by evaporation would commence to flow in from north and south toward the trade-wind or evaporating region, to restore the level.

305. On the other hand, the winds have taken this vapor, borne it off to the extra-tropical regions, and precipitated it (§ 129), we will suppose, where precipitation is in excess of evaporation. Here is another alteration of sea level by elevation instead of by depression; and hence we have the motive power for a surface current from each pole toward the equator, the object of which is only to supply the demand for evaporation in the trade-wind regions—demand for evaporation being taken here to mean the difference between evaporation and precipitation for any part of the sea.

306. Now imagine this sea of uniform temperature (§ 301) to be suddenly stricken with the invisible wand of heat and cold, and its waters brought to the various temperatures at which they at this instant are standing. This change of temperature would make a change of specific gravity in the waters, which would destroy the equilibrium of the whole ocean, upon which (§ 275) a set of currents (§ 277) would immediately commence to flow, viz., a current of cold and heavy water to the warm, and a current of warm and lighter to the cold.

The motive power of these would be difference of specific gravity due to difference of temperature in fresh water.

307. We have now traced (§ 303 and 306) the effect of two agents, which, in a sea of fresh water, would tend to create currents, and to beget a system of aqueous circulation; but a set of currents and a system of circulation which, it is readily perceived, would be quite different from those which we find in the salt sea. One of these agents would be employed (§ 305) in restoring, by means of one or more polar currents, the water that is taken from one part of the ocean by evaporation, and deposited in another by

precipitation. The other agent would be employed in restoring, by the forces due difference of specific gravity (§ 306), the equilibrium, which has been disturbed by heating, and of course expanding, the waters of the torrid zone on one hand, and by cooling, and consequently contracting, those of the frigid zone on the other. This agency would, if it were not modified by others, find expression in a system of currents and counter currents, or rather in a set of surface currents of warm and light water, from the equator toward the poles, and in another set of under currents of cooler, dense, and heavy water from the poles toward the equator.

308. Such, keeping out of view the influence of the winds, which we may suppose would be the same, whether the sea were salt or fresh, would be the system of oceanic circulation were the sea all of fresh water. But fresh water, in cooling, begins to expand near the temperature of 40°, and expands more and more till it reaches the freezing point, and ceases to be fluid. This law of expansion by cooling would impart a peculiar feature to the system of oceanic circulation were the waters all fresh, which it is not necessary to notice further than to say it can not exist in seas of salt water, for salt water (§ 31) contracts as its temperature is lowered to its freezing point. Hence, in consequence of its salts, changes of temperature derive increased power to disturb the equilibrium of the ocean.

309. If this train of reasoning be good, we may infer that, in a system of oceanic circulation, the dynamical force to be derived from difference of temperature, where the waters are all fresh, would be quite feeble; and that, were the sea not salt, we should probably have no such current in it as the Gulf Stream.

So far we have been reasoning hypothetically, to show what would be the chief agents, exclusive of the winds, in disturbing the equilibrium of the ocean, were its waters fresh and not salt. And whatever disturbs equilibrium there may be regarded as the *primum mobile* in any system of marine currents.

Let us now proceed another step in the process of explaining and illustrating the effect of the salts of the sea in the system of oceanic circulation. To this end, let us suppose this imaginary ocean of fresh water suddenly to become that which we have, viz., an ocean of salt water, which contracts as its temperature is lowered (§ 308) till it reaches 28° or thereabout.

310. Let evaporation now commence in the trade-wind region, as it was supposed to do (§ 304) in the case of the fresh-water seas, and as it actually goes on in nature—and what takes place? Why, a lowering of the sea level, as before. But as the vapor of salt water is fresh, or nearly so, fresh water only is taken up from the ocean; that which remains behind is therefore more salt. Thus, while the level is lowered in the *salt* sea, the equilibrium is destroyed because of the saltness of the water; for the water that remains after the evaporation takes place is, on account of the solid matter held in solution, specifically heavier than it was before any portion of it was converted into vapor.

311. The vapor is taken from the surface water; the surface water thereby becomes more salt, and, under certain conditions, heavier; when it becomes heavier, it sinks; and hence we have, due to the salts of the sea, a vertical circulation, viz., a descent of heavier—because salter and cooler—water from the surface, and an ascent of water that is lighter—because it is not so salt—from the depths below.

312. This vapor, then, which is taken up from the evaporating regions (§ 126), is carried by the winds through their channels of circulation, and poured back into the ocean where the regions of precipitation are; and by the regions of precipitation I mean those parts of the ocean, as in the polar basins, where the ocean receives more fresh water in the shape of rain, snow, &c., than it returns to the atmosphere in the shape of vapor.

313. In the precipitating regions, therefore, the level is destroyed, as before explained, by elevation; and in the evaporating regions, by depression; which, as already stated (§ 305), gives rise to a system of surface currents, moved by gravity alone, from the poles toward the equator.

But we are now considering the effects of evaporation and precipitation in giving impulse to the circulation of the ocean where its waters are *salt*.

314. The fresh water that has been taken from the evaporating regions is deposited upon those of precipitation, which, for illustration merely, we will locate in the north polar basin. Among the sources of supply of fresh water for this basin we must include not only the precipitation which takes place over the basin itself, but also the amount of fresh water discharged into it by the

rivers of the great hydrographical basins of Arctic Europe, Asia, and America.

315. This fresh water, being emptied into the Polar Sea and agitated by the winds, becomes mixed with the salt; but as the agitation of the sea by the winds extends to no great depth (§ 302), it is only the upper layer of salt water, and that to a moderate depth, which becomes mixed with the fresh. The specific gravity of this upper layer, therefore, is diminished just as much as the specific gravity of the sea water in the evaporating regions was increased. And thus we have a surface current of saltish water from the poles toward the equator, and an under current of water salter and heavier from the equator to the poles. This under current supplies, in a great measure, the salt which the upper current, freighted with fresh water from the clouds and rivers, carries back.

316. Thus it is to the salts of the sea that we owe that feature in the system of oceanic circulation which causes an under current to flow from the Mediterranean into the Atlantic (§ 252), and another (§ 245) from the Red Sea into the Indian Ocean. And it is evident, since neither of these seas is salting up, that just as much, or nearly just as much salt as the under current brings out, just so much the upper currents carry in.

317. We now begin to perceive what a powerful impulse is derived from the salts of the sea in giving effective and active circulation to its waters.

318. Hence we infer that the currents of the sea, by reason of its saltness, attain their maximum of volume and velocity. Hence, too, we infer that the transportation of warm water from the equator toward the frozen regions of the poles, and of cold water from the frigid toward the torrid zone, is facilitated; and consequently here, in the saltness of the sea, have we not an agent by which climates are mitigated—by which they are softened and rendered much more salubrious than it would be possible for them to be were the waters of the ocean deprived of their property of saltness?

319. This property of saltness imparts to the waters of the ocean another peculiarity, by which the sea is still better adapted for the regulation of climates, and it is this: by evaporating fresh water from the salt in the tropics, the surface water becomes heavier than the average of sea water (§ 127). This heavy wa-

ter is also warm water; it sinks, and being a good retainer, but a bad conductor of heat, this warm water is employed in transporting through under currents heat for the mitigation of climates in far-distant regions. Now this also is a property which a sea of fresh water could not have. Let the winds take up their vapor from a sheet of fresh water, and that at the bottom is not disturbed, for there is no change in the specific gravity of that at the surface by which that at the bottom may be brought to the top; but let evaporation go on, though never so gently, from salt water, and the specific gravity of that at the top will soon be so changed as to bring that from the very lowest depths of the sea speedily to the top.

320. If these inferences as to the influence of the salts upon the currents of the sea be correct, the same cause which produces an under current from the Mediterranean, and an under current from the Red Sea into the ocean, should produce an under current from the ocean into the north Polar basin. In each case, the hypothesis with regard to the part performed by the salt, in giving vigor to the system of oceanic circulation, requires that, counter to the surface current of water with less salt, there should be an under current of water with more salt in it.

That such is the case with regard both to the Mediterranean and the Red Sea, has been amply shown in other parts of this work (§ 252 and 239), and abundantly proved by other observers.

321. That there is a constant current setting out of the Arctic Ocean through Davis's and other straits thereabout, which connect it with the Atlantic Ocean, is generally admitted. Lieutenant De Haven, United States Navy, when in command of the American expedition in search of Sir John Franklin, was frozen up with his vessels in the main channel of Wellington Straits; and during the nine months that he was so frozen, his vessels, holding their place in the ice, were drifted with it bodily for more than a thousand miles toward the south.

The ice in which they were bound was of sea water, and the currents by which they were drifted were of sea water—only, it may be supposed, the latter were not quite so salt as the sea water generally is. The same phenomenon is repeated in the Sound, where (§ 252) an under current of salt water runs in, and an upper current of brackish water (§ 36 and 51) runs out.

322. Then, since there is salt always flowing out of the north polar basin, we infer that there must be salt always flowing into it, else it would either become fresh, or the whole Atlantic Ocean would be finally silted up with salt.

It might be supposed, were there no evidence to the contrary, that this salt was supplied to the Polar seas from the Atlantic around North Cape, and from the Pacific through Behring's Straits, and through no other channels.

323. But, fortunately, Arctic voyagers, who have cruised in the direction of Davis's Straits, have afforded us, by their observations (§ 281), proof positive as to the fact of this other source for supplying the Polar seas with salt. They tell us of an under current setting from the Atlantic toward the Polar basin. They describe huge icebergs, with tops high up in the air, and of course the bases of which extend far down into the depths of the ocean, ripping and tearing their way, with terrific force and awful violence, through the surface ice or against a surface current, on their way into the Polar basin.

Passed Midshipman S. P. Griffin, who commanded the brig Rescue in the American searching expedition after Sir John Franklin, informs me that, on one occasion, the two vessels were endeavoring, when in Baffin's Bay, to warp up to the northward against a strong surface current, which of course was setting to the south; and that while so engaged, an iceberg, with its top many feet above the water, came "drifting up" from the south, and passed by them "like a shot." Although they were stemming a surface current against both the berg and themselves, such was the force and velocity of the under current, that it carried the berg to the northward faster than the crew could warp the vessel against a surface but counter current.

Captain Duncan, master of the English whale-ship Dundee, says, at page 76 of his interesting little narrative:*

"*December* 18*th* (1826). It was awful to behold the immense icebergs working their way to the northeast from us, and not one drop of water to be seen; they were working themselves right through the middle of the ice."

And again, at page 92, &c.:

* Arctic Regions; Voyage to Davis's Strait, by Dorea Duncan, Master of the Ship Dundee, 1826, 1827.

"*February* 23*d*. Latitude 68° 37′ north, longitude about 63° west.

"The dreadful apprehensions that assailed us yesterday, by the near approach of the iceberg, were this day most awfully verified. About three P.M., the iceberg came in contact with our floe, and in less than one minute it broke the ice; we were frozen in quite close to the shore; the floe was shivered to pieces for several miles, causing an explosion like an earthquake, or one hundred pieces of heavy ordnance fired at the same moment. The iceberg, with awful but majestic grandeur (in height and dimensions resembling a vast mountain), came almost up to our stern, and every one expected it would have run over the ship. . . . .

"The iceberg, as before observed, came up very near to the stern of our ship; the intermediate space between the berg and the vessel was filled with heavy masses of ice, which, though they had been previously broken by the immense weight of the berg, were again formed into a compact body by its pressure. The berg was drifting at the rate of about four knots, and by its force on the mass of ice, was pushing the ship before it, as it appeared, to inevitable destruction."

"*Feb.* 24*th*. The iceberg still in sight, but driving away fast to the northeast."

"*Feb.* 25*th*. The iceberg that so lately threatened our destruction had driven completely out of sight to the northeast from us."

324. Now, then, whence, unless from the difference of specific gravity due sea water of different degrees of saltness, can we derive a motive power with force sufficient to give such tremendous masses of ice such a velocity?

325. What is the temperature of this under current? Be that what it may, it is probably above the freezing point of sea water. Suppose it to be at 32°. (Break through the ice in the northern seas, and the temperature of the surface water is always 28°. At least Lieutenant De Haven so found it in his long imprisonment, and it may be supposed that, as it was with him, so it generally is.) Assuming, then, the water of the surface current which runs out with the ice to be all at 28°, we observe that it is not unreasonable to suppose that the water of the under current, inasmuch as it comes from the south, and therefore from warmer latitudes,

is probably not so cold; and if it be not so cold, its temperature, before it comes out again, must be reduced to 28°, or whatever be the average temperature of the outer but surface current.

Moreover, if it be true, as some philosophers have suggested, that there is in the depths of the ocean a line from the equator to the poles along which the water is of the same temperature all the way, then the question may be asked, Should we not have in the depths of the ocean a sort of isothermal floor, as it were, on the upper side of which all the changes of temperature are due to agents acting from above, and on the lower side of which, the changes, if any, are due to agents acting from below?

326. This under Polar current water, then, as it rises to the top, and is brought to the surface by the agitation of the sea in the Arctic regions, gives out its surplus heat and warms the atmosphere there till the temperature of this warm under current water is lowered to the requisite degree for going out on the surface. Hence the water-sky of those regions.

327. And the heat that it loses in falling from its normal temperature, be that what it may, till it reaches the temperature of 28°, is so much caloric set free in the Polar regions, to temper the air and mitigate the climate there. Now is not this one of those modifications of climate which may be fairly traced back to the effect of the saltness of the sea in giving energy to its circulation?

Moreover, if there be a deep sea in the Polar basin, which serves as a receptacle for the waters brought into it by this under current, which, because it comes from toward the equatorial regions, comes from a milder climate, and is therefore warmer, we can easily imagine why there might be an open sea in the Polar regions—why Lieutenant De Haven, in his instructions, was directed to look for it; and why both he and Captain Penny, of one of the English searching vessels, found it there.

328. And in accounting for this polynia, we see that its existence is not only consistent with the hypothesis with which we set out, touching a perfect system of oceanic circulation, but that it may be ascribed, in a great degree at least, if not wholly, to the effect produced by the salts of the sea upon the mobility and circulation of its waters.

Here, then, is an office which the sea performs in the economy of the universe by virtue of its saltness, and which it could not perform were its waters altogether fresh. And thus philosophers have a clew placed in their hands which will probably guide them to one of the many hidden reasons that are embraced in the true answer to the question, "Why is the sea salt?"

329. SEA SHELLS.—We find in sea water other matter besides common salt. Lime is dissolved by the rains and the rivers, and emptied in vast quantities into the ocean. Out of it, coral islands and coral reefs of great extent — marl-beds, shell-banks, and infusorial deposits of enormous magnitude have been constructed by the inhabitants of the deep. These creatures are endowed with the power of secreting, apparently for their own purposes only, solid matter, which the waters of the sea hold in solution. But this power was given to them that they also might fulfill the part assigned them in the economy of the universe. For to them, probably, has been allotted the important office of assisting in giving circulation to the ocean, of helping to regulate the climates of the earth, and of preserving the purity of the sea.

330. The better to comprehend how such creatures may influence currents and climates, let us suppose the ocean to be perfectly at rest—that throughout, it is in a state of complete equilibrium—that, with the exception of those tenants of the deep which have the power of extracting from it the solid matter held in solution, there is no agent in nature capable of disturbing that equilibrium—and that all these fish, &c., have suspended their secretions, in order that this state of a perfect aqueous equilibrium and repose throughout the sea might be attained.

In this state of things—the waters of the sea being in perfect equilibrium—a single mollusk or coralline, we will suppose, commences his secretions, and abstracts from the sea water (§ 293) solid matter for his cell. In that act, this animal has destroyed the equilibrium of the whole ocean, for the specific gravity of that portion of water from which this solid matter has been abstracted is altered. Having lost a portion of its solid contents, it has become specifically lighter than it was before; it must, therefore, give place to the pressure which the heavier water exerts to push it aside and to occupy its place, and it must consequently travel about and mingle with the waters of the other parts of the ocean until its proportion of solid matter is returned to it, and until it attains the exact degree of specific gravity due sea water generally.

331. How much solid matter does the whole host of marine plants and animals abstract from sea water daily? Is it a thousand pounds, or a thousand millions of tons? No one can say. But, whatever be its weight, it is so much of the power of gravity applied to the dynamical forces of the ocean. And this power is derived from the salts of the sea, through the agency of sea-shells and other marine animals, that of themselves scarcely possess the power of locomotion. Yet they have power to put the whole sea in motion, from the equator to the poles, and from top to bottom.

332. Those powerful and strange equatorial currents (§ 270), which navigators tell us they encounter in the Pacific Ocean, to what are they due? Coming from sources unknown, they are lost in the midst of the ocean. They are due, no doubt, to some extent, to the effects of precipitation and evaporation, and the change of heat produced thereby. But we have yet to inquire, How far may they be due to the derangement of equilibrium arising from the change of specific gravity caused by the secretions of the myriads of marine animals that are continually at work in those parts of the ocean? These abstract from sea water solid matter enough to build continents of. And, also, we have to inquire as to the extent to which equilibrium in the sea is disturbed by the salts which evaporation leaves behind.

Thus, when we consider the salts of the sea in one point of view, we see the winds and the marine animals operating upon the waters, and, in certain parts of the ocean, deriving from the solid contents of the same those very principles of antagonistic forces which hold the earth in its orbit, and preserve the harmonies of the universe.

In another point of virw, we see how the sea-breeze and the sea-shell, in performing their appointed offices, act so as to give rise to a reciprocating motion in the waters; and thus they impart to the ocean dynamical forces also for its circulation.

333. The sea-breeze plays upon the surface; it converts only fresh water into vapor, and leaves the solid matter behind. The surface water thus becomes specifically heavier, and sinks. On the other hand, the little marine architect below, as he works upon his coral edifice at the bottom, abstracts from the water

there a portion of its solid contents; it therefore becomes specifically lighter, and up it goes, ascending to the top with increased velocity, to take the place of the descending column, which, by the action of the winds, has been sent down loaded with fresh food and materials for the busy little mason in the depths below.

334. Seeing, then, that the inhabitants of the sea, with their powers of secretion, are competent to exercise at least some degree of influence in disturbing equilibrium, are not these creatures entitled to be regarded as agents which have their offices to perform in the system of oceanic circulation, and do not they belong to its physical geography? It is immaterial how great or how small that influence may be supposed to be; for, be it great or small, we may rest assured it is not a chance influence, but it is an influence exercised—if exercised at all—by design, and according to the commandment of Him whose "voice the winds and the sea obey." Thus God speaks through sea-shells to the ocean.

335. It may therefore be supposed that the arrangements in the economy of nature are such as to require that the various kinds of marine animals, whose secretions are calculated to alter the specific gravity of sea water, to destroy its equilibrium, to beget currents in the ocean, and to control its circulation, should be distributed according to order.

336. Upon this supposition—the like of which nature warrants throughout her whole domain—we may conceive how the marine animals of which we have been speaking may impress other features upon the physical relations of the sea by assisting also to regulate climates, and to adjust the temperature of certain latitudes. For instance, let us suppose the waters in a certain part of the torrid zone to be 70°, but, by reason of the fresh water which has been taken from them in a state of vapor, and consequently by reason of the proportionate increase of salts, these waters are heavier than waters that may be cooler, but not so salt (§ 35).

This being the case, the tendency would be for this warm, but salt and heavy water, to flow off as an under current toward the Polar or some other regions of lighter water.

Now if the sea were not salt, there would be no coral islands to beautify its landscape and give variety to its features; sea-shells and marine insects could not operate upon the specific gravity of its waters, nor give variety to its climates; neither could evaporation give dynamical force to its circulation, and they, ceasing to contract as their temperature falls below 40°, would give but little impulse to its currents, and thus its circulation would be torpid, and its bosom lack animation.

337. This under current may be freighted with heat to temper some hyperborean region or to soften some extra-tropical climate (§ 64), for we know that such is among the effects of marine currents. At starting, it might have been, if you please, so loaded with solid matter, that, though its temperature were 70°, yet, by reason of the quantity of such matter held in solution, its specific gravity might have been greater even than that of extra-tropical sea water generally at 28°.

338. Notwithstanding this, it may be brought into contact, by the way, with those kinds and quantities of marine organisms that shall abstract solid matter enough to reduce its specific gravity, and, instead of leaving it greater than common sea water at 28°, make it less than common sea water at 40°; consequently, in such a case, this warm sea water, when it comes to the cold latitudes, would be brought to the surface through the instrumentality of shell-fish, and various other tribes that dwell far down in the depths of the ocean. Thus we perceive that these creatures, though they are regarded as being so low in the scale of creation, may nevertheless be regarded as agents of much importance in the terrestrial economy; for we perceive that they are capable of spreading over certain parts of the ocean those benign mantles of warmth which temper the winds, and modify, more or less, all the marine climates of the earth.

339. The makers of nice astronomical instruments, when they have put the different parts of their machinery together, and set it to work, find, as in the chronometer, for instance, that it is subject in its performance to many irregularities and imperfections—that in one state of things there is expansion, and in another state contraction among cogs, springs, and wheels, with an increase or diminution of rate. This defect the makers have sought to overcome; and, with a beautiful display of ingenuity, they have attached to the works of the instrument a contrivance which has had the effect of correcting these irregularities, by counteracting

the tendency of the instrument to change its performance with the changing influences of temperature.

This contrivance is called a *compensation;* and a chronometer that is well regulated and properly compensated will perform its office with certainty, and preserve its rate under all the vicissitudes of heat and cold to which it may be exposed.

340. In the clock-work of the ocean and the machinery of the universe, order and regularity are maintained by a system of compensations. A celestial body, as it revolves around its sun, flies off under the influence of centrifugal force; but immediately the forces of compensation begin to act; the planet is brought back to its elliptical path, and held in the orbit for which its mass, its motions, and its distance were adjusted. Its compensation is perfect.

341. So, too, with the salts and the shells of the sea in the machinery of the ocean; from them are derived principles of compensation the most perfect; through their agency the undue effects of heat and cold, of storm and rain, in disturbing the equilibrium, and producing thereby currents in the sea, are compensated, regulated, and controlled.

342. The dews, the rains, and the rivers are continually dissolving certain minerals of the earth, and carrying them off to the sea. This is an accumulating process; and if it were not *compensated,* the sea would finally become as the Dead Sea is, saturated with salt, and therefore unsuitable for the habitation of many fish of the sea.

The sea-shells and marine insects afford the required *compensation.* They are the conservators of the ocean. As the salts are emptied into the sea, these creatures secrete them again and pile them up in solid masses, to serve as the bases of islands and continents, to be in the process of ages upheaved into dry land, and then again dissolved by the dews and rains, and washed by the rivers away into the sea.

343. The question as to whence the salts of the sea were originally derived, of course has not escaped the attention of philosophers. Some have advanced the idea—Darwin, the poet, among others—that they came originally from the land, and were washed into the sea by the rivers and the rains. There seems to be plausibility in this idea; but there is reason for questioning it, as will

be seen by the arguments advanced and the facts stated in the Appendix to the second edition.—(See Appendix F.)

344. Thus we behold sea-shells and animalculæ in a new light. In every department of nature there is to be found this self-adjusting principle—this beautiful and exquisite system of *compensation*, by which the operations of the grand machinery of the universe are maintained in the most perfect order.

[For another view of the origin of the salts of the sea, adopted upon more matured reflection, see Appendix F.]

344. Thus we behold sea-shells and animalculæ in a new light. May we not now cease to regard them as beings which have little or nothing to do in maintaining the harmonies of creation? On the contrary, do we not see in them the principles of the most admirable compensation in the system of oceanic circulation? We may even regard them as regulators, to some extent, of climates in parts of the earth far removed from their presence. There is something suggestive, both of the grand and the beautiful, in the idea that, while the insects of the sea are building up their coral islands in the perpetual summer of the tropics, they are also engaged in dispensing warmth to distant parts of the earth, and in mitigating the severe cold of the Polar winter.

Surely an hypothesis which, being followed out, suggests so much design, such perfect order and arrangement, and so many beauties for contemplation and admiration as does this, which, for the want of a better, I have ventured to offer with regard to the solid matter of the sea water, its salts and its shells—surely such an hypothesis, though it be not based entirely on the results of actual observation, can not be regarded as wholly vain or as altogether profitless. **(See Appendix G.)**

CHAPTER IX.

THE EQUATORIAL CLOUD-RING.

345. SEAFARING people have, as if by common consent, divided the ocean off into regions, and characterized them according to the winds; *e. g.*, there are the "trade-wind regions," the "variables," the "horse latitudes," the "doldrums," &c. The "horse latitudes" are the belts of calms and light airs (§ 101) which border the Polar edge of the northeast trades. They were so called from the circumstance that vessels formerly bound from New England to the West Indies, with a deck load of horses, were often so delayed in this calm belt of Cancer, that, for the want of water for their animals, they were compelled to throw a portion of them overboard.

346. The "equatorial doldrums" is another of these calm places (§ 104). Besides being a region of calms and baffling winds, it is a region noted for its rains and clouds, which make it one of the most oppressive and disagreeable places at sea. The emigrant ships from Europe for Australia have to cross it. They are often baffled in it for two or three weeks; then the children and the passengers who are of delicate health suffer most. It is a frightful grave-yard on the way-side to that golden land.

347. A vessel bound into the southern hemisphere from Europe or America, after clearing the region of variable winds and crossing the "horse latitudes," enters the northeast trades. Here the mariner finds the sky sometimes mottled with clouds, but for the most part clear. Here, too, he finds his barometer rising and falling under the ebb and flow of a regular atmospherical tide, which gives a high and low barometer every day with such regularity

that the time of day within a few minutes may be told by it. The rise and fall of this tide, measured by the barometer, amounts to about one tenth (0.1) of an inch, and it occurs daily and every where between the tropics; the maximum about 10h. 30m. A.M., the minimum between 4h. and 5h. P.M., with a second maximum and minimum about 10 P.M. and 5 A.M.* The diurnal variation of the needle changes also with the turning of these invisible tides. Continuing his course toward the equinoctial line, he observes his thermometer to rise higher and higher as he approaches it; at last, entering the region of equatorial calms and rains, he feels the weather to become singularly close and oppressive; he discovers here that the elasticity of feeling which he breathed from the trade-wind air has forsaken him; he has entered the doldrums, and is under the "cloud-ring."

Escaping from this gloomy region, and entering the southeast trades beyond, his spirits revive, and he turns to his log-book to see what changes are recorded there. He is surprised to find that, notwithstanding the oppressive weather of the rainy latitudes, both his thermometer and barometer stood, while in them, lower than in the clear weather on either side of them; that just before entering and just before leaving the rainy parallels, the mercury of the thermometer and barometer invariably stands higher than it does when within them, even though they include the equator. In crossing the equatorial doldrums he has passed a ring of clouds that encircles the earth.

348. I find in the journal of the late Commodore Arthur Sinclair, kept on board the United States frigate Congress during a cruise to South America in 1817–18, a picture of the weather under this *cloud-ring* that is singularly graphic and striking. He encountered it in the month of January, 1818, between the parallel of 4° north and the equator, and between the meridians of 19° and 23° west. He says of it:

"This is certainly one of the most unpleasant regions in our globe. A dense, close atmosphere, except for a few hours after a thunder-storm, during which time torrents of rain fall, when the air becomes a little refreshed; but a hot, glowing sun soon heats it again, and but for your awnings, and the little air put in circu-

* See paper on Meteorological Observations in India, by Colonel Sykes, Philosophical Transactions for 1850, part 2d, page 297.

lation by the continual flapping of the ship's sails, it would be almost insufferable. No person who has not crossed this region can form an adequate idea of its unpleasant effects. You feel a degree of lassitude unconquerable, which not even the sea-bathing, which every where else proves so salutary and renovating, can dispel. Except when in actual danger of shipwreck, I never spent twelve more disagreeable days in the professional part of my life than in these calm latitudes.

"I crossed the line on the 17th of January, at eight A. M., in longitude 21° 20′, and soon found I had surmounted all the difficulties consequent to that event; that the breeze continued to freshen and draw round to the south-southeast, bringing with it a clear sky and most heavenly temperature, renovating and refreshing beyond description. Nothing was now to be seen but cheerful countenances, exchanged as by enchantment from that sleepy sluggishness which had borne us all down for the last two weeks."

349. One need not go to sea to perceive the grand work which the clouds perform in collecting moisture from the crystal vaults of the sky, in sprinkling it upon the fields, and making the hills glad with showers of rain. Winter and summer, "the clouds drop fatness upon the earth." This part of their office is obvious to all, and I do not propose to consider it now. But the sailor at sea observes phenomena and witnesses operations in the terrestrial economy which tell him that, in the beautiful and exquisite adjustments of the grand machinery of the atmosphere, the clouds have other important offices to perform besides those merely of dispensing showers, of producing the rains, and of weaving mantles of snow for the protection of our fields in winter. As important as are these offices, the philosophical mariner, as he changes his sky, is reminded that the clouds have commandments to fulfill, which, though less obvious, are not therefore the less benign in their influences, or the less worthy of his notice. He beholds them at work in moderating the extremes of heat and cold, and in mitigating climates. At one time they spread themselves out; they cover the earth as with a mantle; they prevent radiation from its crust, and keep it warm. At another time, they interpose between it and the sun; they screen it from his scorching rays, and protect the tender plants from his heat, the land from the drought; or, like a garment, they overshadow the sea, defending its

waters from the intense forces of evaporation. Having performed these offices for one place, they are evaporated and given up to the sunbeam and the winds again, to be borne on their wings away to other places which stand in need of like offices.

Familiar with clouds and sunshine, the storm and the calm, and all the phenomena which find expression in the physical geography of the sea, the right-minded mariner, as he contemplates "the cloud without rain," ceases to regard it as an empty thing; he perceives that it performs many important offices; he regards it as a great moderator of heat and cold—as a "compensation" in the atmospherical mechanism which makes the performance of the grand machine perfect.

350. Marvelous are the offices and wonderful is the constitution of the atmosphere. Indeed, I know of no subject more fit for profitable thought on the part of the truth-loving, knowledge-seeking student, be he seaman or landsman, than that afforded by the atmosphere and its offices. Of all parts of the physical machinery, of all the contrivances in the mechanism of the universe, the atmosphere, with its offices and its adaptations, appears to me to be the most wonderful, sublime, and beautiful. In its construction, the perfection of knowledge is involved. The perfect man of Uz, in a moment of inspiration, thus demands of his comforters: "But where shall wisdom be found, and where is the place of understanding? The depth saith, it is not in me; and the sea saith, it is not with me. It can not be gotten for gold, neither shall silver be weighed for the price thereof. No mention shall be made of coral or of pearls, for the price of wisdom is above rubies.

"Whence, then, cometh wisdom, and where is the place of understanding? Destruction and Death say, we have heard the fame thereof with our ears.

"God understandeth the way thereof, and he knoweth the place thereof; for he looketh to the ends of the earth, and seeth under the whole heaven; *to make the weight for the winds;* and he weigheth the waters by measure. When he made a decree for the rain, and a way for the lightning of the thunder; then did he see it, and declare it; he prepared it, yea, and searched it out."*

When the pump-maker came to ask Galileo to explain how it was that his pump would not lift water higher than thirty-two

* Job, chapter xxviii.

feet, the philosopher thought, but was afraid to say, it was owing to the "weight of the winds;" and though the fact that the air has weight is here so distinctly announced, philosophers never knew it until within comparatively a recent period, and then it was proclaimed by them as a great discovery. Nevertheless, the fact was set forth as distinctly in the book of nature as it is in the book of revelation; for the infant, in availing itself of atmospherical pressure to suck the milk from its mother's breast, unconsciously proclaimed it.

351. Both the thermometer and the barometer (§ 347) stand lower under this cloud-ring than they do on either side of it. After having crossed it, and referred to the log-book to refresh his mind as to the observations there entered with regard to it, the attentive navigator may perceive how this belt of clouds, by screening the parallels over which he may have found it to hang from the sun's rays, not only promotes the precipitation which takes place within these parallels at certain periods, but how, also, the rains are made to change the places upon which they are to fall; and how, by traveling with the calm belt of the equator up and down the earth, this cloud-ring shifts the surface from which the heating rays of the sun are to be excluded; and how, by this operation, tone is given to the atmospherical circulation of the world, and vigor to its vegetation.

Having traveled with the calm belt to the north or south, the cloud-ring leaves the sky about the equator clear; the rays of the torrid sun pour down upon the crust of the earth there, and raise its temperature to a scorching heat. The atmosphere dances (§ 205–6), and the air is seen trembling in ascending and descending columns, with busy eagerness to conduct the heat off and deliver it to the regions aloft, where it is required to give momentum to the air in its general channels of circulation. The dry season continues; the sun is vertical; and finally the earth becomes parched and dry; the heat accumulates faster than the air can carry it away; the plants begin to wither, and the animals to perish. Then comes the mitigating cloud-ring. The burning rays of the sun are intercepted by it. The place for the absorption and reflection, and the delivery to the atmosphere of the solar heat, is changed; it is transferred from the upper surface of the earth to the upper surface of the clouds.

352. Radiation from the land and the sea below the cloud-belt

is thus interrupted, and the excess of heat in the earth is delivered to the air, and by absorption carried up to the clouds, and there transferred to their vapors to prevent excess of precipitation.

353. In the mean time, the trade-winds north and south are pouring into this cloud-covered receiver, as the calm and rain-belt of the equator may be called, fresh supplies in the shape of ceaseless volumes of heated air, which loaded to saturation with vapor, has to rise above and get clear of the clouds before it can commence the process of cooling by radiation. In the mean time, also, the vapors which the trade-winds bring from the north and the south, expanding and growing cooler as they ascend, are being condensed on the lower side of the cloud stratum, and their latent heat is set free, to check precipitation and prevent a flood.

354. While this process and these operations are going on upon the nether side of the cloud-ring, one not less important is going on upon the upper side. There, from sunrise to sunset, the rays of the sun are pouring down without intermission. Every day, and all day long, they operate with ceaseless activity upon the upper surface of the cloud stratum. When they become too powerful, and convey more heat to the cloud vapors than the cloud vapors can reflect and give off to the air above them, then, with a beautiful elasticity of character, the clouds absorb the surplus heat. They melt away, become invisible, and retain, in a latent and harmless state, until it is wanted at some other place and on some other occasion, the heat thus imparted.

355. We thus have an insight into the operations which are going on in the equatorial belt of precipitation, and this insight is sufficient to enable us to perceive that exquisite indeed are the arrangements which Nature has provided for supplying this calm belt with heat, and for pushing the snow-line there high up above the clouds, in order that the atmosphere may have room to expand, to rise up, overflow, and course back into its channels of healthful circulation. As the vapor is condensed and formed into drops of rain, a twofold object is accomplished: coming from the cooler regions of the clouds, the rain-drops are cooler than the air and earth below; they descend, and by absorption take up the heat which has been accumulating in the earth's crust during the dry season, and which can not now escape by radiation. Thus this cloud-ring modifies the climate of all places beneath it; overshadowing, at different seasons, all parallels from 5° south to 15° north.

356. In the process of condensation, these rain-drops, on the other hand, have set free a vast quantity of latent heat, which has been gathered up with the vapor from the sea by the trade-winds and brought hither. The caloric thus liberated is taken by the air and carried up aloft still farther, to keep, at the proper distance from the earth, the line of perpetual congelation. Were it possible to trace a thermal curve in the upper regions of the air to represent this line, we should no doubt find it mounting sometimes at the equator, sometimes on this side, and sometimes on that of it, but always so mounting as to overleap this cloud-ring. This thermal line would not ascend always over the same parallels: it would ascend over those between which this ring happens to be; and the distance of this ring from the equator is regulated according to the seasons.

357. If we imagine the atmospherical equator to be always where the calm belt is which separates the northeast from the southeast trade-winds, then the loop in the thermal curve, which should represent the line of perpetual congelation in the air, would be always found to stride this equator; and it may be supposed that a thermometer, kept sliding on the surface of the earth so as always to be in the middle of this rain-belt, would show very nearly the same temperature all the year round; and so, too, would a barometer the same pressure.

358. *Its Office.*—Returning and taking up the train of contemplation as to the office which this belt of clouds, as it encircles the earth, performs in the system of oceanic adaptations, we may see how the cloud-ring and calm zone which it overshadows perform the office both of ventricle and auricle in the immense atmospherical heart, where the heat and the forces which give vitality and power to the system are brought into play—where dynamical strength is gathered, and an impulse given to the air sufficient to send it thence through its long and tortuous channels of circulation.

359. Thus this ring, or band, or belt of clouds is stretched around our planet to regulate the quantity of precipitation in the rain-belt beneath it; to preserve the due quantum of heat on the face of the earth; to adjust the winds; and send out for distribution to the four corners, vapors in proper quantities to make up to each river-basin, climate, and season, its quota of sunshine, cloud, and moisture. Like the balance-wheel of a well-constructed chro-

nometer, this cloud-ring affords the grand atmospherical machine the most exquisitely arranged *self-compensation.* If the sun fail in his supply of heat to this region, more of its vapors are condensed, and heat is discharged from its latent store-houses in quantities just sufficient to keep the machine in the most perfect compensation. If, on the other hand, too much heat be found to accompany the rays of the sun as they impinge upon the upper circumference of this belt, then again on that side are the means of self-compensation ready at hand; so much of the cloud-surface as may be requisite is then resolved into invisible vapor—for of invisible vapor are made the vessels wherein the surplus heat from the sun is stored away and held in the latent state until it is called for, when instantly it is set free, and becomes an obvious and active agent in the grand design.

360. That the thermometer stands *invariably* lower (§ 351) beneath this cloud-belt than it does on either side of it, has not, so far as my researches are concerned, been made to appear by actual observation, for the observations in my possession have not yet been *fully* discussed concerning the temperature of the air. But that the temperature of the air at the surface under this cloud-ring is lower, is a theoretical deduction as susceptible of demonstration as is the rotation of the earth on its axis. Indeed, Nature herself has hung a thermometer under this cloud-belt that is more perfect than any that man can construct, and its indications are not to be mistaken.

361. Where do the vapors which form this cloud-ring, and which are here condensed and poured down into the sea as rain, come from? They come from the trade-wind regions (§ 115); under the cloud-ring they rise up; as they rise up, they expand; and as they expand, they grow cool, form clouds, and then are condensed into rains; moreover, it requires no mercurial instrument of human device to satisfy us that the air which brings the vapor for these clouds can not take it up and let it down at the same temperature. Precipitation and evaporation are the converse of each other; and the same air can not precipitate and evaporate, take up and let down water, at one and the same temperature. As the temperature of the air is raised, its capacity for receiving and retaining water in the state of vapor is increased; as the temperature of the air is lessened, its capacity for retaining that moist-

ure is diminished. These are physical laws, and therefore, when we see water dripping from the atmosphere, we need no instrument to tell us that the elasticity of the vapor so condensed, and falling in drops, is less than was its elasticity when it was taken up from the surface of the ocean as water, and went up into the clouds as vapor.

362. Hence we infer that, when the vapors of sea water are condensed, the heat which was necessary to sustain them in the vapor state, and which was borrowed from the ocean, is parted with, and that therefore they were subjected, in the act of condensation, to a lower temperature than they were in the act of evaporation. Ceaseless precipitation goes on under this cloud-ring. Evaporation under it is suspended almost entirely. We know that the trade-winds encircle the earth; that they blow perpetually; that they come from the north and the south, and meet each other near the equator; therefore we infer that this line of meeting extends around the world. By the rainy seasons of the torrid zone we can trace the declination of this cloud-ring stretched like a girdle round about the earth: it travels up and down the ocean as from north to south and back.

363. It is broader than the belt of calms out of which it rises. As the air, with its vapors, rises up in this calm belt and ascends, these vapors are condensed into clouds (§ 361), and this condensation is followed by a turgid intumescence, which causes the clouds to overflow the calm belt, as it were, both to the north and the south. The air flowing off in the same direction assumes the character of winds that form the upper currents that are counter (Plate I.) to the trade-winds. These currents carry the clouds still farther to the north and south, and thus make the cloud-ring broader. At least, we infer such to be the case, for the rains are found to extend out into the trade-winds, and often to a considerable distance both to the north and the south of the calm belt.

364. Were this cloud-ring luminous, and could it be seen by an observer from one of the planets, it would present to him an appearance not unlike the rings of Saturn do to us. Such an observer would remark that this cloud-ring of the earth has a motion contrary to that of the axis of our planet itself—that while the earth was revolving rapidly from west to east, he would observe the cloud-ring to go slowly, but only relatively, from east to west. As the winds which bring the cloud-vapor to this region of calms

rise up with it, the earth is slipping from under them; and thus the cloud-ring, though really moving from west to east with the earth, goes relatively slower than the earth, and would therefore appear to require a longer time to complete a revolution.

365. But, unlike the rings of Saturn through the telescope, the outer surface, or the upper side to us, of this cloud-ring would appear exceedingly jagged, rough, and uneven.

366. The rays of the sun, playing upon this peak and then upon that of the upper cloud-surface, melt away one set of elevations and create another set of depressions. The whole stratum is, it may be imagined, in the most turgid state; it is in continued throes when viewed from above; the heat which is liberated from below in the process of condensation, the currents of warm air ascending from the earth, and of cool descending from the sky, all, we may well conceive, tend to keep the upper cloud-surface in a perpetual state of agitation, upheaval, and depression.

367. Imagine in such a cloud-stratum an electrical discharge to take place; the report, being caught up by the cloud-ridges above, is passed from peak to peak, and repeated from valley to valley, until the last echo dies away in the mutterings of the distant thunder. How often do we hear the voice of the loud thunder rumbling and rolling away above the cloud-surface, like the echo of artillery discharged among the hills!

Hence we perceive or infer that the clouds intercept the progress of sound, as well as of light and heat, through the atmosphere, and that this upper surface is often like Alpine regions, which echo back and roll along with rumbling noise the mutterings of the distant thunder.

368. It is by trains of reasoning like this that we are continually reminded of the interest which attaches to the observations which the mariner is called on to make. There is no expression uttered by Nature which is unworthy of our most attentive consideration—for no physical fact is too bald for observation—and mariners, by registering in their logs the kind of lightning, whether sheet, forked, or streaked, and the kind of thunder, whether rolling, muttering, or sharp, may be furnishing facts which will throw much light on the features and character of the clouds in different latitudes and seasons. Physical facts are the language of Nature, and every expression uttered by her is worthy of our most attentive consideration.

CHAPTER X.

ON THE GEOLOGICAL AGENCY OF THE WINDS.

To appreciate the Offices of the Winds and Waves, Nature must be regarded as a Whole, § 369.—Level of the Dead Sea, 370.—Evidences that at former Geological Periods more Rain fell than now falls upon the Dead Sea and other inland Basins, 371.—Where Vapor for the Rains in the Basin of the American Lakes comes from, 375.—The Effect produced by the Upheaval of Mountains across the course of vapor-bearing Winds, 376.—The Agencies by which the Drainage of Hydrographic Basins may be cut off from the Sea, 380.—Utah an Example, 382.—Effect of the Andes upon vapor-bearing Winds, 383.—Geological Age of the Andes and Dead Sea compared, 391.—Ranges of dry Countries and little Rain, 393.—Rain and Evaporation in the Mediterranean, 399.—Evaporation and Precipitation in the Caspian Sea equal, 404.—The Quantity of Moisture the Atmosphere keeps in Circulation, 407.—Where Vapor for the Rains that feed the Nile come from, 409.—Lake Titicaca, 420.

369. Properly to appreciate the various offices which the winds and the waves perform, we must regard nature as a whole, for all the departments thereof are intimately connected. If we attempt to study in one of them, we often find ourselves tracing clews which lead us off insensibly into others, and, before we are aware, we discover ourselves exploring the chambers of some other department.

The study of drift takes the geologist out to sea, and reminds him that a knowledge of waves, winds, and currents, of navigation and hydrography, are closely and intimately connected with his favorite pursuit.

The astronomer directs his telescope to the most remote star, or to the nearest planet in the sky, and makes an observation upon it. He can not reduce this observation, nor make any use of it, until he has availed himself of certain principles of optics; until he has consulted the thermometer, gauged the atmosphere, and considered the effect of heat in changing its powers of refraction. In order to adjust the pendulum of his clock to the right length, he has to measure the water of the sea and weigh the earth. He, too, must therefore go into the study of the tides; he must examine the earth's crust, and consider the matter of which it is composed, from pole to pole, circumference to centre; and in doing this, he finds himself, in his researches, right alongside of the navigator, the geologist, and the meteorologist, with a host of other good fellows, each one holding by the same thread, and following it up into the same labyrinth—all, it may be, with different objects in view, but nevertheless, each thread will be sure to lead them where there are stores of knowledge for all, and instruction for each one in particular. And thus, in undertaking to explore the physical geography of the sea, I have found myself standing side by side with the geologist on the land, and with him, far away from the sea-shore, engaged in considering some of the phenomena which the inland basins of the earth—those immense indentations on its surface that have no sea-drainage—present for contemplation and study.

370. Among the most interesting of these is that of the Dead Sea. Lieutenant Lynch, of the United States Navy, has run a level from that sea to the Mediterranean, and finds the former to be about one thousand three hundred feet below the general sea-level of the earth. In seeking to account for this great difference of water level, the geologist examines the neighboring region, and calls to his aid the forces of elevation and depression which are supposed to have resided in the neighborhood; he then points to them as the agents which did the work. Truly they are mighty agents, and they have diversified the surface of the earth with the most towering monuments of their power. But is it necessary to suppose that they resided in the vicinity of this region? May they not have come from the sea, and been, if not in this case, at least in the case of other inland basins, as far removed as the other hemisphere? This is a question which I do not pretend to answer definitely. But the inquiry as to the geological agency of the winds in such cases is a question which my investigations have suggested. It has its seat in the sea, and therefore I propound it as one which, in accounting for the formation of this or that inland basin, is worthy, at least, of consideration.

371. Is there any evidence that the annual amount of precipitation upon the water-shed of the Dead Sea, at some former period, was greater than the annual amount of evaporation from it now is? If yea, from what part of the sea did the vapor that supplied the excess of that precipitation come, and what has cut off

that supply? The mere elevation and depression of the lake basin (§ 370) would not cut it off.

372. If we establish the fact that the Dead Sea at a former period did send a river to the ocean, we carry along with it the admission that when that sea overflowed into that river, then the water that fell from the clouds over the Dead Sea basin was more than the winds could convert into vapor and carry away again; the river carried off the excess to the ocean whence it came (§ 116).

373. In the basin of the Dead Sea, in the basin of the Caspian, of the Sea of Aral, and in the other inland basins of Asia, we are entitled to infer that the precipitation and evaporation are at this time exactly equal. Were it not so, the level of these seas would be rising or sinking. If the precipitation were in excess, these seas would be gradually becoming fuller; and if the evaporation were in excess, they would be gradually drying up; but observation does not show, nor history tell us, that either is the case. As far as we know, the level of these seas is as permanent as that of the ocean, and it is difficult to realize the existence of subterranean channels between them and the great ocean. Were there such a channel, the Dead Sea being the lower, it would be the recipient of ocean waters; and we can not conceive how it should be such a recipient without ultimately rising to the level of its feeder.

374. It may be that the question suggested by my researches has no bearing upon the Dead Sea; that local elevations and subsidences alone were concerned in placing the level of its waters where it is. But is it probable that, throughout all the geological periods, during all the changes which have taken place in the distribution of land and water surface over the earth, the winds, which in the general channels of circulation pass over the Dead Sea, have alone been unchanged? Throughout all ages, periods, and formations, is it probable that the winds have brought us just as much moisture to that sea as they now bring, and have just taken up as much water from it as they now carry off? Obviously and clearly not. The salt-beds, the water-marks, the geological formations, and other facts traced by Nature's own hand upon the tablets of the rock—all indicate plainly enough that not only the Dead Sea, but the Caspian also, had upon them, in former periods, more abundant rains than they now have. Where

did the vapor for those rains come from? and what has stopped the supply? Surely not the elevation or depression of the Dead Sea basin.

375. My researches with regard to the winds have suggested the probability (§ 121) that the vapor which is condensed into rains for the lake valley, and which the St. Lawrence carries off to the Atlantic Ocean, is taken up by the southeast trade-winds of the Pacific Ocean. Suppose this to be the case, and that the winds which bring this vapor arrive with it in the lake country at a mean dew-point of 50°. This would make the southwest winds the rain winds for the lakes generally, as well as for the Mississippi Valley; they are also, speaking generally, the rain winds of Europe, and, I have no doubt, of extra-tropical Asia also.

376. Now suppose a certain mountain range, hundreds of miles to the southwest of the lakes, but across the path of these winds, were to be suddenly elevated, and its crest pushed up into the regions of snow, having a mean temperature of 30° Fahrenheit. The winds, in passing that range, would be subjected to a mean dew-point of 30°; and, not meeting with any more evaporating surface between such range and the lakes (§ 125), they would have no longer any moisture to deposit at the supposed lake temperature of 50°; for they could not yield their moisture to any thing above 30°. Consequently, the amount of precipitation in the lake country would fall off; the winds which feed the lakes would cease to bring as much water as the lakes now give to the St. Lawrence. In such a case, that river and the Niagara would drain them to the level of their bed; evaporation would be increased by reason of the dryness of the atmosphere and the want of rain, and the lakes would sink to that level at which, as in the case of the Caspian Sea, the precipitation and evaporation would finally become equal.

377. There is a self-regulating principle that would bring about this equality; for as the water in the lakes becomes lower, the area of its surface would be diminished, and the amount of vapor taken from it would consequently become less and less as the surface was lowered, until the amount of water evaporated would become equal to the amount rained down again, precisely in the same way that the amount of water evaporated from the sea is exactly equal to the whole amount poured back into it by the

rains, the fogs, and the dews.* Thus the great lakes of this continent would remain inland seas at a permanent level; the salt brought from the soil by the washings of the rivers and rains would cease to be taken off to the ocean as it now is; and finally, too, the great American lakes, in the process of ages, would become first brackish, and then briny.

378. Now suppose the water-basins which hold the lakes to be over a thousand fathoms (six thousand feet) deep. We know they are not more than four hundred and twenty feet deep; but suppose them to be six thousand feet deep. The process of evaporation, after the St. Lawrence had gone dry, might go on until one or two thousand feet or more were lost from the surface, and we should then have another instance of the level of an inland water-basin being far below the sea-level, as in the case of the Dead Sea; or it would become a rainless district, when the lakes themselves would go dry.

379. Or let us take another case for illustration. Corallines are at work about the Gulf Stream; they have built up the Florida Reefs on one side, and the Bahama Banks on the other. Suppose they should build up a dam across the Florida Pass, and obstruct the Gulf Stream; and that, in like manner, they were to connect Cuba with Yucatan, by damming up the Yucatan Pass, so that the waters of the Atlantic should cease to flow into the Gulf of Mexico. What should we have?

The depth of the marine basin which holds the waters of that Gulf is, in the deepest part, about a mile. The officers of the United States ship Albany have run a line of deep-sea soundings from west to east across the Gulf; the greatest depth they reported was about six thousand feet. Subsequent experiments, however, induce the belief that the depth is not quite so great.

We should therefore have, by stopping up the channels between the Gulf and the Atlantic, not a sea-level in the Gulf, but we should have a mean level between evaporation and precipitation. If the former were in excess, the level of the Gulf waters would sink down until the surface exposed to the air would be just sufficient to return to the atmosphere, as vapor, the amount of water discharged by the rivers—the Mississippi and others—into the Gulf. As the waters were lowered, the extent of evaporating

* The quantity of dew in England is about five inches during a year.—*Glaisher*.

surface would grow less and less, until Nature should establish the proper ratio between the ability of the air to take up and the capacity of the clouds to let down. Thus we might have a sea whose level would be much farther below the water-level of the ocean than is the Dead Sea.

380. There is still another process, besides the two already alluded to, by which the drainage of these inland basins may, through the agency of the winds, have been cut off from the great salt seas, and that is by the elevation of continents from the bottom of the sea in distant regions of the earth, and the substitution caused thereby of dry land instead of water for the winds to blow upon.

381. Now suppose that a continent should rise up in that part of the ocean, wherever it may be, that supplies the clouds with the vapor that makes the rain for the hydrographic basin of the great American lakes. What would be the result? Why, surely, fewer clouds and less rain, which would involve a change of climate in the lake country; an increase of evaporation from it, because a decrease of precipitation upon it; and, consequently, a diminution of cloudy screens to protect the waters of the lakes from being sucked up by the rays of the sun; and consequently, too, there would follow a low stage for water-courses, and a lowering of the lake-level would ensue.

So far, I have instanced these cases only hypothetically; but, both in regard to the hydrographical basins of the Mexican Gulf and American lakes, I have confined myself strictly to analogies. Mountain ranges have been upheaved across the course of the winds, and continents have been raised from the bottom of the sea; and, no doubt, the influence of such upheavals has been felt in remote regions by means of the winds, and the effects which a greater or less amount of moisture brought by them would produce.

382. In the case of the Salt Lake of Utah, we have an example of drainage that has been cut off, and an illustration of the process by which Nature equalizes the evaporation and precipitation. To do this, in this instance, she is salting up the basin which received the drainage of this inland water-shed. Here we have the appearance, I am told, of an old channel by which the water used to flow from this basin to the sea. Supposing there was such a time and such a water-course, the water returned through it to

the ocean was the amount by which the precipitation used to exceed the evaporation over the whole extent of country drained through this now dry bed of a river. The winds have had something to do with this; they are the agents which used to bring more moisture from the sea to this water-shed than they took away; and they are the agents which now carry off from that valley more moisture than is brought to it, and which, therefore, are making a salt-bed of places that used to be covered by water. In like manner, there is evidence that the great American lakes formerly had a drainage with the Gulf of Mexico. Steamers have been actually known, in former years, and in times of freshets, to pass from the Mississippi River over into the lakes. At low water, the bed of a dry river can be traced between them. Now the Salt Lake of Utah is to the southward and westward of our northern lake basin; that is the quarter (§ 214) whence the rain winds have been supposed to come. May not the same cause which lessened the precipitation or increased the evaporation in the Salt Lake water-shed, have done the same for the water-shed of the great American system of lakes?

If the mountains to the west—the Sierra Nevada, for instance—stand higher now than they formerly did, and if the winds which fed the Salt Lake valley with precipitation had, as (§ 212) I suppose they have, to pass the summits of the mountains, it is easy to perceive why the winds should not convey as much vapor across them now as they did when the summit of the range was lower and not so cool.

383. The Andes, in the trade-wind region of South America, stand up so high, that the wind, in order to cross them, has to part with all its moisture (§ 133), and consequently there is, on the west side, a rainless region. Now suppose a range of such mountains as these to be elevated across the track of the winds which supply the lake country with rains; it is easy to perceive how the whole country watered by the vapor which such winds bring, would be converted into a rainless region.

I have used these hypothetical cases to illustrate a position which any philosopher, who considers the geological agency of the winds, may with propriety consult, when he is told of an inland basin the water-level of which, it is evident, was once higher than it now is; and that position is that, though the evidences of a higher water-level be unmistakable and conclusive, it does not follow, therefore, that there has been a subsidence of the lake basin itself, or an upheaval of the water-shed drained by it.

384. The cause which has produced this change in the water-level, instead of being local and near, may be remote; it may have its seat in the obstructions to "the winds in his circuits," which have been interposed in some other quarter of the world, which obstructions may prevent the winds from taking up or from bearing off their wonted supplies of moisture for the region whose water-level has been lowered.

385. Having therefore, I hope, made clear the meaning of the question proposed, by showing the manner in which winds may become important geological agents, and having explained how the upheaving of a mountain range in one part of the world may, through the winds, bear upon the physical geography of the sea, affect climates, and produce geological phenomena in another, I return to the Dead Sea and the great inland basins of Asia, and ask, How far is it possible for the elevation of the South American continent, and the upheaval of its mountains, to have had any effect upon the water-level of those seas? There are indications (§ 374) that they all once had a higher water-level than they now have, and that formerly the amount of precipitation was greater than it now is; then what has become of the sources of vapor? What has diminished its supply? Its supply would be diminished (§ 381) by the substitution of dry land in those parts of the ocean which used to supply that vapor; or the quantity of vapor deposited in the hydrographical basins of those seas would have been lessened if a snow-capped range of mountains (§ 376) had been elevated across the path of these winds, between the places where they were supplied with vapor and these basins.

386. A chain of evidence which it would be difficult to set aside is contained in the chapters beginning severally at p. 66, 97, and 104, going to show that the vapor which supplies the extra-tropical regions of the north with rains comes, in all probability, from the trade-wind regions of the southern hemisphere.

387. Now if it be true that the trade-winds from that part of the world take up there the water which is to be rained in the extra-tropical north, the path ascribed to the southeast trades of Africa and America, after they descend and become the prevail-

ing southwest winds of the northern hemisphere, should pass over a region of less precipitation generally than they would do if, while performing the office of southeast trades, they had blown over water instead of land. The southeast trade-winds, with their load of vapor, whether great or small, take, after ascending in the equatorial calms, a northeasterly direction; they continue to flow in the upper regions of the air in that direction until they cross the tropic of Cancer. The places of least rain, then, between this tropic and the pole, should be precisely those places which depend for their rains upon the vapor which the winds that blow over southeast trade-wind Africa and America convey.

388. Now, if we could trace the path of the winds through the extra-tropical regions of the northern hemisphere, we should be able to identify the track of these Andean winds by the foot-prints of the clouds; for the path of the winds which depend for their moisture upon such sources of supply as the dry land of Central South America and Africa can not lie through a country that is watered well.

389. It is a remarkable coincidence, at least, that the countries in the extra-tropical regions of the north that are situated to the northeast of the southeast trade-winds of South Africa and America—that these countries, over which theory makes these winds to blow, include all the great deserts of Asia, and the districts of least precipitation in Europe. A line from the Galapagos Islands through Florence in Italy, another from the mouth of the Amazon through Aleppo in Holy Land (Plate VII.), would, after passing the tropic of Cancer, mark upon the surface of the earth the route of these winds; this is that "lee country" (§ 137) which, if such be the system of atmospherical circulation, ought to be scantily supplied with rains. Now the hyetographic map of Europe, in Johnston's beautiful *Physical Atlas*, places the region of least precipitation between these two lines (Plate VII.).

390. It would seem that Nature, as if to reclaim this "lee" land from the desert, had stationed by the way-side of these winds a succession of inland seas, to serve them as relays for supplying with moisture this thirsty air. There is the Mediterranean Sea, the Caspian Sea, and the Sea of Aral, all of which are situated exactly in this direction, as though these sheets of water were designed, in the grand system of aqueous arrangements, to supply

with fresh vapor, winds that had already left rain enough behind them to make an Amazon and an Oronoco of.

391. Now that there has been such an elevation of land out of the water, we infer from the fact that the Andes were once covered by the sea, for their tops are now crowned with the remains of marine animals. When they and their continent were submerged—admitting that Europe in general outline was then as it now is—it can not be supposed, if the circulation of vapor were then such as it is supposed now to be, that the climates of that part of the Old World which is under the lee of those mountains were then as scantily supplied with moisture as they now are. When the sea covered South America, the winds had nearly all the waters which now make the Amazon to bring away with them, and to distribute among the countries situated along the route (Plate VII.) ascribed to them.

392. If ever the Caspian Sea exposed a larger surface for evap oration than it now does—and no doubt it did; if the precipitation in that valley ever exceeded the evaporation from it, as it does in all valleys drained into the open sea, then there must have been a change of hygrometrical condition there. And admitting the vapor-springs for that valley to be situated in the direction supposed, the rising up of a continent from the bottom of the sea, or the upheaval of a range of mountains in certain parts of America, Africa, or Spain, across the route of the winds which brought the rain for the Caspian water-shed, might have been sufficient to rob them of the moisture which they were wont to carry away and precipitate upon this great inland basin. See how the Andes have made Atacama a desert, and of Western Peru a rainless country; these regions have been made rainless simply by the rising up of a mountain range between them and the vapor-springs in the ocean which feed with moisture the winds that blow over these now rainless regions.

393. That part of Asia, then, which is under the lee of southern trade-wind Africa, lies to the north of the tropic of Cancer, and between two lines, the one passing through Cape Palmas and Medina, the other through Aden and Delhi. Being extended to the equator, they will include that part of it which is crossed by the continental southeast trade-winds of Africa, after they have traversed the greatest extent of land surface (Plate VII.).

394. The range which lies between the two lines that represent the course of the American winds with their vapors, and the two lines which represent the course of the African winds with their vapors, is the range which is under the lee of winds that have, for the most part, traversed water-surface, or the ocean, in their circuit as southeast trade-winds. But a bare inspection of Plate VII. will show that the southeast trade-winds which cross the equator between longitude 15° and 50° west, and which are supposed to blow over into this hemisphere between these two ranges, have traversed land as well as water ; and the Trade-wind Chart* shows that it is precisely those winds which, in the summer and fall, are converted into southwest monsoons for supplying the whole extent of Guinea with rains to make rivers of. Those winds, therefore, it would seem, leave much of their moisture behind them, and pass along to their channels in the grand system of circulation, for the most part, as dry winds. Moreover, it is not to be supposed that the channels through which the winds blow that cross the equator at the several places named, are as sharply defined in nature as the lines suggested, or as Plate VII. would represent them to be.

395. The whole region of the extra-tropical Old World that is included within the ranges marked, is the region which has most land to windward of it in the southern hemisphere. Now it is a curious *coincidence*, at least, that all the great extra-tropical deserts of the earth, with those regions in Europe and Asia which have the least amount of precipitation upon them, should lie within this range. That they are situated under the lee of the southern continents, and have but little rain, may be a coincidence, I admit ; but that these deserts of the Old World are placed where they are is no coincidence—no accident : they are placed where they are, and as they are, by design ; and in being so placed, it was intended that they should subserve some grand purpose in the terrestrial economy. Let us see, therefore, if we can discover any other marks of that design—any of the purposes to be subserved by such an arrangement—and trace any connection between that arrangement and the supposition which I maintain as to the place where the winds that blow over those regions derive their vapors.

396. It will be remarked at once that all the inland seas of Asia, and all those of Europe except the semi-fresh-water gulfs of

* Series of Maury's Wind and Current Charts.

the north, are within this range. The Persian Gulf and the Red Sea, the Mediterranean, the Black, and the Caspian, all fall within it. And why are they planted there? Why are they arranged to the northeast and southwest under this lee, and in the very direction in which theory makes this breadth of thirsty winds to prevail? Clearly and obviously, one of the purposes in the divine economy was, that they might replenish with vapor the winds which are almost vaporless when they arrive at these regions in the general system of circulation. And why should these winds be almost vaporless? They are almost vaporless because their route, in the general system of circulation, is such, that they are not brought into contact with a water-surface from which the needful supplies of vapor are to be had; or, being obtained, the supplies have since been taken away by the cool tops of mountain ranges over which these winds have had to pass.

397. In the Mediterranean, the evaporation is greater than the precipitation. Upon the Red Sea there never falls a drop of rain; it is all evaporation. Are we not, therefore, entitled to regard the Red Sea as a make-weight, thrown in to regulate the proportion of cloud and sunshine, and to dispense rain to certain parts of the earth in due season and in proper quantities? Have we not, in these two facts, evidence conclusive that the winds which blow over these two seas come, for the most part, from a dry country—from regions which contain few or no pools to furnish supplies of vapor?

398. Indeed, so scantily supplied with vapor are the winds which pass in the general channels of circulation over the water-shed and sea-basin of the Mediterranean, that they take up there more water as vapor than they deposit. But, throwing out of the question what is taken up from the surface of the Mediterranean itself, these winds deposit more water on the water-shed whose drainage leads into that sea than they take up from it again. The excess is to be found in the rivers which discharge into the Mediterranean; but so thirsty are the winds which blow across the bosom of that sea, that they not only take up again all the water that those rivers pour into it, but they are supposed by philosophers (§ 252) to create a demand for an immense current from the Atlantic to supply the waste.

399. It is estimated that three* times as much water as the

* *Vide* article "Physical Geography," Encyclopædia Britannica.

Mediterranean receives from its rivers is evaporated from its surface. This may be an over-estimate, but the fact that evaporation from it is in excess of the precipitation, is made obvious by the current which the Atlantic sends into it through the Straits of Gibraltar; and the difference, we may rest assured, whether it be much or little, is carried off to modify climate elsewhere—to refresh with showers and make fruitful some other part of the earth.

400. The great inland basin of Asia, in which are Aral and the Caspian Seas, is situated on the route which this hypothesis requires these thirsty winds from southeast trade-wind Africa and America to take; and so scant of vapor are these winds when they arrive in this basin, that they have no moisture to leave behind; just as much as they pour down they take up again and carry off. We know (§ 116) that the volume of water returned by the rivers, the rains, and the dews, into the whole ocean, is exactly equal to the volume which the whole ocean gives back to the atmosphere; as far as our knowledge extends, the level of each of these two seas is as permanent as that of the great ocean itself. Therefore, the volume of water discharged by rivers, the rains, and the dews, into these two seas, is exactly equal to the volume which these two seas give back as vapor to the atmosphere.

401. These winds, therefore, do not begin permanently to lay down their load of moisture, be it great or small, until they cross the Oural Mountains. On the steppes of Issam, after they have supplied the Amazon and the other great equatorial rivers of the south, we find them first beginning to lay down more moisture than they take up again. In the Obi, the Yenesi, and the Lena, is to be found the volume which contains the expression for the load of water which these winds have brought from the southern hemisphere, from the Mediterranean, and the Red Sea; for in these almost hyperborean river-basins do we find the first instance in which, throughout the entire range assigned these winds, they have, after supplying the Amazon, &c., left more water behind them than they have taken up again and carried off. The low temperatures of Siberian Asia are quite sufficient to extract from these winds the remnants of vapor which the cool mountain-tops and mighty rivers of the southern hemisphere have left in them.

402. Here I may be permitted to pause, that I may call attention to another remarkable coincidence, and admire the marks of

design, the beautiful and exquisite adjustments that we see here provided, to insure the perfect workings of the great aqueous and atmospherical machine. This coincidence—may I not call it cause and effect?—is between the hygrometrical conditions of all the countries within, and the hygrometrical conditions of all the countries without, the range included within the lines which I have drawn (Plate VII.) to represent the route in the northern hemisphere of the southeast trade-winds *after* they have blown their course over the land in South Africa and America. Both to the right and left of this range are countries included between the same parallels in which it is, yet these countries all receive more water from the atmosphere than they give back to it again; they all have rivers running into the sea. On the one hand, there is in Europe the Rhine, the Elbe, and all the great rivers that empty into the Atlantic; on the other hand, there are in Asia the Ganges, and all the great rivers of China; and in North America, in the latitude of the Caspian Sea, is our great system of fresh-water lakes; all of these receive from the atmosphere immense volumes of water, and pour it back into the sea in streams the most magnificent.

403. It is remarkable that none of these copiously-supplied water-sheds have, to the southwest of them in the trade-wind regions of the southern hemisphere, any considerable body of land; they are, all of them, under the lee of evaporating surfaces, of ocean waters in the trade-wind regions of the south. Only those countries in the extra-tropical north which I have described as lying under the lee of trade-wind South America and Africa are scantily supplied with rains. Pray examine Plate VII. in this connection. It tends to confirm the views taken in Chapter V., p. 115.

404. The surface of the Caspian Sea is about equal to that of our lakes; in it, evaporation is just equal to the precipitation. Our lakes are between the same parallels, and about the same distance from the western coast of America that the Caspian Sea is from the western coast of Europe; and yet the waters discharged by the St. Lawrence give us an idea of how greatly the precipitation upon it is in excess of the evaporation. To windward of the lakes, and in the trade-wind regions of the southern hemisphere, is no land; but to windward of the Caspian Sea, and in the trade-wind region of the southern hemisphere, there is land. Therefore, supposing the course of the vapor-distributing

winds to be such as I maintain it to be, ought they not to carry more water from the ocean to the American lakes than it is possible for them to carry from the land—from the interior of South Africa and America—to the valley of the Caspian Sea?

405. In like manner (§ 228), extra-tropical New Holland and South Africa have each land—not water—to the windward of them in the trade-wind regions of the northern hemisphere, where, according to this hypothesis, the vapor for their rains ought to be taken up: they are both countries of little rain; but extra-tropical South America has, in the trade-wind region to windward of it in the northern hemisphere, a great extent of ocean, and the amount of precipitation (§ 141) in extra-tropical South America is wonderful. The coincidence, therefore, is remarkable, that the countries in the extra-tropical regions of this hemisphere, which lie to the northeast of large districts of land in the trade-wind regions of the other hemisphere, should be scantily supplied with rains; and likewise, that those so situated in the extra-tropical south, with regard to land in the trade-wind region of the north, should be scantily supplied with rains.

Having thus remarked upon the coincidence, let us turn to the evidences of design, and contemplate the beautiful harmony displayed in the arrangement of the land and water, as we find them along this conjectural "wind-road." (Plate VII.)

406. Those who admit design among terrestrial adaptations, or have studied the economy of cosmical arrangements, will not be loth to grant that by design the atmosphere keeps in circulation a certain amount of moisture; that the water of which this moisture is made is supplied by the aqueous surface of the earth, and that it is to be returned to the seas again through rivers and the process of precipitation; that a permanent increase or decrease of the quantity of water thus put and kept in circulation by the winds would be followed by a corresponding change of hygrometrical conditions, which would draw after it permanent changes of climate; and that permanent changes of climate would involve the ultimate well-being of myriads of organisms, both in the vegetable and animal kingdoms.

407. The quantity of moisture that the atmosphere keeps in circulation is, no doubt, just that quantity which is best suited to the well-being, and most adapted to the proper development of

the vegetable and animal kingdoms; and that quantity is dependent upon the arrangement and the proportions that we see in nature between the land and the water—between mountain and desert, river and sea. If the seas and evaporating surfaces were changed, and removed from the places they occupy to other places, the principal places of precipitation probably would also be changed: whole families of plants would wither and die for want of cloud and sunshine, dry and wet, in proper proportions and in due season; and, with the blight of plants, whole tribes of animals would also perish. Under such a chance arrangement, man would no longer be able to rely upon the early and the latter rain, or to count with certainty upon the rains being sent in due season for seed-time and harvest. And that the rain will be sent in due season, we are assured from on high; and when we recollect who it is that "sendeth" it, we feel the conviction strong within us that He that sendeth the rain has the winds for his messengers; and that they may do his bidding, the land and the sea were arranged, both as to position and relative proportions, where they are, and as they are.

408. It should be borne in mind that the southeast trade-winds, after they rise up at the equator (Plate I.), have to overleap the northeast trade-winds. Consequently, they do not touch the earth until near the tropic of Cancer (see the bearded arrows, Plate VII.)—more frequently to the north than to the south of it; but for a part of every year, the place where these vaulting southeast trades first strike the earth, after leaving the other hemisphere, is very near this tropic. On the equatorial side of it, be it remembered, the northeast trade-winds blow; on the polar side, what were the southeast trades, and what are now the prevailing southwesterly winds of our hemisphere, prevail. Now examine Plate VII., and it will be seen that the upper half of the Red Sea is north of the tropic of Cancer; the lower half is to the south of it; that the latter is within the northeast trade-wind region; the former, in the region where the southwest passage winds are the prevailing winds.

409. The River Tigris is probably evaporated from the upper half of this sea by these winds; while the northeast trade-winds take up from the lower half those vapors which feed the Nile with rain, and which the clouds deliver to the cold demands of the

Mountains of the Moon. Thus there are two "wind-roads" crossing this sea: to the windward of it, each road runs through a rainless region; to the leeward there is, in each case, a river to cross.

410. The Persian Gulf lies, for the most part, in the track of the southwest winds; to the windward of the Persian Gulf is a desert; to the leeward, the River Indus. This is the route by which theory would require the vapor from the Red Sea and Persian Gulf to be conveyed; and this is the direction in which we find indications that it is conveyed. For to leeward do we find, in each case, a river, telling to us, by signs not to be mistaken, that it receives more water from the clouds than it gives back to the winds.

411. Is it not a curious circumstance, that the winds which travel the road suggested from the southern hemisphere should, when they touch the earth on the polar side of the tropic of Cancer, be so thirsty, more thirsty, much more, than those which travel on either side of their path, and which are supposed to have come from southern seas, not from southern lands?

412. The Mediterranean has to give those winds three times as much vapor as it receives from them (§ 399); the Red Sea gives them as much as they can take, and receives nothing back in return but a little dew (§ 238); the Persian Gulf also gives more than it receives. What becomes of the rest? Doubtless it is given to the winds, that they may bear it off to distant regions, and make lands fruitful, that but for these sources of supply would be almost rainless, if not entirely arid, waste, and barren.

413. These seas and arms of the ocean now present themselves to the mind as counterpoises in the great hygrometrical machinery of our planet. As sheets of water placed where they are, to balance the land in the trade-wind region of South America and South Africa, they now present themselves. When the foundations of the earth were laid, we know who it was that "measured the waters in the hollow of his hand, and meted out the heavens with a span, and comprehended the dust of the earth in a measure, and weighed the mountains in scales, and the hills in a balance;" and hence we know also that they are arranged both according to proportion and to place.

414. Here, then, we see harmony in the winds, design in the mountains, order in the sea, arrangement in the dust, and form for the desert. Here are signs of beauty and works of grandeur; and

we may now fancy that, in this exquisite system of adaptations and compensations, we can almost behold, in the Red and Mediterranean Seas, the very waters that were held in the hollow of the Almighty hand when he weighed the Andes and balanced the hills of Africa in his comprehensive scales.

415. In that great inland basin of Asia which holds the Caspian Sea, and embraces an area of one million and a half of geographical square miles, we see the water-surface so exquisitely adjusted that it is just sufficient, and no more, to return to the atmosphere as vapor exactly as much moisture as the atmosphere lends in rain to the rivers of that basin.

416. Thus we are entitled to regard (§ 390) the Mediterranean, the Red Sea, and Persian Gulf as relays, distributed along the route of these thirsty winds from the continents of the other hemisphere, to supply them with vapors, or to restore to them that which they have left behind to feed the sources of the Amazon, the Niger, and the Congo.

The hypothesis that the winds from South Africa and America do take the course through Europe and Asia which I have marked out for them (Plate VII.), is supported by so many coincidences, to say the least, that we are entitled to regard it as probably correct, until a train of coincidences as striking can be adduced to show that such is not the case.

417. Returning once more to a consideration of the geological agency of the winds in accounting for the depression of the Dead Sea, we now see the fact most strikingly brought out before us, that if the Straits of Gibraltar were to be barred up, so that no water could pass through them, we should have a great depression of water-level in the Mediterranean. Three times as much water is evaporated from that sea as is returned to it through the rivers. A portion of water evaporated from it is probably rained down and returned to it through the rivers; but, supposing it to be barred up, as the demand upon it for vapor would exceed the supply by rains and rivers, it would commence to dry up. As it sinks down, the area exposed for evaporation would decrease, and the supplies to the rivers would diminish, until finally there would be established between the evaporation and precipitation an equilibrium, as in the Dead and Caspian Seas; but, for aught we know, the water-level of the Mediterranean might, before this equilibrium

were attained, have to reach a stage far below that of the Dead Sea level.

The Lake Tadjura is now in the act of attaining such an equilibrium. There are connected with it the remains of a channel by which the water ran into the sea; but the surface of the lake is now five hundred feet below the sea-level, and it is salting up. If not in the Dead Sea, do we not, in the valley of this lake, find outcropping some reason for the question, What have the winds had to do with the phenomena before us?

418. The winds, in this sense, are geological agents of great power. It is not impossible but that they may afford us the means of comparing, directly, geological events which have taken place in one hemisphere, with geological events in another: *e.g.*, the tops of the Andes were once at the bottom of the sea. Which is the oldest formation, that of the Dead Sea or the Andes? If the former be the older, then the climate of the Dead Sea must have been hygrometrically very different from what it now is.

419. In regarding the winds as geological agents, we can no longer consider them as the type of instability. We should rather treat them in the light of ancient and faithful chroniclers, which, upon being rightly consulted, will reveal to us truths that Nature has written upon their wings in characters as legible and enduring as any with which she has ever engraved the history of geological events upon the tablet of the rock.

420. The waters of Lake Titicaca, which receives the drainage of the great inland basin of the Andes, are only brackish, not salt. Hence we may infer that this lake has not been standing long enough to become briny, like the waters of the Dead Sea; consequently, it belongs to a more recent period. On the other hand, it will also be interesting to hear that my friend, Captain Lynch, informs me that, in his exploration of the Dead Sea, he saw what he took to be the dry bed of a river that once flowed from it. And thus we have two more links, stout and strong, to add to the chain of circumstantial evidence going to sustain the testimony of this strange and fickle witness which I have called up from the sea to testify in this presence concerning the works of Nature, and to tell us which be the older—the Andes, watching the stars with their hoary heads, or the Dead Sea, sleeping upon its ancient beds of crystal salt.

CHAPTER XI.

THE DEPTHS OF THE OCEAN.

The Depth of blue Water unknown, § 421.—Results of former Methods of Deep-sea Soundings not entitled to Confidence, 422.—Attempts by Sound and Pressure, 423.—The Myths of the Sea, 424.—Common Opinion as to its Depths, 425.—Interesting Subject, 427.—The deepest Soundings reported, 428.—Plan adopted in the American Navy, 429.—Soundings to be made from a Boat, 431.—Why the Sounding-twine will not stop running out when the Plummet reaches Bottom, 432.—Indications of under Currents, 433.—Rate of Descent, 434.—Brooke's Deep-sea Sounding Apparatus, 437.—The greatest Depths at which Bottom has been found, 438.

421. Until the commencement of the plan of deep-sea soundings, as now conducted in the American Navy, the bottom of what the sailors call "blue water" was as unknown to us as is the interior of any of the planets of our system. Ross and Dupetit Thouars, with other officers of the English, French, and Dutch navies, had attempted to fathom the deep sea, some with silk threads, some with spun-yarn (coarse hemp threads twisted together), and some with the common lead and line of navigation. All of these attempts were made upon the supposition that when the lead reached the bottom, either a shock would be felt, or the line, becoming slack, would cease to run out.

422. The series of systematic experiments recently made upon this subject shows that there is no reliance to be placed on such a supposition, for the shock caused by striking bottom can not be communicated through very great depths, and therefore it does not follow that the line will become slack and cease to run out when the plummet reaches the bottom. Furthermore, the lights of experience show that, as a general rule, the under currents of the deep sea have force enough to take the line out long after the plummet has ceased to do so. Consequently, there is but little reliance to be placed upon deep-sea soundings of former methods, when the depths reported exceeded eight or ten thousand feet.

423. Attempts to fathom the ocean, both by sound and pressure, had been made, but in "blue water" every trial was only a failure

repeated. The most ingenious and beautiful contrivances for deep-sea soundings were resorted to. By exploding heavy charges of powder in the deep sea, when the winds were hushed and all was still, the echo or reverberation from the bottom might, it was held, be heard, and the depth determined from the rate at which sound travels through water. But, though the explosion took place many feet below the surface, echo was silent, and no answer was received from the bottom. Ericsson and others constructed deep-sea leads having a column of air in them, which, by compression, would show the aqueous pressure to which they might be subjected. This was found to answer well for ordinary purposes, but in the depths of "blue water," where the pressure would be equal to several hundred atmospheres, the trial was more than this instrument could stand.

Mr. Baur, an ingenious mechanician of New York, constructed, according to a plan which I furnished him, a deep-sea sounding apparatus. To the lead was attached, upon the principle of the screw propeller, a small piece of clock-work for registering the number of revolutions made by the little screw during the descent; and, it having been ascertained by experiment in shoal water that the apparatus, in descending, would cause the propeller to make one revolution for every fathom of perpendicular descent, hands provided with the power of self-registration were attached to a dial, and the instrument was complete. It worked beautifully in moderate depths, but failed in blue water, from the difficulty of hauling it up if the line used were small, and from the difficulty of getting it down if the line used were large enough to give the requisite strength for hauling up.

424. But, notwithstanding these failures, there was encouragement, for greater difficulties had been overcome in other departments of physical research. Astronomers had measured the volumes and weighed the masses of the most distant planets, and increased thereby the stock of human knowledge. Was it creditable to the age that the depths of the sea should remain in the category of an unsolved problem? It was a sealed volume, abounding in knowledge and instruction that might be both useful and profitable to man. The seal which covered it was of rolling waves many thousand feet in thickness. Could it not be broken? Curiosity had always been great, yet neither the enterprise nor the

ingenuity of man had as yet proved itself equal to the task. No one had succeeded in penetrating, and bringing up from beyond the depth of two or three hundred fathoms below the aqueous covering of the earth, any specimens of solid matter for the study of philosophers.

The sea, with its myths, has suggested attractive themes to all people in all ages. Like the heavens, it affords an almost endless variety of subjects for pleasing and profitable contemplation, and there has remained in the human mind a longing to learn more of its wonders and to understand its mysteries. The Bible often alludes to them. Are they past finding out? How deep is it? and what is at the bottom of it? Could not the ingenuity and appliances of the age throw some light upon these questions?

The government was liberal and enlightened; times seemed propitious; but when or how to begin, after all these failures, with this interesting problem, was one of the difficulties first to be overcome.

425. It was a common opinion, derived chiefly from a supposed physical relation, that the depths of the sea are about equal to the heights of the mountains. But this conjecture was, at best, only a speculation. Though plausible, it did not satisfy. There were, in the depths of the sea, untold wonders and inexplicable mysteries. Therefore the contemplative mariner, as in mid ocean he looked down upon the gentle bosom of the sea, continued to experience sentiments akin to those which fill the mind of the devout astronomer when, in the stillness of the night, he looks out upon the stars, and wonders.

426. Nevertheless, the depths of the sea still remained as fathomless and as mysterious as the firmament above. Indeed, telescopes of huge proportions and of vast space-penetrating powers had been erected here and there by the munificence of individuals, and attempts made with them to gauge the heavens and sound out the regions of space. Could it be more difficult to sound out the sea than to gauge the blue ether and fathom the vaults of the sky? The result of the astronomical undertakings* lies in the discovery that what, through other instruments of less power, appeared as clusters of stars, were, by these of larger powers, separated into groups, and what had been reported as nebulæ could now be re-

* See the works of Herschel and Ross, and their telescopes.

solved into clusters; that, in certain directions, the abyss beyond these faint objects is decked with other nebulæ, which these great instruments may bring to light, but can not resolve; and that there are still regions and realms beyond, which the rays of the brightest sun in the sky have neither the intensity nor the force to reach, much less to penetrate.

427. So, too, with the bottom of the sea, and the knowledge-seeking mariner. Though nothing thence had been brought to light, exploration had invested the subject with additional interest, and increased the desire to know more. In this state of the case, the idea of a common twine thread for a sounding-line, and a cannon ball for a sinker, was suggested. It was a beautiful conception; for, besides its simplicity, it had in its favor the greatest of recommendations—it could be readily put into practice.

Well-directed attempts to fathom the ocean began now to be made, and the public mind was astonished at the vast depths that were at first reported.

428. Lieutenant Walsh, of the United States schooner "Taney," reported a cast with the deep-sea lead at thirty-four thousand feet without bottom. His sounding-line was an iron wire more than eleven miles in length. Lieutenant Berryman, of the United States brig "Dolphin," reported another unsuccessful attempt to fathom mid ocean with a line thirty-nine thousand feet in length. Captain Denham, of her Britannic majesty's ship "Herald," reported bottom in the South Atlantic at the depth of forty-six thousand feet; and Lieutenant J. P. Parker, of the United States frigate "Congress," afterward, in attempting to sound near the same region, let go his plummet, and saw a line fifty thousand feet long run out after it as though the bottom had not been reached.

The three last-named attempts were made with the sounding twine of the American Navy, which has been introduced in conformity with a very simple plan for sounding out the depths of the ocean. It involved for each cast only the expenditure of a cannon ball, and twine enough to reach the bottom. This plan was introduced as a part of the researches conducted at the National Observatory, and which have proved so fruitful and beneficial, concerning the winds and currents, and other phenomena of the ocean. These researches had already received the approbation of the Congress of the United States; for that body, in a spirit worthy of the representatives of a free and enlightened people, had authorized the Secretary of the Navy to employ three public vessels to assist in perfecting the discoveries, and in conducting the investigations connected therewith.

429. The plan of deep-sea soundings finally adopted, and now in practice, is this: Every vessel of the Navy that will, when she puts to sea, is, if she desires it, furnished with a sufficient quantity of sounding-twine, carefully marked at every length of one hundred fathoms—six hundred feet—and wound on reels of ten thousand fathoms each. It is made the duty of the commander to avail himself of every favorable opportunity to try the depth of the ocean, whenever he may find himself out upon "blue water." For this purpose he is to use a cannon ball of thirty-two pounds as a plummet. Having one end of the twine attached to it, the cannon ball is to be thrown overboard from a boat, and suffered to take the twine from the reel as fast as it will.

The reel is made to turn easily. A silk thread, or the common wrapping-twine of the shops would, it was thought, be strong enough for this purpose; for it was supposed there would be no strain upon the line, except the very slight one required to drag it down, and the twine having nearly the specific gravity of sea water, this strain would, it was imagined, be very slight. Moreover, when the shot reached the bottom, the line, it was thought (§ 421), would cease to run out; then breaking it off, and seeing how much remained upon the reel, the depth of the sea could be ascertained at any place and time, simply at the expense of one cannon ball and a few pounds of common twine.

430. But practical difficulties that were not suspected at all were lurking in the way, and afterward showed themselves at every attempt to sound; and it was before these practical difficulties had been fairly overcome that the great soundings (§ 428) were reported. In the first place, it was discovered that the line, once started and dragged down into the depths of the ocean, never would cease to run out (§ 422), and, consequently, that there was no means of knowing when, if ever, the shot had reached the bottom. And, in the next place, it was ascertained that the ordinary twine (§ 427) would not do; that the sounding-line, in going down, was really subjected to quite a heavy strain, and that, consequently, the twine to be used must be strong; it must be subjected to

a test which required it to bear a weight of at least sixty pounds freely suspended in the air. So we had to go to work anew, and make several hundred thousand fathoms of sounding-twine especially for the purpose. It was small, and stood the test required, a pound of it measuring about six hundred feet in length.

431. The officers intrusted with the duty soon found that the soundings could not be made from the vessel with any certainty as to the depth. It was necessary that a boat should be lowered, and the trial be made from it; the men with their oars keeping the boat from drifting, and maintaining it in such a position that the line should be "up and down" the while.

432. That the line would continue to run out after the cannon ball had reached bottom, was explained by the conjecture that there is in the ocean, as in the air, a system of currents and counter currents one above the other, and that it was one or more of these submarine currents, operating upon the bight of the line, which caused it to continue to run out after the shot had reached the bottom. In corroboration of this conjecture, it was urged, with a truth-like force of argument, that it was these under currents, operating with a swigging force upon the bights of the line—for there might be several currents running in different directions, and operating upon it at the same time—which caused it to part whenever the reel was stopped and the line held fast in the boat.

433. A powerful train of circumstantial evidence was this (and it was derived from a source wholly unexpected), going to prove the existence of that system of oceanic circulation which the climates, and the offices, and the adaptations of the sea require, and which its inhabitants (§ 293) in their mute way tell us of.

This system of circulation commenced on the third day of creation, with the "gathering together of the waters," which were "called seas," and doubtless will continue as long as sea water shall possess the properties of saltness and fluidity.

434. In making these deep-sea soundings, the practice is to time the hundred fathom marks as they successively go out; and by always using a line of the same size and "make," and a sinker of the same shape and weight, we at last established the law of descent. Thus the mean of our experiments gave us, for the sinker and twine used,

2 m. 21 s.	as the average time of descent from	400 to	500 fathoms.
3 m. 26 s.	" " "	1000 to	1100 "
4 m. 29 s.	" " "	1800 to	1900 "

435. Now, by aid of the law here indicated, we could tell very nearly when the ball ceased to carry the line out, and when, of course, it began to go out in obedience to the current and drift alone; for currents would sweep the line out at a uniform rate, while the cannon ball would drag it out at a decreasing rate.

436. The development of this law certainly was an achievement, for it enabled us to show that the depth of the sea at the places named (§ 428) was not as great as reports made it. These researches were interesting; the problem in hand was important, and it deserved every effort that ingenuity could suggest for reducing it to a satisfactory solution.

437. As yet, no specimens of the bottom had been brought up. The line was too small, the shot was too heavy, and it could not be weighed. In this state of the case, Passed Midshipman J. M. Brooke, United States Navy, who, at the time, was associated with me on duty at the Observatory, proposed a contrivance by which the shot, on striking the bottom, would detach itself from the line, and send up a specimen of the bottom. This beautiful contrivance, called Brooke's Deep-sea Sounding Apparatus, is represented in Plates II. and III. opposite.

A is a cannon ball, having a hole through it for the rod B. Plate II. represents the rod, B; the slings, D D, with the shot slung, and in the act of being lowered down. Plate III. represents the apparatus in the act of striking the bottom, and shows how the shot is detached, and how specimens of the bottom are brought up, by adhering to a little soap or tallow,* called "arming," in the cup, C, at the lower end of the rod, B. With this contrivance specimens of the bottom have been brought up from the depth of more than two miles.

438. The greatest depths at which the bottom of the sea has been reached with the plummet are in the North Atlantic Ocean, and the places where it has been fathomed do not show it to be deeper than twenty-five thousand feet.

The deepest place in this ocean (Plate XI.) is probably between the parallels of 35° and 40° north latitude, and immediately to the

* A Stellwagen cup is found to answer better.

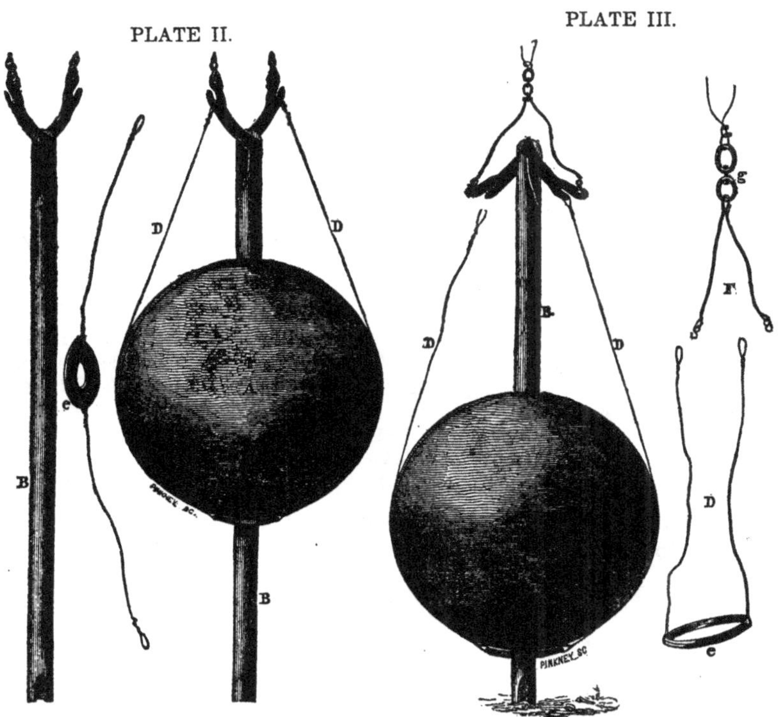

BROOKE'S DEEP-SEA SOUNDING APPARATUS.

southward of the Grand Banks of Newfoundland. No satisfactory deep-sea soundings, either in the Pacific or Indian Oceans, have as yet been made by those who are co-operating in this admirable plan of research.* A few have been made in the South Atlantic, but not enough to justify deduction as to its depths or the shape of its floor.

* Since the above was written, I have received a letter from Captain Ringgold, commanding the Surveying Expedition in the Pacific, informing me that, on his way out, he had obtained, in the southern hemisphere, a deep-sea sounding, with bottom at the depth of eight thousand fathoms. The notes and details of this cast have not yet been received.

CHAPTER XII.

THE BASIN OF THE ATLANTIC.

439. The Basin of the Atlantic, according to the deep-sea soundings made by the American Navy, in the manner described in the foregoing chapter, is shown on Plate XI. This plate refers chiefly to that part of the Atlantic which is included within our hemisphere.

440. In its entire length, the basin of this sea is a long trough, separating the Old World from the New, and extending probably from pole to pole.

This ocean-furrow was scored into the solid crust of our planet by the Almighty hand, that there the waters which "he called seas" might be gathered together, so as to "let the dry land appear," and fit the earth for the habitation of man.

From the top of Chimborazo to the bottom of the Atlantic, at the deepest place yet reached by the plummet in the North Atlantic, the distance, in a vertical line, is nine miles.

Could the waters of the Atlantic be drawn off, so as to expose to view this great sea-gash, which separates continents, and extends from the Arctic to the Antarctic, it would present a scene the most rugged, grand, and imposing. The very ribs of the solid earth, with the foundations of the sea, would be brought to light, and we should have presented to us at one view, in the empty cradle of the ocean, "a thousand fearful wrecks," with that dreadful array of dead men's skulls, great anchors, heaps of pearl and inestimable stones, which, in the poet's eye, lie scattered in the bottom of the sea, making it hideous with sights of ugly death.

441. To measure the elevation of the mountain-top above the sea, and to lay down upon our maps the mountain ranges of the earth, is regarded in geography as an important thing, and rightly so. Equally important is it, in bringing the physical geography of the sea regularly within the domains of science, to present its orography, by mapping out the bottom of the ocean so as to show the depressions of the solid parts of the earth's crust there below the sea-level.

442. Plate XI. presents the second attempt at such a map. It relates exclusively to the bottom of that part of the Atlantic Ocean which lies north of 10° south. It is stippled with four shades; the darkest (that which is nearest the shore-line) shows where the water is less than six thousand feet deep; the next, where it is less than twelve thousand feet; the third, where it is less than eighteen thousand; and the fourth, or lightest, where it is not over twenty-four thousand feet deep. The blank space south of Nova Scotia and the Grand Banks includes a district within which very deep water has been reported, but from casts of the deep-sea lead which upon discussion do not appear satisfactory.

The deepest part of the North Atlantic (§ 438) is probably somewhere between the Bermudas and the Grand Banks, but how deep it may be yet remains for the cannon ball and sounding-twine to determine.

443. The waters of the Gulf of Mexico are held in a basin about a mile deep in the deepest part.

444. THE BOTTOM OF THE ATLANTIC, or its depressions below the sea-level, are given, perhaps, on this plate with as much accuracy as the best geographers have been enabled to show on a map the elevations above the sea-level of the interior either of Africa or Australia.

445. "What is to be the use of these deep-sea soundings?" is a question that often occurs; and it is as difficult to be answered in categorical terms as Franklin's question, "What is the use of a new-born babe?" Every physical fact, every expression of nature, every feature of the earth, the work of any and all of those agents which make the face of the world what it is, and as we see it, is interesting and instructive. Until we get hold of a group of physical facts, we do not know what practical bearings they may have, though right-minded men know that they contain many

precious jewels, which science or the expert hand of philosophy will not fail to bring out, polished, and bright, and beautifully adapted to man's purposes. Already we are obtaining practical answers to this question as to the use of deep-sea soundings; for as soon as they were announced to the public, they forthwith assumed a practical bearing in the minds of men with regard to the question of a submarine telegraph across the Atlantic.

446. There is at the bottom of this sea, between Cape Race in Newfoundland and Cape Clear in Ireland, a remarkable steppe, which is already known as the telegraphic plateau. A company is now engaged with the project of a submarine telegraph across the Atlantic. It is proposed to carry the wires along this plateau from the eastern shores of Newfoundland to the western shores of Ireland. The great circle distance between these two shore-lines is one thousand six hundred miles, and the sea along the route is probably nowhere more than ten thousand feet deep. This company, it is understood, consists of men of enterprise and wealth, who, should the inquiries that they are now making prove satisfactory, are prepared to undertake the establishment forthwith of a submarine telegraph across the Atlantic.

447. It was upon this plateau that Brooke's sounding apparatus (§ 437) brought up its first trophies from the bottom of the sea. These specimens Lieutenant Berryman and his officers judged to be clay; but they took the precaution to label them, carefully to preserve them, and, on their return to the United States, to send them to the proper bureau. They were divided: a part was sent for examination to Professor Ehrenberg, of Berlin, and a part to Professor Bailey, of West Point—eminent microscopists both. I have not heard from the former, but the latter, in November, 1853, thus responded:

448. "I am greatly obliged to you for the deep soundings you sent me last week, and I have looked at them with great interest. They are exactly what I have wanted to get hold of. The bottom of the ocean at the depth of *more than two miles* I hardly hoped ever to have a chance of examining; yet, thanks to Brooke's contrivance, we have it clean and free from grease, so that it can at once be put under the microscope. I was greatly delighted to find that *all* these deep soundings are filled with microscopic shells; not a particle of sand or gravel exists in them. They are

chiefly made up of perfect little calcareous shells (*Foraminiferæ*), and contain, also, a small number of silicious shells (*Diatomaceæ*).

"It is not probable that these animals lived at the depths where these shells are found, but I rather think that they inhabit the waters near the surface; and when they die, their shells settle to the bottom. With reference to this point, I shall be very glad to examine bottles of water from various depths which were brought home by the Dolphin, and any similar materials, either 'bottom,' or water from other localities. I shall study them carefully. . . . . The results already obtained are of very great interest, and have many important bearings on geology and zoology. . . . . .

"I hope you will induce as many as possible to collect soundings with Brooke's lead, in all parts of the world, so that we can map out the animalculæ as you have the whales. Get your whalers also to collect mud from pancake ice, &c., in the Polar regions: this is always full of interesting microscopic forms."

449. These little mites of shells seem to form but a slender clew indeed by which the chambers of the deep are to be threaded, and mysteries of the ocean revealed; yet the results are suggestive; in right hands and to right minds, they are guides to both light and knowledge.

The first noticeable thing the microscope gives of these specimens is, that all of them are of the animal, not one of the mineral kingdom.

450. The ocean teems with life, we know. Of the four elements of the old philosophers—fire, earth, air, and water—perhaps the sea most of all abounds with living creatures. The space occupied on the surface of our planet by the different families of animals and their remains is inversely as the size of the individual. The smaller the animal, the greater the space occupied by his remains. Though not invariably the case, yet this rule, to a certain extent, is true, and will, therefore, answer our present purposes, which are simply those of illustration. Take the elephant and his remains, or a microscopic animal and his, and compare them. The contrast, as to space occupied, is as striking as that of the coral reef or island with the dimensions of the whale. The grave-yard that would hold the corallines is larger than the grave-yard that would hold the elephants.

451. We notice another practical bearing in this group of phys-

ical facts that Brooke's apparatus fished up from the bottom of the deep sea. Bailey, with his microscope (§ 448), could not detect a single particle of sand or gravel among these little mites of shells. They were from the great telegraphic plateau (§ 446), and the inference is that there, if any where, the waters of the sea are at rest. There was not motion enough there to abrade these very delicate organisms, nor current enough to sweep them about and mix up with them a grain of the finest sand, nor the smallest particle of gravel torn from the loose beds of debris that here and there strew the bottom of the sea. This plateau is not too deep for the wire to sink down and rest upon, yet it is not so shallow that currents, or icebergs, or any abrading force can derange the wire after it is once lodged.

452. As Professor Bailey remarks, the animalculæ, whose remains Brooke's lead has brought up from the bottom of the deep sea, probably did not live or die there. They would have had no light there, and, had they lived there, their frail little textures would have been subjected in their growth to a pressure upon them of a column of water twelve thousand feet high, equal to the weight of four hundred atmospheres. They probably lived and sported near the surface, where they could feel the genial influence of both light and heat, and were buried in the lichen caves below after death.

453. Brooke's lead and the microscope, therefore, it would seem, are about to teach us to regard the ocean in a new light. Its bosom, which so teems with animal life; its face, upon which time writes no wrinkles—makes no impression—are, it would now seem, as obedient to the great law of change as is any department whatever, either of the animal or the vegetable kingdom. It is now suggested that, henceforward, we should view the surface of the sea as a nursery teeming with nascent organisms, its depths as the cemetery for families of living creatures that outnumber the sands on the sea-shore for multitude.

Where there is a nursery, hard by there will be found also a grave-yard—such is the condition of the animal world. But it never occurred to us before to consider the surface of the sea as one wide nursery, its every ripple a cradle, and its bottom one vast burial-place.

454. On those parts of the solid portions of the earth's crust

which are at the bottom of the atmosphere, various agents are at work, leveling both upward and downward. Heat and cold, rain and sunshine, the winds and the streams, all assisted by the forces of gravitation, are unceasingly wasting away the high places on the land, and as perpetually filling up the low.

But in contemplating the leveling agencies that are at work upon the solid portions of the crust of our planet which are at the bottom of the sea, one is led, at first thought, almost to the conclusion that these leveling agents are powerless there.

455. In the deep sea there are no abrading processes at work; neither frosts nor rains are felt there, and the force of gravitation is so paralyzed down there that it can not use half its power, as on the dry land, in tearing the overhanging rock from the precipice and casting it down into the valley below.

When considering the bottom of the ocean, we have, in the imagination, been disposed to regard the waters of the sea as a great cushion, placed between the air and the bottom of the ocean to protect and defend it from these abrading agencies of the atmosphere. The geological clock may, we thought, strike new periods; its hands may point to era after era; but, so long as the ocean remains in its basin, so long as its bottom is covered with blue water, so long must the deep furrows and strong contrasts in the solid crust below stand out bold, ragged, and grand. Nothing can fill up the hollows there; no agent now at work, that we know of, can descend into its depths, and level off the floors of the sea.

456. But it now seems that we forgot these oceans of animalculæ, that make the surface of the sea sparkle and glow with life. They are secreting from its surface solid matter for the very purpose of filling up those cavities below. These little marine insects are building their habitations at the surface, and when they die, their remains, in vast multitudes, sink down and settle upon the bottom. They are the atoms of which mountains are formed—plains spread out. Our marl-beds, the clay in our river-bottoms, large portions of many of the great basins of the earth, are composed of the remains of just such little creatures as these, which the ingenuity of Brooke and the industry of Berryman have enabled us to fish up from the depth of more than two miles (twelve thousand feet) below the sea-level.

These *foraminiferæ*, therefore, when living, may have been preparing the ingredients for the fruitful soil of a land that some earthquake or upheaval, in ages far away in the future, may be sent to cast up from the bottom of the sea for man's use.

The study of these "sunless treasures," recovered with so much ingenuity from the rich bottom of the sea, suggests new views concerning the physical economy of the ocean.

457. In the chapter on the *Salts of the Sea*, p. 150, I endeavored to show how sea-shells and marine insects may, by reason of the offices which they perform, be regarded as compensations in that exquisite system of physical machinery by which the harmonies of nature are preserved.

But the treasures of the lead and revelations of the microscope present the insects of the sea in a new and still more striking light. We behold them now serving not only as compensations by which the motions of the water in its channels of circulation are regulated and climates softened, but acting also as checks and balances by which the equipoise between the solid and the fluid matter of the earth is preserved.

Should it be established that these microscopic creatures live at the surface, and are only buried at the bottom of the sea, we may then view them as conservators of the ocean; for, in the offices which they perform, they assist to preserve its *status* by maintaining the purity of its waters.

It is admitted (§ 343) that the salts of the sea come from the land, and that they consist of the soluble matter which the rains wash out from the fields, and which the rivers bring down to the sea.

The waters of the Mississippi and the Amazon, together with all the streams and rivers of the world, both great and small, hold in solution large quantities of lime, soda, iron, and other matter. They discharge annually into the sea an amount of this soluble matter which, if precipitated and collected into one solid mass, would no doubt surprise and astonish the boldest speculator with its magnitude.

458. This soluble matter can not be evaporated. Once in the ocean, there it must remain; and as the rivers are continually pouring in fresh supplies of it, the sea, it has been argued, must continue to become more and more salt.

Now the rivers convey to the sea this solid matter mixed with fresh water, which, being lighter than that of the ocean, remains for a considerable time at or near the surface. Here the microscopic organisms of the deep-sea lead are continually at work, secreting this same lime and soda, &c., and extracting from the sea water all this solid matter as fast as the rivers bring it down and empty it into the sea.

Thus we haul up from the deep sea specimens of dead animals, and recognize in them the remains of creatures which, though invisible to the naked eye, have nevertheless assigned to them a most important office in the physical economy of the universe, viz., that of regulating the saltness of the sea (§ 342).

This view suggests many contemplations. Among them, one in which the ocean is presented as a vast chemical bath, in which the solid parts of the earth are washed, filtered, and precipitated again as solid matter, but in a new form, and with fresh properties.

Doubtless it is only a re-adaptation, though it may be in an improved form, of old, and, perhaps, effete matter, to the uses and well-being of man.

These are speculations merely; they may be fancies without foundation, but idle they are not, I am sure; for when we come to consider the agents by which the physical economy of this our earth is regulated, by which this or that result is brought about and accomplished in this beautiful system of terrestrial arrangements, we are utterly amazed at the offices which have been performed, the work which has been done, by the animalculæ of the water.

459. But whence come the little calcareous shells which Brooke's lead has brought up, in proof of its sounding, from the depth of two miles and a quarter? Did they live in the surface waters immediately above? or is their *habitat* in some remote part of the sea, whence, at their death, the currents were sent forth as pall-bearers, with the command to deposit their remains where the plummet found them?

460. In this view, these little organisms become doubly interesting. When dead, the descent of the shell to its final resting-place would not, it may be supposed, be very rapid. It would partake of the motion of the sea water in which it lived and died, and probably be carried along with it in its channels of circulation for many a long mile.

The microscope, under the eye of Ehrenberg, has enabled us (§ 158) to put tallies on the wings of the wind, to learn of them somewhat concerning its "circuits."

Now, may not these shells, which were so fine and impalpable that the officers of the Dolphin took them to be a mass of unctuous clay—may not, I say, these, with other specimens of soundings yet to be collected, be all converted by the microscope into tallies for the waters of the different parts of the sea, by which the channels through which the circulation of the ocean is carried on are to be revealed?

Suppose, for instance, that the dwelling-place of the little shells which compose this specimen from that part of the ocean be ascertained, by referring to living types, to be the Gulf of Mexico or some other remote region; that the *habitat* and the burial-place, in every instance, be far removed from each other—by what agency, except through that of currents, can we suppose these little creatures—themselves not having the powers of locomotion—to come from the place of their birth, or to travel to that of their burial?

Man can never see—he can only touch the bottom of the deep sea, and then only with the plummet. Whatever it brings up thence is to the philosopher matter of powerful interest; for by such information alone as he may gather from a most careful examination of such matter, the amount of human knowledge concerning nearly all that portion of our planet which is covered by the sea must depend.

Every specimen of bottom from the deep sea is, therefore, to be regarded as probably containing something precious in the way of contribution to the sources of human knowledge.

CHAPTER XIII.

THE WINDS.

461. Plate VIII. is a chart of the winds, based on information derived from the Pilot Charts, one of the series of Maury's Wind and Current Charts. The object of this chart is to make the student acquainted with the prevailing direction of the wind in every part of the ocean.

The arrows of the plate are supposed to fly with the wind; the half bearded and half feathered arrows denoting monsoons or periodic winds; the dotted bands, the regions of calm and baffling winds.

462. Monsoons, properly speaking, are winds which blow one half of the year from one direction, and the other half from an opposite, or nearly an opposite direction.

Let us commence the study of Plate VIII. by examining the trade-wind region; that, also, is the region in which monsoons are most apt to be found.

463. The belt or zone of the southeast trade-winds is broader, it will be observed, than the belt or zone of northeast trades. This phenomenon is explained by the fact that there is more land in the northern hemisphere, and that most of the deserts of the earth—as the great deserts of Asia and Africa—are situated in the rear, or behind the northeast trades; so that, as these deserts become more or less heated, there is a call—a pulling back, if you

please—upon these trades to turn about and restore the equilibrium which the deserts destroy. There being no, or few such regions in the rear of the southeast trades, the trade-wind force prevails, and carries them over into the northern hemisphere.

464. By resolving the forces which it is supposed are the principal forces that put these winds in motion, viz., calorific action of the sun and diurnal rotation of the earth, we are led to the conclusion that the latter is much the greater of the two in its effects upon those of the northern hemisphere. But not to such an extent is it greater in its effects upon those of the southern. We see by the plate that those two opposing currents of wind are so unequally balanced that the one recedes before the other, and that the current from the southern hemisphere is larger in volume; *i. e.*, it moves a greater zone or belt of air. The southeast trade-winds discharge themselves over the equator—*i. e.*, across a great circle—into the region of equatorial calms, while the northeast trade-winds discharge themselves into the same region over a parallel of latitude, and consequently over a small circle. If, therefore, we take what obtains in the Atlantic as the type of what obtains entirely around the earth, as it regards the trade-winds, we shall see that the southeast trade-winds keep in motion more air than the northeast do, by a quantity at least proportioned to the difference between the circumference of the earth at the equator and at the parallel of latitude of 9° north. For if we suppose that those two perpetual currents of air extend the same distance from the surface of the earth, and move with the same velocity, a greater volume from the south would flow across the equator in a given time than would flow from the north over the parallel of 9° in the same time; the ratio between the two quantities would be as radius to the secant of 9°. Besides this, the quantity of land lying within and to the north of the region of the northeast trade-winds is much greater than the quantity within and to the south of the region of the southeast trade-winds. In consequence of this, the mean level of the earth's surface within the region of the northeast trade-winds is, it may reasonably be supposed, somewhat above the mean level of that part which is within the region of the southeast trade-winds. And as the northeast trade-winds blow under the influence of a greater extent of land surface than the southeast trades do, the former are more obstructed in their course

than the latter by the forests, the mountain ranges, unequally heated surfaces, and other such like inequalities.

465. As already stated, the investigations show that the momentum of the southeast trade-winds is sufficient to push the equatorial limits of their northern congeners back into the northern hemisphere, and to keep them, at a mean, as far north as the ninth parallel of north latitude. Besides this fact, they also indicate that while the northeast trade-winds, so called, make an angle in their general course of about 23° with the equator (east-northeast), those of the southeast make an angle of 30° or more with the equator (southeast by east). I speak of those in the Atlantic, thus indicating that the latter approach the equator more directly in their course than do the others, and that, consequently, the effect of the diurnal rotation of the earth being the same for like parallels, north and south, the calorific influence of the sun exerts more power in giving motion to the southern than to the northern system of Atlantic trade-winds.

466. That such is actually the case is rendered still more probable from this consideration: All the great deserts are in the northern hemisphere, and the land surface is also much greater on our side of the equator. The action of the sun upon these unequally absorbing and radiating surfaces in and behind, or to the northward of the northeast trades, tends to retard these winds, and to draw large volumes of the atmosphere, that otherwise would be moved by them, back to supply the partial vacuum made by the heat of the sun, as it pours down its rays upon the vast plains of burning sands and unequally heated land surfaces in our overheated hemisphere. The northwest winds of the southern are also —it may be inferred—stronger than the southwest winds of the northern hemisphere.

467. The investigations that have taken place show that the influence of the land upon the normal directions of the wind at sea is an immense influence. It is frequently traced for a thousand miles or more out upon the ocean. For instance, the action of the sun's rays upon the great deserts and arid plains of Africa, in the summer and autumnal months, is such as to be felt nearly across the Atlantic Ocean between the equator and the parallel of 13° north. Between this parallel and the equator, the trade-winds are turned back by the heated plains of Africa, and are caused to

blow a regular southwardly monsoon for several months. They bring the rains which divide the season in these parts of the African coast. The region of the ocean embraced by the monsoons is cuneiform in its shape, having its base resting upon Africa, and its apex stretching over till within 10° or 15° of the mouth of the Amazon.

468. Indeed, when we come to study the effects of South America and Africa (as developed by the Wind and Current Charts) upon the winds at sea, we should be led to the conclusion—had the foot of civilized man never trod the interior of these two continents—that the climate of one is humid; that its valleys are, for the most part, covered with vegetation, which protects its surface from the sun's rays; while the plains of the other are arid and naked, and, for the most part, act like furnaces in drawing the winds from the sea to supply air for the ascending columns which rise from its overheated plains.

469. Pushing these facts and arguments still farther, these beautiful and interesting researches seem already sufficient almost to justify the assertion that, were it not for the Great Desert of Sahara, and other arid plains of Africa, the western shores of that continent, within the trade-wind region, would be almost, if not altogether, as rainless and sterile as the desert itself.

These investigations, with their beautiful developments, eagerly captivate the mind; giving wings to the imagination, they teach us to regard the sandy deserts, and arid plains, and the inland basins of the earth, as compensations in the great system of atmospherical circulation. Like counterpoises to the telescope, which the astronomer regards as incumbrances to his instrument, these wastes serve as make-weights, to give certainty and smoothness of motion—facility and accuracy to the workings of the machine.

470. When we travel out upon the ocean, and get beyond the influence of the land upon the winds, we find ourselves in a field particularly favorable for studying the general laws of atmospherical circulation. Here, beyond the reach of the great equatorial and polar currents of the sea, there are no unduly heated surfaces, no mountain ranges, or other obstructions to the circulation of the atmosphere—nothing to disturb it in its natural courses. The sea, therefore, is the field for observing the operations of the general laws which govern the movements of the great aerial ocean. Ob-

servations on the land will enable us to discover the exceptions. But from the sea we shall get the rule. Each valley, every mountain range and local district, may be said to have its own peculiar system of calms, winds, rains, and droughts. But not so the surface of the broad ocean; over it the agents which are at work are of a uniform character.

471. RAIN-WINDS are the winds which convey the vapor from the sea, where it is taken up, to other parts of the earth, where it is let down either as snow, hail, or rain. As a general rule, the trade-winds (§ 126) may be regarded as the evaporating winds; and when, in the course of their circuit, they become monsoons, or the variables of either hemisphere, they then generally become also the rain-winds—especially the monsoons—for certain localities. Thus the southwest monsoons of the Indian Ocean are the rain-winds for the west coast of the Peninsula (§ 139). In like manner, the African monsoons of the Atlantic are the winds which feed the springs of the Niger and the Senegal with rains.

472. Upon every water-shed which is drained into the sea, the precipitation may be considered as greater than the evaporation, for the whole extent of the shed so drained, by the amount of water which runs off through the river into the sea. In this view, all rivers may be regarded as immense rain-gauges, and the volume of water annually discharged by any one, as an expression of the quantity which is annually evaporated from the sea, carried back by the winds, and precipitated throughout the whole extent of the valley that is drained by it. Now, if we knew the rain-winds from the dry, for each locality and season generally throughout such a basin, we should be enabled to determine, with some degree of probability at least, as to the part of the ocean from which such rains were evaporated. And thus, notwithstanding all the eddies caused by mountain chains, and other uneven surfaces, we might detect the general course of the atmospherical circulation over the land as well as the sea, and make the general courses of circulation in each valley as obvious to the mind of the philosopher as is the current of the Mississippi, or of any other great river, to his senses.

473. These investigations as to the rain-winds at sea indicate that the vapors which supply the sources of the Amazon with rain are taken up from the Atlantic Ocean by the northeast and south-

east trade-winds; and many circumstances, some of which have already been detailed (§ 226), tend to show that the winds which feed the Mississippi with rains get their vapor in the southeast trade-wind region of the other hemisphere. For instance, we know from observation that the trade-wind regions of the ocean, beyond the immediate vicinity of the land, are, for the most part, rainless regions, and that the trade-wind zones may be described, in a hyetographic sense, as the evaporating regions (§ 32). They also show, or rather indicate as a general rule, that, leaving the polar limits of the two trade-wind systems, and approaching the nearest pole, the precipitation is greater than the evaporation until the point of maximum cold is reached.

And we know, also, that, as a *general* rule, the southeast and northeast trade-winds which come from a lower and go to a higher temperature are the evaporating winds, *i. e.*, they evaporate more than they precipitate; while those winds which come from a higher and go to a lower temperature are the rain-winds, *i. e.*, they precipitate more than they evaporate. That such is the case, not only do researches indicate, but reason teaches, and philosophy tells.

These views, therefore, suggest the inquiry as to the sufficiency of the Atlantic, after supplying the sources of the Amazon and its tributaries with their waters, to supply also the sources of the Mississippi and the St. Lawrence, and of all the rivers, great and small, of North America and Europe.

A careful study of the rain-winds (§ 32), in connection with the *Wind and Current Charts*, will probably indicate to us the "springs in the ocean" which supply the vapors for the rains that are carried off by those great rivers. "All the rivers run into the sea; yet the sea is not full; unto the place from whence the rivers come, thither they return again."

474. Monsoons (§ 462) are, for the most part, formed of trade-winds. When a trade-wind is turned back or diverted by overheated districts from its regular course at stated seasons of the year, it is regarded as a monsoon. Thus the African monsoons of the Atlantic (Plate VIII.), the monsoons of the Gulf of Mexico, and the Central American monsoons of the Pacific, are, for the most part, formed of the northeast trade-winds, which are turned back to restore the equilibrium which the overheated plains of

Africa, Utah, Texas, and New Mexico have disturbed. When the monsoons prevail for five months at a time, for it takes about a month for them to change and become settled, then both they and the trade-winds, of which they are formed, are called monsoons.

475. The northeast and the southwest monsoons of the Indian Ocean afford an example of this kind. A force is exerted upon the northeast trade-winds of that sea by the disturbance which the heat of summer creates in the atmosphere over the interior plains of Asia, which is more than sufficient to neutralize the forces which cause those winds to blow as trade-winds ; it turns them back ; and were it not for the peculiar conditions of the land about that ocean, what are now called the northeast monsoons would blow the year round ; there would be no southwest monsoons ; and the northeast winds, being perpetual, would become all the year, what in reality for five months (§ 474) they are, viz., northeast trade-winds.

476. The agents which produce monsoons reside (§ 475) on the land. These winds are caused by the rarefaction of the air over large districts of country situated on the polar edge, or near the polar edge of the trade-winds. Thus the monsoons of the Indian Ocean are caused by the intense heat which the rays of a cloudless sun produce during the summer time upon the Desert of Cobi and the burning plains of Central Asia. When the sun is north of the equator, the force of his rays, beating down upon these wide and thirsty plains, is such as to cause the vast superincumbent body of air to expand and ascend. There is, consequently, a rush of air, especially from toward the equator, to restore the equilibrium ; and in this case, the force which tends to draw the northeast trade-winds back becomes greater than the force which is acting to propel them forward. Consequently, they obey the stronger power, turn back, and become the famous southwest monsoons of the Indian Ocean, which blow from May to September inclusive.

477. Of course, the vast plains of Asia are not brought up to monsoon heat *per saltum*, or in a day. They require time both to be heated up to this point and to be cooled down again. Hence there is a conflict for a few weeks about the change of the monsoon, when neither the trade-wind nor the monsoon force has fairly lost or gained the ascendency. This debatable period

amounts to about a month at each change. So that the monsoons of the Indian Ocean prevail really for about five months each way, viz., from May to September from the southwest, in obedience to the influence of the overheated plains, and from November to March inclusive from the northeast, in obedience to the trade-wind force.

478. The monsoon season may be always known by referring to the cause which produces these winds. Thus, by recollecting where the thirsty and overheated plains are which cause the monsoons, we know at once that these winds are rushing with greatest force toward these plains at the time that is the hottest season of the year upon them.

479. The influence of these heated plains upon the winds at sea is felt for a thousand miles and more. Thus, though the Desert of Cobi and the sun-burnt plains of Asia are, for the most part, north of latitude 30°, their influence in making monsoons is felt south of the equator (Plate VIII.). So, too, with the great Desert of Sahara and the African monsoons of the Atlantic; also, with the Salt Lake country and the Mexican monsoons on one side, and those of Central America in the Pacific on the other. The influence of the deserts of Arabia upon the winds is felt in Austria and other parts of Europe, as the observations of Kriel, Lamont, and others show. (See Appendix H.)

480. It would appear, therefore, that these desert countries exercise a powerful influence in checking, and consequently in weakening, the force of the northeast trade-winds. There are no such extensive influences at work checking the southeast trades. On the contrary, these are accelerated; for the same forces that serve to draw the northeast trade-winds back, or retard them, tend also to draw the southeast trade-winds on, or to accelerate them. Hence the ability of the southeast trade-winds to push themselves over into the northern hemisphere.

481. Hence, also, we infer that, between certain parallels of latitude in the northern hemisphere, the sun's rays, by reason of the great extent of land surface, operate with much more intensity than they do between corresponding parallels in the southern; and that, consequently, the mean summer temperature on shore, north of the equator, is higher than it is south: a beautiful physical fact which the winds have revealed, in corroboration of what

observations with the thermometer had already induced meteorologists to suspect.

482. It appears, from what has been said (§ 474), that it is the rays of the sun operating upon the land, not upon the water, which causes the monsoons. Now let us turn to Plate VIII., and examine into this view. The monsoon regions are marked with half-bearded and half-feathered arrows; and we perceive, looking at the northern hemisphere, that all of Europe, some of Africa, most of Asia, and nearly the whole of North America, are to the north, or on the polar side of the northeast trade-wind zone; whereas but a small part of Australia, less of South America, and still less of South Africa, are situated on the polar side of the zone of southeast trade-winds. In other words, there are no great plains on the polar side of the southeast trade-winds upon which the rays of the sun, in the summer of the other hemisphere, can play with force enough to rarefy the air sufficiently to materially interrupt these winds in their course. But, besides the vast area of such plains in the northern hemisphere, on the polar side of its trade-wind belt, the heat of which is sufficient (§ 479) to draw these trade-winds back, there are numerous other districts in the extra-tropical regions of our hemisphere the summer heat of which, though it be not sufficient to turn the northeast trade-winds back, and make a monsoon of them, yet may be sufficient to weaken them in their force, and, by retarding them (§ 480), draw the southeast trade-winds over into the northern hemisphere.

483. Now, as this interference from the land takes place in the summer only, we might infer, without appealing to actual observation, that the position of these trade-wind zones is variable; that is, that the equatorial edge of the southeast trade-wind zone is farther to the north in our summer, when the northeast trades are most feeble, than it is in winter, when they are strongest.

484. We have here, then, at work upon these trade-wind zones, a force now weak, now strong, which, of course, would cause these zones to vibrate up and down the ocean, and within certain limits, according to the season of the year. These limits are given on Plate VIII. for spring and autumn. During the latter season these zones reach their extreme northern declination, and in our spring their utmost limits toward the south.

485. The Calm Belts.—There is between the two systems of

trade-winds a region of calms, known as the equatorial calms. It has a mean average breadth of about six degrees of latitude. In this region, the air which is brought to the equator by the northeast and southeast trades ascends. This belt of calms always separates these two trade-wind zones, and travels up and down with them. If we liken this belt of equatorial calms to an immense atmospherical trough, extending, as it does, entirely around the earth, and if we liken the northeast and southeast trade-winds to two streams discharging themselves into it, we shall see that we have two currents perpetually running in at the bottom, and that, therefore, we must have as much air as the two currents bring in at the bottom to flow out at the top. What flows out at the top is carried back north and south by these upper currents, which are thus proved to exist and to flow counter to the trade-winds.

Using still farther this mode of illustration: if we liken the calm belt of Cancer and the calm belt of Capricorn each to a great atmospherical trough extending around the earth also, we shall see that in this case the currents are running in at the top and out at the bottom (§ 101).

486. The belt of equatorial calms is a belt of constant precipitation. Captain Wilkes, of the Exploring Expedition, when he crossed it in 1838, found it to extend from 4° north to 12° north. He was ten days in crossing it, and during those ten days rain fell to the depth of 6.15 inches, or at the rate of eighteen feet and upward during the year. In the summer months this belt of calms is found between the parallels of 8° and 14° of north latitude, and in the spring between 5° south and 4° north. (*Vide* Plate VIII.)

487. This calm belt carries with it the rainy seasons of the torrid zone, always, in its motions from south to north and back, arriving at certain parallels at stated periods of the year; consequently, by attentively considering Plate VIII., one can tell what places within the range of this zone have, during the year, two rainy seasons, what one, and what are the rainy months for each locality.

Were the northeast and the southeast trades, with the belt of equatorial calms, of different colors, and visible to an astronomer in one of the planets, he might, by the motion of these belts or girdles alone, tell the seasons with us. He would see them at one season going north, then appearing stationary, and then commencing their return to the south. But, though he would observe (§ 131) that they follow the sun in his annual course, he would remark that they do not change their latitude as much as the sun does his declination; he would, therefore, discover that their extremes of declination are not so far asunder as the tropics of Cancer and Capricorn, though in certain seasons the changes from day to day are very great. He would observe that these zones of winds and calms have their tropics or stationary nodes, about which they linger near three months at a time; and that they pass from one of their tropics to the other in a little less than another three months. Thus he would observe the whole system of belts to go north from the latter part of May till some time in August. Then they would stop and remain stationary till winter, in December; when again they would commence to move rapidly over the ocean, and down toward the south, until the last of February or the first of March; then again they would become stationary, and remain about this, their southern tropic, till May again.

488. THE HORSE LATITUDES.—Having completed the physical examination of the equatorial calms and winds, if the supposed observer should now turn his telescope toward the poles of our earth, he would observe a zone of calms bordering the northeast trade-winds on the north (§ 100), and another bordering the southeast trade-winds on the south (§ 106). These calm zones also would be observed to vibrate up and down with the trade-wind zones, partaking (§ 130) of their motions, and following the declination of the sun.

On the polar side of each of these two calm zones there would be a broad band extending up into the polar regions, the prevailing winds within which are the opposites of the trade-winds, viz., southwest in the northern and northwest in the southern hemisphere.

489. The equatorial edge of these calm belts is near the tropics, and their average breadth is 10° or 12°. On one side of these belts (§ 101) the winds blow perpetually toward the equator; on the other, their prevailing direction is toward the poles. They are called (§ 101) the "horse latitudes" by seamen.

490. Along the polar borders of these two calm belts (§ 129) we have another region of precipitation, though generally the rains here are not so constant as they are in the equatorial calms. The

precipitation near the tropical calms is nevertheless sufficient to mark the seasons; for whenever these calm zones, as they go from north to south with the sun, leave a given parallel, the rainy season of that parallel, if it be in winter, is said to commence. Hence we may explain the rainy season in Chili at the south, and in California at the north.

491. THE WESTERLY WINDS.—To complete the physical examination of the earth's atmosphere, which we have supposed an astronomer in one of the planets to have undertaken according to the facts developed by the *Wind and Current Charts*, it remains for him to turn his telescope upon the southwest passage winds of the northern hemisphere, pursue them into the arctic regions, and see theoretically how they get there, and, being there, what becomes of them.

From the parallel of 40° up toward the north pole, the prevailing winds, as already remarked, are the southwest passage winds (Plate VIII.), or, as they are more generally called by mariners, the "westerly" winds; these, in the Atlantic, prevail over the "easterly" winds in the ratio of about two to one.

Now if we suppose, and such is probably the case, these "westerly" winds to convey in two days a greater volume of atmosphere toward the arctic circle than those "easterly" winds can bring back in one, we establish the necessity for an upper current by which this difference may be returned to the tropical calms of our hemisphere (§ 109). Therefore there must be some place in the polar regions (§ 112) at which these southwest winds cease to go north, and from which they commence their return to the south, and this locality must be in a region peculiarly liable to calms. It is another atmospherical node in which the motion of the air is upward, with a decrease of barometric pressure. It is marked P, Plate I.

If we now return to the calm belt of the northern tropic, and trace theoretically a portion of air that, in its circuit, shall fairly represent the average course of these southwest passage winds, we shall see (§ 113) that it approaches the pole in a loxodromic curve; that as it approaches the pole, it acquires, from the spiral convolutions of this curve which represents its path, a whirling motion, in a direction *contrary* to that of the hands of a watch; and that the portion of atmosphere whose path we are following would gradually contract its gyrations, until it would finally ascend, turning against the hands of a watch as it whirls around.

In the southern hemisphere a like process is going on; only there, the northwest passage wind would, as it arrives near the antarctic calms, acquire a motion with the sun, or in the direction of the hands of a watch.

PLATE IV.

ISOTHERMAL CHART
OF THE
ATLANTIC OCEAN
FOR MARCH AND SEPTEMBER.
March.
September.
PINKNEY SC
BRITISH ISLES
NORTH SEA
Newfoundland
New York
UNITED STATES
Azores
Madeira
Canary Is.
GULF OF MEXICO
Cuba
Hayti
CARRIBEAN SEA
Panama
Monrovia
GULF OF GUINEA
FRANCE
SPAIN
MEDITERRANEAN SEA
BRAZIL
St Helena
Rio Janeiro
Buenos Ayers
C. of Good Hope
Cape Horn
September
March

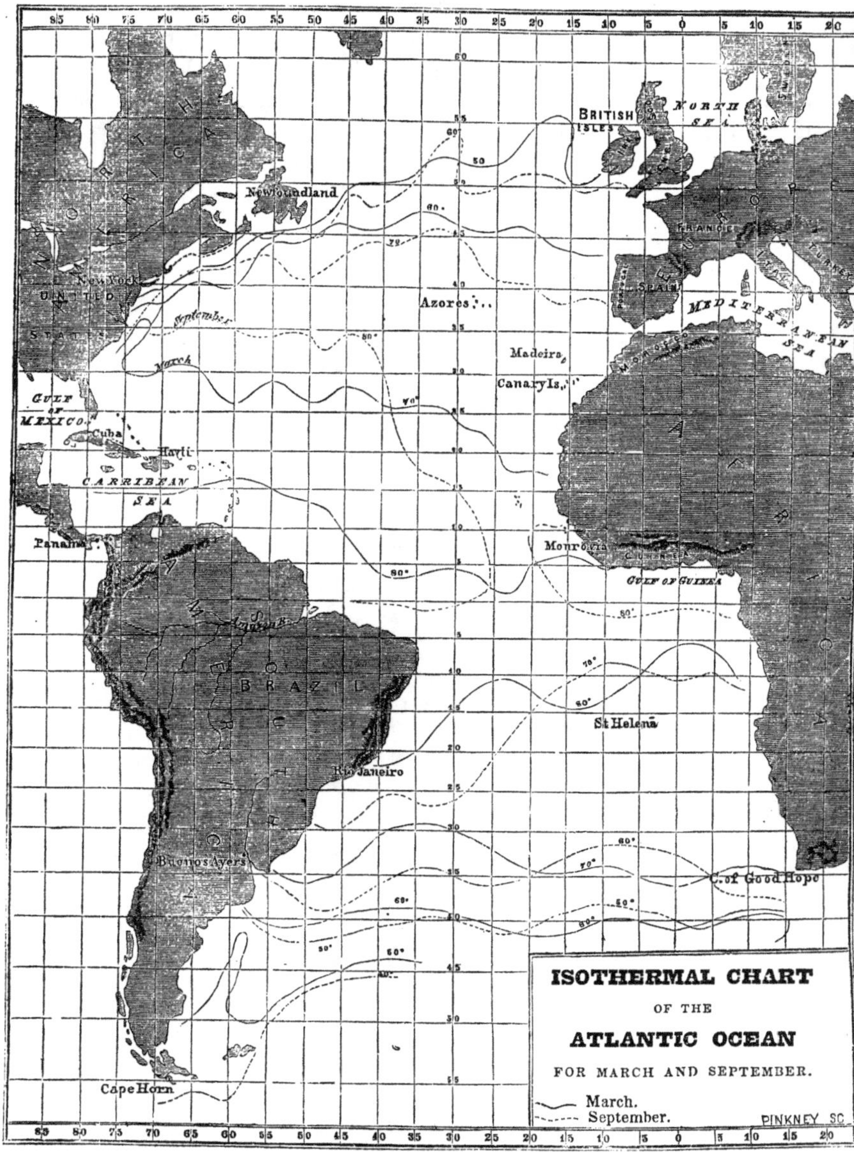

CHAPTER XIV.

THE CLIMATES OF THE OCEAN.

Gulf Stream likened to the Milky Way, § 492.—March and September the hottest Months in the Sea, 496.—How the Isothermal Lines move up and down the Ocean, 498.—A Line of invariable Temperature, 508.—How the western Half of the Atlantic is heated up, 509.—The Relation between a Shore-line in one part of the World and Climates in another, 512.—The Climate of Patagonia, 516.—The Summer of the northern Hemisphere warmer than the Summer of the southern, indicated by the Sea, 521.—How the cold Waters from Davis's Straits press upon the Gulf Stream, 522.—How the different Isotherms travel from North to South with the Seasons, 523.—The Polar and Equatorial Drift, 524.

492. Thermal charts, showing the temperature of the surface of the Atlantic Ocean by actual observations made indiscriminately all over it, and at all times of the year, have been published by the National Observatory. The isothermal lines which these charts enable us to draw, and some of which are traced on Plate IV., afford the navigator and the philosopher much valuable and interesting information touching the circulation of the oceanic waters, including the phenomena of the cold and warm sea currents; they also cast light upon the climatology of the sea, its hyetographic peculiarities, and the climatic conditions of various regions of the earth; they show that the profile of the coast-line of intertropical America assists to give expression to the mild climate of Southern Europe; they also increase our knowledge concerning the Gulf Stream, for it enables us to mark out, for the mariner's guidance, the "Milky Way" in the ocean, the waters of which teem, and sparkle, and glow with life and incipient organisms as they run across the Atlantic. In them are found the clusters and nebulæ of the sea which stud and deck the great highway of ships on their voyage between the Old World and the New; and these lines assist to point out for the navigator their limits and his way. They show this *via lactea* to have a vibratory motion that calls to mind the graceful wavings of a pennon as it floats gently to the breeze. Indeed, if we imagine the head of the Gulf Stream to be hemmed in by the land in the Straits of Bemini, and to be stationary there, and then liken the tail of the Stream itself to an im-

mense pennon floating gently in the current, such a motion as such a streamer may be imagined to have—very much such a motion—do my researches show the tail of the Gulf Stream to have. Running between banks of cold water (§ 1), it is pressed now from the north, now from the south, according as the great masses of sea matter on either hand may change or fluctuate in temperature.

493. In September, when the waters in the cold regions of the north have been tempered, and made warm and light by the heat of summer, its limits on the left (Plate VI) are as denoted by the line of arrows; but after this great sun-swing, the waters on the left side begin to lose their heat, grow cold, become heavy, and press the hot waters of this stream within the channel marked out for them.

494. Thus it acts like a pendulum, slowly propelled by heat on one side and repelled by cold on the other. In this view, it becomes the chronograph of the sea, keeping time for its inhabitants, and marking the seasons for the great whales; and there it has been for all time vibrating to and fro, swinging from north to south and from south to north, a great self-regulating, self-compensating pendulum.

495. In seeking information concerning the climates of the ocean, it is well not to forget this remarkable contrast between its climatology and that of the land, viz.: on the land, February and August are considered the coldest and the hottest months; but to the inhabitants of the sea, the annual extremes of cold and heat occur in the months of March and September. On the dry land, after the winter "is past and gone," the solid parts of the earth continue to receive from the sun more heat in the day than they radiate at night, consequently there is an accumulation of caloric, which continues to increase until August. The summer is now at its height; for, with the close of this month, the solid parts of the earth's crust and the atmosphere above begin to dispense with their heat faster than the rays of the sun can impart fresh supplies, and, consequently, the climates which they regulate grow cooler and cooler until the dead of winter again.

496. But at sea a different rule seems to prevail. Its waters are the store-houses in which the surplus heat of summer is stored away against the severity of winter, and its waters continue to grow warmer for a month after the weather on shore has begun

to get cool. This brings the highest temperature to the sea in September, the lowest in March. Plate IV. is intended to show the extremes of heat and cold to which the *waters*—not the ice—of the sea are annually subjected, and therefore the isotherms of 40°, 50°, 60°, 70°, and 80° have been drawn for March and September, the months of extreme heat and extreme cold to the inhabitants of the "great deep." Corresponding isotherms for any other month will fall between these, taken by pairs. Thus the isotherm of 70° for July will fall nearly between the same isotherms (70°) for March and September.

497. A careful study of this plate, and the contemplation of the benign influences of the sea upon the climates which we enjoy, suggest many beautiful thoughts; for by such study we get a glimpse into the arrangements and the details of that exquisite machinery in the ocean which enables it to perform all its offices, and to answer with fidelity its marvelous adaptations.

498 How, let us inquire, does the isotherm of 80°, for instance, get from its position in March to its position in September? Is it wafted along by currents, that is, by water which, after having been heated near the equator to 80°, then flows to the north with this temperature? Or is it carried there simply by the rays of the sun, as the snow-line is carried up the mountain in summer? We have reason to believe that it is carried from one parallel to another by each of these agents acting together, but mostly through the instrumentality of currents, for currents are the chief agents for distributing heat to the various parts of the ocean. The sun with his rays would, were it not for currents, raise the water in the torrid zone to blood heat; but before that can be done, they run off with it to the poles, softening, and mitigating, and tempering climates by the way. The provision for this is as beautiful as it is benign; for, to answer a physical adaptation, it is provided by a law of nature that when the temperature of water is raised, it shall expand; as it expands, it must become lighter, and just in proportion as its specific gravity is altered, just in that proportion is equilibrium in the sea destroyed. Arrived at this condition, it is ordained that this hot water shall obey another law of nature, which requires it to run away, and hasten to restore that equilibrium. Were these isothermal lines moved only by the rays of the sun, they would slide up and down the ocean like so many paral-

lels of latitude—at least there would be no breaks in them, like that which we see in the isotherm of 80° for September. It appears from this line that there is a part of the ocean near the equator, and about midway the Atlantic, which, with its waters, never does attain the temperature of 80° in September. Moreover, this isotherm of 80° will pass, in the North Atlantic, from its extreme southern to its extreme northern declination—nearly two thousand miles—in about three months. Thus it travels at the rate of about twenty-two miles a day. Surely, without the aid of currents, the rays of the sun could not drive it along that fast.

499. Being now left to the gradual process of cooling by evaporation, atmospherical contact, and radiation, it occupies the other eight or nine months of the year in slowly returning south to the parallel whence it commenced to flow northward. As it does not cool as rapidly as it was heated, the disturbance of equilibrium by alteration of specific gravity is not so sudden, nor the current which is required to restore it so rapid. Hence the slow rate of movement at which this line travels on its march south.

500. Between the meridians of 25° and 30° west, the isotherm of 60° in September ascends as high as the parallel of 56°. In October it reaches the parallel of 50° north. In November it is found between the parallels of 45° and 47°, and by December it has nearly reached its extreme southern descent between these meridians, which it accomplishes in January, standing then near the parallel of 40°. It is all the rest of the year in returning northward to the parallel whence it commenced its flow to the south in September.

501. Now it will be observed that this is the season—from September to December—immediately succeeding that in which the heat of the sun has been playing with greatest activity upon the polar ice. Its melted waters, which are thus put in motion in June, July, and August, would probably occupy the fall months in reaching the parallels indicated. These waters, though cold, and rising gradually in temperature as they flow south, are probably fresher, and if so, probably lighter than the sea water; and therefore it may well be that both the warmer and cooler systems of these isothermal lines are made to vibrate up and down the ocean principally by a gentle surface current in the season of quick motion, and in the season of the slow motion principally by a grad-

ual process of calorific absorption on the one hand, and by a gradual process of cooling on the other.

502. We have precisely such phenomena exhibited by the waters of the Chesapeake Bay as they spread themselves over the sea in winter. At this season of the year, the charts show that water of very low temperature is found projecting out and overlapping the usual limits of the Gulf Stream. The outer edge of this cold water, though jagged, is circular in its shape, having its centre near the mouth of the Bay. The waters of the Bay, being fresher than those of the sea, may, therefore, though colder, be lighter than the warmer waters of the ocean. And thus we have repeated here, though on a smaller scale, the phenomenon as to the flow of cold waters from the north, which force the surface isotherm of 60° from latitude 56° to 40° during three or four months.

503. Changes in the color or depth of the water, and the shape of the bottom, &c., would also cause changes in the temperature of certain parts of the ocean, by increasing or diminishing the capacities of such parts to absorb or radiate heat; and this, to some extent, would cause a bending, or produce irregular curves in the isothermal lines.

504. After a careful study of this plate, and the Thermal Charts of the Atlantic Ocean, from which the materials for this plate were derived, I am led to infer that the mean temperature of the atmosphere between the parallels of 56° and 40° north, for instance, and over that part of the ocean in which we have been considering the fluctuations of the isothermal line of 60°, is at least 60° of Fahrenheit, and upward, from January to August, and that the heat which the waters of the ocean derive from this source—atmospherical contact and radiation—is one of the causes which move the isotherm of 60° from its January to its September parallel.

505. It is well to consider another of the causes which are at work upon the currents in this part of the ocean, and which tend to give the rapid southwardly motion to the isotherm of 60°. We know the mean dew-point must always be below the mean temperature of any given place, and that, consequently, as a general rule, at sea the mean dew-point due the isotherm of 60° is higher than the mean dew-point along the isotherm of 50°, and this, again, higher than that of 40°—this than 30°, and so on. Now suppose, merely for the sake of illustration, that the mean dew-point for

each isotherm be 5° lower than the mean temperature, we should then have the atmosphere which crosses the isotherm of 60°, with a mean dew-point of 55°, gradually precipitating its vapors until it reaches the isotherm of 50°, with a mean dew-point of 45° ; by which difference of dew-point the total amount of precipitation over the entire zone between the isotherms of 60° and 50° has exceeded the total amount of evaporation from the same surface. The prevailing direction of the winds to the north of the fortieth parallel of north latitude is from the southward and westward (Plate VIII.); in other words, it is from the higher to the lower isotherms. Passing, therefore, from a higher to a lower temperature over the ocean, the total amount of vapor deposited by any given volume of atmosphere, as it is blown from the vicinity of the tropical toward that of the polar regions, is greater than that which is taken up again.

506. The area comprehended on Plate VIII. between the isotherms of 40° and 50° Fahrenheit is less than the area comprehended between the isotherms 50° and 60°, and this, again, less than the area between this last and 70°, for the same reason that the area between the parallels of latitude 50° and 60° is less than the area between the parallels of latitude 40° and 50° ; therefore, more rain to the square inch ought to fall upon the ocean between the colder isotherms of 10° difference, than between the warmer isotherms of the same difference. This is an interesting and an important view, therefore let me make myself clear : the aqueous isotherm of 50°, in its extreme northern reach, touches the parallel of 60° north. Now between this and the equator there are but three isotherms, 60°, 70°, and 80°, with the common difference of 10°. But between the isotherm of 40° and the pole, there are at least five others, viz., 40°, 30°, 20°, 10°, 0°, with a common difference of 10°. Thus, to the north of the isotherm 50°, the vapor which would saturate the atmosphere from zero, and perhaps far below, to near 40°, is deposited, while to the south of 50° the vapor which would saturate it from the temperature of 50° up to that of 80° can only be deposited. At least, such would be the case if there were no irregularities of heated plains, mountain ranges, land, &c., to disturb the laws of atmospherical circulation as they apply to the ocean.

507. Having therefore, theoretically, at sea more rain in high

latitudes, we should have more clouds; and therefore it would require a longer time for the sun, with his feeble rays, to raise the temperature of the cold water, which, from September to January, has brought the isotherm of 60° from latitude 56° to 40°, than it did for these cool surface currents to float it down. After this southward motion of the isotherm of 60° has been checked in December by the cold, and after the sources of the current which brought it down have been bound in fetters of ice, it pauses in the long nights of the northern winter, and scarcely commences its return till the sun recrosses the equator, and increases its power as well in intensity as in duration.

Thus, in studying the physical geography of the sea, we have the effects of night and day, of clouds and sunshine, upon its currents and its climates, beautifully developed. These effects are modified by the operations of certain powerful agents which reside upon the land; nevertheless, feeble though those of the former class may be, a close study of this plate will indicate that they surely exist.

508. Now, returning toward the south: we may, on the other hand, infer that the mean atmospherical temperature for the parallels between which the isotherm of 80° fluctuates is below 80°, at least for the nine months of its slow motion. This vibratory motion suggests the idea that there is, probably, somewhere between the isotherm of 80° in August and the isotherm of 60° in January, a line or belt of invariable or nearly invariable temperature, which extends on the surface of the ocean from one side of the Atlantic to the other. This line or band may have its cycles also, but they are probably of long and uncertain periods.

509. The fact has been pretty clearly established by the discoveries to which the wind and current charts have led, that the western half of the Atlantic Ocean is heated up, not by the Gulf Stream alone, as is generally supposed, but by the great equatorial caldron to the west of longitude 35°, and to the north of Cape St. Roque, in Brazil. The lowest reach of the 80° isotherm for September—if we except the remarkable equatorial flexure (Plate IV.) which actually extends from 40° north to the line—to the west of the meridian of Cape St. Roque, is above its highest reach to the east of that meridian. And now that we have the fact, how obvious, beautiful, and striking is the cause!

Cape St. Roque is in 5° south. Now study the configuration of the Southern American Continent from this Cape to the Windward Islands of the West Indies, and take into account also certain physical conditions of these regions: the Amazon, always at a high temperature because it runs from west to east, is pouring an immense volume of warm water into this part of the ocean. As this water and the heat of the sun raise the temperature of the ocean along the equatorial sea-front of this coast, there is no escape for the liquid element, as it grows warmer and lighter, except to the north. The land on the south prevents the tepid waters from spreading out in that direction as they do to the east of 35° west, for here there is a space, about 18 degrees of longitude broad, in which the sea is clear both to the north and south.

510. They must consequently flow north. A mere inspection of the plate is sufficient to make obvious the fact that the warm waters which are found east of the usual limits assigned the Gulf Stream, and between the parallels of 30° and 40° north, do not come from the Gulf Stream, but from this great equatorial caldron, which Cape St. Roque blocks up on the south, and which forces its overheated waters up to the fortieth degree of north latitude, not through the Caribbean Sea and Gulf Stream, but over the broad surface of the left bosom of the Atlantic Ocean.

511. Here we are again tempted to pause and admire the beautiful revelations which, in the benign system of terrestrial adaptation, these researches into the physics of the sea unfold and spread out before us for contemplation. In doing this, we shall have a free pardon from those at least who delight "to look through nature up to nature's God."

What two things in nature can be apparently more remote in their physical relations to each other, than the climate of Western Europe and the profile of a coast-line in South America? Yet this plate reveals to us not only the fact that these relations between the two are the most intimate, but makes us acquainted with the arrangements by which such relations are established.

512. The barrier which the South American shore-line opposes to the escape, on the south, of the hot waters from this great equatorial caldron of St. Roque, causes them to flow north, and in September, as the winter approaches, to heat up the western half of the Atlantic Ocean, and to cover it with a mantle of warmth

above summer heat as far up as the parallel of 40°. Here heat to temper the winter climate of Western Europe is stored away as in an air-chamber to furnace-heated apartments; and during the winter, when the fire of the solar rays sinks down, the westwardly winds and eastwardly currents are sent to perform their office in this benign arrangement. Though unstable and capricious to us they seem to be, they nevertheless "fulfill His commandments" with regularity and perform their offices with certainty. In tempering the climates of Europe with heat in winter that has been bottled away in the waters of the ocean during summer, they are to be regarded as the flues and the regulators for distributing at the right time, and at the right places, in the right quantities.

513. By March, when "the winter is past and gone," the furnace which had been started by the rays of the sun in the previous summer, and which, by autumn, had heated up the ocean in our hemisphere, has gone down. The caldron of St. Roque, ceasing in activity, has failed in its supplies, and the chambers of warmth upon the northern sea, having been exhausted of their heated water, which has been expended in the manner already explained, have contracted their limits. The surface of heated water which, in September, was spread out over the western half of the Atlantic, from the equator to the parallel of 40° north, and which raised this immense area to the temperature of 80° and upward, is not to be found in early spring on this side of the parallel of 8° north.

514. The isotherm of 80° in March, after quitting the Caribbean Sea, runs parallel with the South American coast toward Cape St. Roque, keeping some 8 or 10 degrees from it. Therefore the heat dispensed over Europe from this caldron falls off in March. But at this season the sun comes forth with fresh supplies; he then crosses the line and passes over into the northern hemisphere; observations show that the process of heating the water in this great caldron for the next winter is now about to commence.

515. In the mean time, so benign is the system of cosmical arrangements, another process of raising the temperature of Europe commences. The land is more readily impressed than the sea by the heat of the solar rays; at this season, then, the summer climate due these transatlantic latitudes is modified by the action of

the sun's rays directly upon the land. The land receives heat from them, but, instead of having the capacity of water for retaining it, it imparts it straightway to the air; and thus the proper climate, because it is the climate which the Creator has, for his own wise purposes, allotted to this portion of the earth, is maintained until the marine caldron of Cape St. Roque is again heated and brought into the state for supplying the means of maintaining the needful temperature in Europe during the absence of the sun in the other hemisphere.

516. In like manner, the Gulf of Guinea forms a caldron and a furnace, and spreads out over the South Atlantic an air-chamber for heating up in winter and keeping warm the extra-tropical regions of South America. Every traveler has remarked upon the mild climate of Patagonia and the Falkland Islands.

"Temperature in high southern latitudes," says a very close observer, who is co-operating with me in collecting materials, "differs greatly from the temperature in northern. In southern latitudes there seem to be no extremes of heat and cold, as at the north. Newport, R. I., for instance, latitude 41° north, longitude 71° west, and Rio Negro, latitude 41° south, and longitude 63° west, as a comparison: in the former, cattle have to be stabled and fed during the winter, not being able to get a living in the fields on account of snow and ice. In the latter, the cattle feed in the fields all winter, there being plenty of vegetation and no use of hay. On the Falkland Islands (latitude 51–2° south), thousands of bullocks, sheep, and horses are running wild over the country, gathering a living all through the winter."

517. The water in the equatorial caldron of Guinea can not escape north—the shore-line will not permit it. It must, therefore, overflow to the south, as that of St. Roque does to the north, carrying to Patagonia and the Falkland Islands, beyond 50° south, the winter climate of Charleston, South Carolina, on our side of the North Atlantic, or of the "Emerald Island" on the other.

All geographers have noticed, and philosophers have frequently remarked upon the conformity, as to the shore-line profile, of equatorial America and equatorial Africa.

518. It is true, we can not now tell the reason, though explanations founded upon mere conjecture have been offered, why there should be this sort of jutting in and jutting out of the shore-line, as

at Cape St. Roque and the Gulf of Guinea, on opposite sides of the Atlantic; but one of the purposes, at least, which this peculiar configuration was intended to subserve, is without doubt now revealed to us.

519. We see that, by this configuration, two cisterns of hot water are formed in this ocean; one of which distributes heat and warmth to western Europe; the other, at the opposite season, tempers the climate of eastern Patagonia.

Phlegmatic must be the mind that is not impressed with ideas of grandeur and simplicity as it contemplates that exquisite design, those benign and beautiful arrangements, by which the climate of one hemisphere is made to depend upon the curve of that line against which the sea is made to dash its waves in the other. Impressed with the perfection of terrestrial adaptations, he who studies the economy of the great cosmical arrangements is reminded that not only is there design in giving shore-lines their profile, the land and the water their proportions, and in placing the desert and the pool where they are, but the conviction is forced upon him also, that every hill and valley, with the grass upon its sides, have each its office to perform in the grand design.

520. March is, in the southern hemisphere, the first month of autumn, as September is with us; consequently, we should expect to find in the South Atlantic as large an area of water of 80° and upward in March, as we should find in the North Atlantic for September. But do we? By no means. The area on this side of the equator is nearly double that on the other.

521. Thus we have the sea as a witness to the fact that the winds (§ 196) had proclaimed, viz., that summer in the northern hemisphere is hotter than summer in the southern, for the rays of the sun raise on this side of the equator double the quantity of sea surface to a given temperature that they do on the other side; at least this is the case in the Atlantic. Perhaps the breadth of the Pacific Ocean, the absence of large islands in the temperate regions north, the presence of New Holland, with Polynesia in the South Pacific, may make a difference there. But of this I can not now speak, for thermal charts of that ocean have not yet been prepared.

522. Pursuing the study of the climates of the sea, let us now turn to Plate VI. Here we see at a glance how the cold waters,

as they come down from the Arctic Ocean through Davis's Straits, press upon the warm waters of the Gulf Stream, and curve their channel into a horse-shoe. Navigators have often been struck with the great and sudden changes in the temperature of the water hereabouts. In the course of a single day's sail in this part of the ocean, changes of 15°, or 20°, and even of 30°, have been observed to take place in the temperature of the sea. The cause has puzzled navigators long, but how obvious is it not now made to appear! This "bend" is the great receptacle of the icebergs which drift down from the north; covering frequently an area of hundreds of miles in extent, its waters differ as much as 20°, 25°, and in rare cases even as much as 30° of temperature from those about it. Its shape and place are variable. Sometimes it is like a peninsula, or tongue of cold water projected far down into the waters of the Gulf Stream. Sometimes the meridian upon which it is inserted into these is to the east of 40°, sometimes to the west of 50° longitude. By its discovery we have clearly unmasked the very seat of that agent which produces the Newfoundland fogs. It is spread out over an area frequently embracing several thousand square miles in extent, covered with cold water, and surrounded on three sides, at least, with an immense body of warm. May it not be that the proximity to each other of these two very unequally heated surfaces out upon the ocean would be attended by atmospherical phenomena not unlike those of the land and sea breezes? These warm currents of the sea are powerful meteorological agents. I have been enabled to trace, in thunder and lightning, the influence of the Gulf Stream in the eastern half of the Atlantic, as far north as the parallel of 55° north; for there, in the dead of winter, a thunder-storm is not unusual.

523. These isothermal lines of 50°, 60°, 70°, 80°, &c., may illustrate for us the manner in which the climates in the ocean are regulated. Like the sun in the ecliptic, they travel up and down the sea in declination, and serve the monsters of the deep for signs and for seasons.

524. It should be borne in mind that the lines of separation, as drawn on Plate IX., between the cool and warm waters, or, more properly speaking, between the channels representing the great polar and equatorial flux and reflux, are not so sharp in nature as this plate would represent them. In the first place, the plate rep-

resents the mean or average limits of these constant flows—polar and equatorial; whereas, with almost every wind that blows, and at every change of season, the line of meeting between their waters is shifted. In the next place, this line of meeting is drawn with a free hand on the plate, as if to represent an average; whereas there is reason to believe that this line in nature is variable and unstable as to position, and as to shape rough and jagged, and oftentimes deeply articulated. In the sea, the line of meeting between waters of different temperatures and density is not unlike the sutures of the skull-bone on a grand scale—very rough and jagged; but on the plate it is a line drawn with a free hand, for the purpose of showing the general direction and position of the channels in the sea, through which its great polar and equatorial circulation is carried on.

525. Now, continuing for a moment our examination of Plate IV., we are struck with the fact that most of the thermal lines there drawn run from the western side of the Atlantic toward the eastern, in a northeastwardly direction, and that, as they approach the shores of this ocean on the east, they again turn down for lower latitudes and warmer climates. This feature in them indicates, more surely than any direct observations upon the currents can do, the presence, along the African shores in the North Atlantic, of a large volume of cooler waters. These are the waters which, having been first heated up in the caldron (§ 509) of St. Roque, in the Caribbean Sea, and Gulf of Mexico, have been made to run to the north, charged with heat and electricity to temper and regulate climates there. Having performed their offices, they have cooled down; but, obedient still to the "Mighty Voice" which the winds and the waves obey, they now return by this channel along the African shore to be again replenished with warmth, and to keep up the system of beneficent and wholesome circulation designed for the ocean.

CHAPTER XV.

THE DRIFT OF THE SEA.

Object of Plate IX., § 528.—The Eastern Edge of the Gulf Stream sometimes visible, 529.—The Polar Drift about Cape Horn, 533.—How the Polar Waters drift into the South Atlantic, and force the Equatorial aside, 535.—How this is accomplished, 537.—A Harbor in a Bend of the Gulf Stream for Icebergs, 539.—Why Icebergs are not found in the North Pacific, 540.—The Womb of the Sea, 541.—Drift of warm Waters out of the Indian Ocean, 543.—A Suggestion from Lieutenant Jansen, of the Dutch Navy, 544.—A Current of warm Water sixteen hundred Miles wide, 545.—The Pulse of the Sea, 546.—How the Gulf Stream beats Time, 547.—The Circulation of the Sea likened to that of the Blood, 548.—The Fish: Number of Vessels engaged in the Fisheries of the Sea, 551.—The Sperm Whale delights in warm Water, 552.—The Torrid Zone impassable to the Right Whale, 553.

526. There is a movement of the waters of the ocean which, though it be a translation, yet does not amount to what is known to the mariner as current, for our nautical instruments and the art of navigation have not been brought to that state of perfection which will enable navigators generally to detect as currents the flow to which I allude as *drift*.

527. If we imagine an object to be set adrift in the ocean at the equator, and if we suppose that it be of such a nature that it would obey only the influence of sea water, and not of the winds, this object, I imagine, would, in the course of time, find its way to the icy barriers about the poles, and again back among the tepid waters of the tropics. Such an object would illustrate the *drift of the sea*, and by its course would indicate the route which the surface waters of the sea follow in their general channels of circulation to and fro between the equator and the poles.

528. The object of Plate IX., therefore, is to illustrate, as far as the present state of my researches enables me to do, the circulation of the ocean, as influenced by *heat* and *cold*, and to indicate the routes by which the overheated waters of the torrid zone escape to cooler regions, on one hand, and on the other, the great channel ways through which the same waters, after having

been deprived of this heat in the extra-tropical or polar regions, return again toward the equator; it being assumed that the drift or flow is from the poles when the temperature of the surface water is *below*, and from the equatorial regions when it is above that due the latitude. Therefore, in a mere diagram, as this plate is, the numerous eddies and local currents which are found at sea are disregarded.

529. Of all the currents in the sea, the Gulf Stream is the best defined; its limits, especially those of the left bank, are always well marked, and, as a rule, those of the right bank, as high as the parallel of the thirty-fifth degree of latitude, are quite distinct, being often visible to the eye. The Gulf Stream shifts its channel (§ 53), but nevertheless its banks are often very distinct. As I write these remarks, the abstract log of the ship Herculean (William M. Chamberlain), from Callao to Hampton Roads, in May, 1854, is received. On the eleventh of that month, being in latitude 33° 39′ north, longitude 74° 56′ west (about one hundred and thirty miles east of Cape Fear), he remarks:

"Moderate breezes, smooth sea, and fine weather. At ten o'clock fifty minutes, entered into the southern (right) edge of the Stream, and in eight minutes the water rose six degrees; the edge of the stream was visible, as far as the eye could see, by the great rippling and large quantities of Gulf weed—more 'weed' than I ever saw before, and I have been many times along this route in the last twenty years."

530. In this diagram, therefore, I have thought it useless to attempt a delineation of any of those currents, as the Rennell Current of the North Atlantic, the "connecting current" of the South, "Mentor's Counter Drift," Rossel's Drift of the South Pacific, &c., which run now this way, now that, and which are frequently not felt by navigators at all.

531. In overhauling the log-books for data for this chart, I have followed vessels with the water thermometer to and fro across the seas, and taken the registrations of it exclusively for my guide, without regard to the reported set of the currents. When, in any latitude, the temperature of the water has appeared too high or too low for that latitude, the inference has been that such water was warmed or cooled, as the case may be, in other latitudes, and that it has been conveyed to the place where found through the great

channels of circulation in the ocean. If too warm, it is supposed (§ 528) that it had its temperature raised in warmer latitudes, and therefore the channel in which it is found leads from the equatorial regions.

532. On the other hand, if the water be too cool for the latitude, then the inference is that it has lost its heat in colder climates, and therefore is found in channels which lead from the polar regions.

The arrow-heads point to the direction in which the waters are supposed to flow. Their rate, according to the best information that I have obtained, is, at a mean, only about four knots a day—rather less than more.

533. Accordingly, therefore, as the immense volume of water in the Antarctic regions is cooled down, it commences to flow north. As indicated by the arrow-heads, it strikes against Cape Horn, and is divided by the continent, one portion going along the west coast as Humboldt's Current (§ 267); the other, entering the South Atlantic, flows up into the Gulf of Guinea, on the coast of Africa. Now, as the waters of this polar flow approach the torrid zone, they grow warmer and warmer, and finally themselves become tropical in their temperature. They do not then, it may be supposed, stop their flow; on the contrary, they keep moving, for the very cause which brought them from the extra-tropical regions now operates to send them back. This cause is to be found in the difference of the specific gravity at the two places. If, for instance, these waters, when they commence their flow from the hyperborean regions, were at 30°, their specific gravity will correspond to that of sea water at 30°. But when they arrive in the Gulf of Guinea or the Bay of Panama, having risen by the way to 80°, or perhaps 85°, their specific gravity becomes such as is due sea water of this temperature; and, since fluids differing in specific gravity can no more balance each other on the same level than can unequal weights in opposite scales, this hot water must now return to restore that equilibrium which it has destroyed in the sea by rising from 30° to 80° or 85°.

534. Hence it will be perceived that these masses of water which are marked as cold are not always cold. They gradually pass into warm; for in traveling from the poles to the equator they partake of the temperature of the latitudes through which they flow, and grow warm.

535. Plate IX., therefore, is only introduced to give general ideas; nevertheless, it is very instructive. See how the influx of cold water into the South Atlantic appears to divide the warm water, and squeeze it out at the sides, along the coasts of South Africa and Brazil. So, too, in the North Indian Ocean, the cold water again compelling the warm to escape along the land at the sides, as well as occasionally in the middle.

536. In the North Atlantic and North Pacific, on the contrary, the warm water appears to divide the cold, and to squeeze it out along the land at the sides. The impression made by the cold current from Baffin's Bay upon the Gulf Stream is strikingly beautiful.

537. Why is it that these polar and equatorial waters should appear now to divide and now to be divided? The Gulf Stream has revealed to us a fact in which the answer is involved. We learn from that stream that cold and warm sea waters are, in a measure (§ 53), like oil and vinegar; that is, there is among the particles of sea water at a high temperature, and among the particles of sea water at a low temperature, a peculiar molecular arrangement that is antagonistic to the free mixing up of cold and hot together. At any rate, that salt waters of different temperatures do not readily intermingle at sea is obvious.

538. Does not this same repugnance exist, at least in degree, between these bodies of cold and warm water of the plate? And if so, does not the phenomenon we are considering resolve itself into a question of masses? The volume of warm water in the North Atlantic is greater than the volume of cold water that meets and opposes it; consequently, the warm thrusts the cold aside, dividing and compelling it *to go round.* The same thing is repeated in the North Pacific, whereas the converse obtains in the South Atlantic. Here the great polar flow, after having been divided by the American Continent, enters the Atlantic, and filling up nearly the whole of the immense space between South America and Africa, seems to press the warm waters of the tropics aside, compelling them to drift along the coast on either hand.

539. Another feature of the sea expressed by this plate is a sort of reflection or recast of the shore-line in the temperature of the water. This feature is most striking in the North Pacific and Indian Ocean. The remarkable intrusion of the cool into the vol-

ume of warm waters to the southward of the Aleutian Islands, is not unlike that which the cool waters from Davis's Straits make in the Atlantic upon the Gulf Stream. As I write, I receive from Captain N. B. Grant the abstract log of the American ship Lady Arbella, bound from Hamburg to New York, in May, 1854. In sailing through this "horse-shoe," or bend in the Gulf Stream (§ 522), he passed, from daylight to noon, twenty-four large "bergs," besides several small ones, "the whole ocean, as far as the eye could reach, being literally covered with them." "I should," he continues, "judge the average height of them above the surface of the sea to be about sixty feet; some five or six of them were at least twice that height, and, with their frozen peaks jutting up in the most fantastic shapes, presented a truly sublime spectacle."

540. This "horse-shoe" of cold in the warm water of the North Pacific, though extending 5 degrees farther toward the south, can not be the harbor for such icebergs. The cradle of those of the Atlantic was perhaps in the Frozen Ocean, for they may have come thence through Baffin's Bay. But in the Pacific there is no nursery for them. The water in Behring's Strait is too shallow to let them pass from that ocean into the Pacific, and the climates of Russian America do not favor the formation of large bergs. But, though we do not find in the North Pacific the physical conditions which generate icebergs like those of the Atlantic, we find them as abundant with fogs. The line of separation between the warm and cold water assures us of these conditions.

541. What beautiful, grand, and benign ideas do we not see expressed in that immense body of warm waters which are gathered together in the middle of the Pacific and Indian Oceans!* It is the womb of the sea. In it, coral islands innumerable have been fashioned, and pearls formed in "great heaps;" there, multitudes of living things, countless in numbers and infinite in variety, are hourly conceived. With space enough to hold the four continents and to spare, its tepid waters teem with nascent organisms.† They sometimes swarm so thickly there that they change

* See Appendix I.

† "It is the realm of reef-building corals, and of the wondrously-beautiful assemblage of animals, vertebrate and invertebrate, that live among them or prey upon them. The brightest and most definite arrangements of color are here displayed. It is the seat of maximum development of the majority of marine genera. It has but few re-

the color of the sea, making it crimson, brown, black, or white,* according to their own hues. These patches of colored water sometimes extend, especially in the Indian Ocean, as far as the eye can reach. The question, "What produces them?" is one that has elicited much discussion in seafaring circles. The Brussels Conference deemed them an object worthy of attention, and recommended special observations with regard to them.

The discolorations of which I speak are no doubt caused by organisms of the sea, but whether wholly animal or wholly vegetable, or whether sometimes the one and sometimes the other, has not been satisfactorily ascertained. I have had specimens of the coloring matter sent to me from the pink-stained patches of the sea. They were animalculæ well defined. Quantities of slimy, red coloring matter are, at certain seasons of the year, washed up along the shores of the Red Sea, which Dr. Ehrenberg, after an examination under the microscope, pronounces to be a very delicate kind of sea weed: from this matter that sea derives its name. So also the Yellow Sea. Along the coasts of China, yellowish colored spots are said not to be uncommon. I know of no examination of this coloring matter, however. In the Pacific Ocean I have often observed these discolorations of the sea. Red patches of water are most frequently met with, but I have also observed white or milky appearances, which at night I have known greatly to alarm navigators, they taking them for shoals.

542. These teeming waters bear off through their several channels the surplus heat of the tropics, and disperse it among the icebergs of the Antarctic. See the immense equatorial flow to the east of New Holland. It is bound for the icy barriers of that unknown sea, there to temper climates, grow cool, and return again, refreshing man and beast by the way, either as the Humboldt Current, or the ice-bearing current which enters the Atlantic around Cape Horn, and changes into warm again as it enters the Gulf of Guinea. It was owing to this great southern flow from the coral regions that Captain Ross was enabled to penetrate so much farther south than Captain Wilkes, on his voyage to the

lations of identity with other provinces. The Red Sea and Persian Gulf are its offsets."—From Professor Forbes's Paper on the "Distribution of Marine Life." Plate 31st, Johnston's Physical Atlas, 2d ed.: Wm. Blackwood & Sons, Edinburgh and London, 1854.

* See Appendix K

Antarctic, and it is upon these waters that that sea is to be penetrated, if ever. The North Pacific, except in the narrow passage between Asia and America, is closed to the escape of these warm waters into the Arctic Ocean. The only outlet for them is to the south. They go down toward the Antarctic regions to dispense their heat and get cool; and the cold of the Antarctic, therefore, it may be inferred, is not so bitter as is the extreme cold of the Frozen Ocean of the north.

543. The warm flow to the south from the middle of the Indian Ocean is remarkable. Masters who return their abstract logs to me mention sea weed, which I suppose to be brought down by this current, as far as 45° south. There it is generally, but not always, about 5 degrees warmer than the ocean along the same parallel on either side.

544. But the most unexpected discovery of all is that of the warm flow along the west coast of South Africa, its junction with the Lagullas current, called, higher up, the Mozambique, and then their starting off as one stream to the southward. The prevalent opinion used to be that the Lagullas current, which has its genesis in the Red Sea (§ 55), doubled the Cape of Good Hope, and then joined the great equatorial current of the Atlantic to feed the Gulf Stream. But my excellent friend Lieutenant Marin Jansen, of the Dutch Navy, suggested to me a few months ago that this was probably not the case. This induced a special investigation, and I found as he suggested, and as is represented on Plate IX. Captain N. B. Grant, in the admirably well-kept abstract log of his voyage from New York to Australia, found this current remarkably developed. He was astonished at the temperature of its waters, and did not know how to account for such a body of warm water in such a place. Being in longitude 14° east and latitude 39° south, he thus writes in his abstract log:

"That there is a current setting to the eastward across the South Atlantic and Indian Oceans is, I believe, admitted by all navigators. The prevailing westerly winds seem to offer a sufficient reason for the existence of such a current, and the almost constant southwest swell would naturally give it a northerly direction. But why the water should be *warmer* here (38° 40′ south) than between the parallels of 35° and 37° south is a problem that, in my mind, admits not of so easy solution, especially if my suspicions are true in regard to the northerly set. I shall look with much interest for a description of the 'currents' in this part of the ocean."

545. In latitude 38° south, longitude 6° east, he found the water at 56°. His course thence was a little to the south of east, to the meridian of 41° east, at its intersection with the parallel of 42° south. Here his water thermometer stood at 50°, but between these two places it ranged at 60° and upward, being as high on the parallel of 39° as 73°. Here, therefore, was a stream—a mighty "river in the ocean"—one thousand six hundred miles across from east to west, having water in the middle of it 23° higher than at the sides. This is truly a Gulf Stream contrast. What an immense escape of heat from the Indian Ocean, and what an influx of warm water into the frozen regions of the south! This stream is not always as broad nor as warm as Captain Grant found it. At its mean stage it conforms more nearly to the limits assigned it in the diagram (Plate IX.).

546. We have, in the volume of heated water reported by Captain Grant, who is a close and accurate observer, an illustration of the sort of *spasmodic* efforts—the heaves and throes—which the sea, in the performance of its ceaseless task, has sometimes to make. By some means, the equilibrium of its waters, at the time of Captain Grant's passage, December—the southern summer—1852, appears to have been disturbed to an unusual extent; hence this mighty rush of overheated waters from the great inter-tropical caldron of the two oceans down toward the south.

Instances of commotion in the sea at uncertain intervals—the making, as it were, of efforts by fits and starts to keep up to time in the performance of its manifold offices—are not unfrequent, nor are they inaptly likened to spasms. The sudden disruption of the ice which arctic voyagers tell of, the immense bergs which occasionally appear in groups near certain latitudes, the variable character of all the currents of the sea—now fast, now slow, now running this way, then that—may be taken as so many signs of the tremendous throes which occur in the bosom of the ocean. Sometimes the sea recedes from the shore, as if to gather strength for a great rush against its barriers, as it did when it fled back to join with the earthquake and overwhelm Callao in 1746, and again Lisbon nine years afterward. The tide-rips in mid ocean, the waves dashing against the shore, the ebb and flow of the tides, may be regarded, in some sense, as the throbbings of the great sea pulse.

547. The motions of the Gulf Stream (§ 53), beating time for the ocean and telling the seasons for the whales, also suggest the idea of a pulse in the sea, which may assist us in explaining some of its phenomena. At one beat there is a rush of warm water from the equator toward the poles, at the next beat a flow from the poles toward the equator. This sort of pulsation is heard also in the howlings of the storm and the whistling of the wind; the needle trembles unceasingly to it, and tells us of magnetic storms of great violence, which at times extend over large portions of the earth's surface; and when we come to consult the records of those exquisitely sensitive anemometers, which the science and ingenuity of the age have placed at the service of philosophers, we find there that the pulse of the atmosphere is never still: in what appears to us the most perfect calm, the recording pens are moving to the pulses of the air.

548. Now if we may be permitted to apply to the Gulf Stream and to the warm flows of water from the Indian Ocean an idea suggested by the functions of the human heart in the circulation of the blood, we perceive how these pulsations of the great sea-heart may perhaps assist in giving circulation to its waters through the immense system of aqueous veins and arteries that run between the equatorial and polar regions. The waters of the Gulf Stream, moving together in a body (§ 1) through such an extent of ocean, and being almost impenetrable to the cold waters on either side—which are, indeed, the banks of this mighty river—may be compared to a wedge-shaped cushion placed between a wall of waters on the right and a wall of waters on the left. If now we imagine the equilibrium of the sea to be disturbed by the heating or cooling of its waters to the right or the left of this stream, or the freezing or thawing of them in any part, or if we imagine the disturbance to take place by the action of any of those agencies which give rise to the motions which we have called the pulsations of the sea, we may conceive how it might be possible for them to force the wall of waters on the left to press this cushion down toward the south, and then again for the wall on the right to press it back again to the north, as (§ 54) we have seen that it is.

Now the Gulf Stream, with its head in the Straits of Florida, and its tail in the midst of the ocean (§ 492), is wedge-shaped; its waters cling together (§ 28), and are pushed to and fro—squeezed, if you please—by a pressure (§ 53), now from the right, then from the left, so as to work the whole wedge along between the cold liquid walls which contain it. May not the velocity of this stream, therefore, be in some sort the result of this working and twisting, this peristaltic force in the sea?

549. In carrying out the views suggested by the idea of pulsations in the sea, and their effects in giving dynamical force to the circulation of its waters, attention may be called to the two lobes of polar waters that stretch up from the south into the Indian Ocean, and which are separated by a feeble flow of tropical waters. Icebergs are sometimes met with in these polar waters as high up as the parallel of the fortieth degree of latitude. Now, considering that this tropical flow in mid ocean is not constant—that many navigators cross the path assigned to it in the plate without finding their thermometer to indicate any increase of heat in the sea; and considering, therefore, that any unusual flow of polar waters, any sudden and extensive disruption of the ice there, sufficient to cause a rush of waters thence, would have the effect of closing for the time this mid-ocean flow of tropical waters, we are entitled to infer that there is a sort of conflict, at times, going on in this ocean between its polar and equatorial flows of water. For instance, a rush of waters takes place from the poles toward the equator. The two lobes close, cut off the equatorial flow between them, and crowd the Indian Ocean with polar waters. They press out the overheated waters; hence the great equatorial flow encountered by Captain Grant.

Thus this opening between the cold-water lobes appears to hold to the chambers of the Indian Ocean, with their heated waters, the relations which the valves and the ventricles of the human heart hold to the circulation of the blood. The closing of these lobes at certain times prevents regurgitation of the warm waters, and compels them to pass through their appointed channels.

550. From this point of view, how many new beauties do not now begin to present themselves in the machinery of the ocean! its great heart not only beating time to the seasons, but palpitating also to the winds and the rains, to the cloud and the sun-

shine, to day and night (§ 507). Few persons have ever taken the trouble to compute how much the fall of a single inch of rain over an extensive region in the sea, or how much the change even of two or three degrees of temperature over a few thousand square miles of its surface, tends to disturb its equilibrium, and consequently to cause an aqueous palpitation that is felt from the equator to the poles. Let us illustrate by an example: The surface of the Atlantic Ocean covers an area of about twenty-five millions of square miles. Now, let us take one fifth of this area, and suppose a fall of rain one inch deep to take place over it. This rain would weigh three hundred and sixty thousand millions of tons; and the salt which, as water, it held in solution in the sea, and which, when that water was taken up as vapor, was left behind to disturb equilibrium, weighed sixteen millions more of tons, or nearly twice as much as all the ships in the world could carry at a cargo each. It might fall in an hour, or it might fall in a day; but, occupy what time it might in falling, this rain is calculated to exert so much force—which is inconceivably great—in disturbing the equilibrium of the ocean. If all the water discharged by the Mississippi River during the year were taken up in one mighty measure, and cast into the ocean at one effort, it would not make a greater disturbance in the equilibrium of the sea than would the fall of rain supposed. Now this is for but one fifth of the Atlantic, and the area of the Atlantic is about one fifth of the sea-area of the world; and the estimated fall of rain was but one inch, whereas the average for the year is (§ 144) sixty inches, but we will assume it for the sea to be no more than thirty inches. In the aggregate, and on an average, then, such a disturbance in the equilibrium of the whole ocean as is here supposed occurs seven hundred and fifty times a year, or at the rate of once in twelve hours. Moreover, when it is recollected that these rains take place now here, now there; that the vapor of which they were formed was taken up at still other places, we shall be enabled to appreciate the better the force and the effect of these pulsations in the sea.

551. Between the hottest hour of the day and the coldest hour of the night there is frequently a change of four degrees in the temperature of the sea.* Let us, therefore, to appreciate the throb-

* *Vide* Admiral Smyth's Memoir of the Mediterranean, p. 125.

bings of the sea-heart, which take place in consequence of the diurnal changes in its temperature, call in the sunshine, the cloud without rain, with day and night, and their heating and radiating processes. And to make the case as strong as to be true to nature we may, let us again select one fifth of the Atlantic Ocean for the scene of operation. The day over it is clear, and the sun pours down his rays with their greatest intensity, and raises the temperature two degrees. At night the clouds interpose, and prevent radiation from this fifth, whereas the remaining four fifths, which are supposed to have been screened by clouds, so as to cut off the heat from the sun during the day, are now looking up to the stars in a cloudless sky, and serve to lower the temperature of the surface waters, by radiation, two degrees. Here, then, is a difference of four degrees, which we will suppose extends only ten feet below the surface. The total and absolute change made in such a mass of sea water by altering its temperature four degrees is equivalent to a change in its volume of three hundred and ninety thousand millions of cubic feet.

552. Do not the clouds, night and day, now present themselves to us in a new light? They are cogs, and rachets, and wheels in that grand and exquisite machinery which governs the sea, and which, amid all the jarrings of the elements, preserves in harmony the exquisite adaptations of the ocean.

553. It seems to be a physical law, that cold-water fish are more edible than those of warm water. Bearing this fact in mind as we study Plate IX., we see at a glance the places which are most favored with good fish-markets. Both shores of North America, the east coast of China, with the west coasts of Europe and South America, are all washed by cold waters, and therefore we may infer that their markets abound with the most excellent fish. The fisheries of Newfoundland and New England, over which nations have wrangled for centuries, are in the cold water from Davis's Strait. The fisheries of Japan and Eastern China, which almost, if not quite, rival these, are situated also in the cold water.

Neither India, nor the east coasts of Africa and South America, where the warm waters are, are celebrated for their fish.

554. Three thousand American vessels, it is said, are engaged in the fisheries. If to these we add the Dutch, French, and En-

glish, we shall have a grand total, perhaps, of not less than six or eight thousand, of all sizes and flags, engaged in this one pursuit. Of all the industrial pursuits of the sea, however, the whale fishery is the most valuable. Wherefore, in treating of the physical geography of the sea, a map for the whales would be useful.

555. The sperm whale is a warm-water fish. The *right* whale delights in cold water. An immense number of log-books of whalers have been discussed at the National Observatory, with the view of detecting the parts of the ocean in which the whales are to be found at the different seasons of the year. Charts showing the result have been published; they form a part of the series of Maury's Wind and Current Charts.

556. In the course of these investigations, the discovery was made that the torrid zone is to the right whale as a sea of fire, through which he can not pass; that the right whale of the northern hemisphere and that of the southern are two different animals; and that the sperm whale has never been known to double the Cape of Good Hope—he doubles Cape Horn.

557. With these remarks, and the explanations given on Plate IX., the parts of the ocean to which the right whale most resorts, and the parts in which the sperm are found, may be seen at a glance.

CHAPTER XVI.

STORMS.

558. Plate V. is constructed from data furnished by the Pilot Charts, as far as they go, that are in process of construction at the National Observatory. For the Pilot Charts, the whole ocean is divided off into districts of five degrees square, *i. e.*, five degrees of latitude by five degrees of longitude, as already explained on page 23. Now, in getting out from the log-books materials for showing, in every district of the ocean, and for every month, how navigators have found the winds to blow, it has been assumed that, in whatever part of one of these districts a navigator may be when he records the direction of the wind in his log, from that direction the wind was blowing at that time all over that district; and this is the only assumption that is permitted in the whole course of investigation.

Now if the navigator will draw, or imagine to be drawn in any such district, twelve vertical columns for the twelve months, and then sixteen horizontal lines through the same for the sixteen points of the compass, *i. e.*, for N., N.N.E., N.E., E.N.E., and so on, omitting the *by*-points, he will have before him a picture of the "Investigating Chart," out of which the "Pilot Charts" are constructed. In this case, the alternate points of the compass only are used; because, when sailing free, the direction of the wind is seldom given for such points as N. *by* E., W. *by* S., &c. Moreover, any attempt, for the present, at greater nicety, would be over-refinement; for navigators do not always make allowance for the aberration of the wind; in other words, they do not allow for the apparent change in the direction of the wind caused by the rate at which the vessel may be moving through the water, and the angle which her course makes with the true direction of the wind. Bearing this explanation in mind, the intelligent navigator will have no difficulty in understanding the wind diagram (Plate V.), and in forming a correct opinion as to the degree of credit due to the fidelity with which the prevailing winds of the year are represented on Plate VIII.

As the compiler wades through log-book after log-book, and scores down in column after column, and upon line after line, mark after mark, he at last finds that, under the month and from the course upon which he is about to make an entry, he has already made four marks or scores, thus (**IIII**). The one that he has now to enter will make the fifth, and he "scores and tallies," and so on until all the abstracts relating to that part of the ocean upon which he is at work have been gone over, and his materials exhausted. These "fives and tallies" are exhibited on Plate V.

Now, with this explanation, it will be seen that in the district marked A (Plate V.) there have been examined the logs of vessels that, giving the direction of the wind for every eight hours, have altogether spent days enough to enable me to record the calms and the prevailing direction of the winds for eight hours, 2,144 times: of these, 285 were for the month of September; and of these 285 observations for September, the wind is reported as prevailing for as much as eight hours at a time: from N., 3 times; from N.N.E., 1; N.E., 2; E.N.E., 1; E., 0; E.S.E., 1; S.E., 4; S.S.E., 2; S., 25; S.S.W., 45; S.W., 93; W.S.W., 24; W., 47; W.N.W., 17; N.W., 15; N.N.W., 1; Calms (the little 0's), 5; total, 285 for this month in this district.

The number expressed in figures denotes the whole number of observations of calms and winds together that are recorded for each month and district.

In C, the wind in May *sets* one third of the time from west. But in A, which is between the same parallels, the favorite quarter for the same month is from S. to S.W., the wind setting one third of the time from that quarter, and only 10 out of 221 times from the west; or, on the average, it blows from the west only 1⅓ day during the month of May.

In B, notice the great "Sun Swing" of the winds in September, indicating that the change from summer to winter, in that region, is sudden and violent; from winter to summer, gentle and gradual.

In some districts of the ocean, more than a thousand observations have been discussed for a single month, whereas, with regard to others, not a single record is to be found in any of the numerous log-books at the National Observatory..

559. TYPHOONS.—The China Seas are celebrated for their furious gales of wind, known among seamen as typhoons and white squalls. These seas are included on the plate (VIII.) as within the region of the monsoons of the Indian Ocean. But the monsoons of the China Seas are not five-month monsoons (§ 475); they do not prevail from the west of south for more than two or three months.

560. Plate V. exhibits the monsoons very clearly in a part of this sea. In the square between 15° and 20° north, 110° and 115° east, there appears to be a system of three monsoons; that is, from northeast in October, November, December, and January; from east in March and April, changing in May; from the southward in June, July, and August, and changing in September. The great disturber of the atmospheric equilibrium is situated among the arid plains of Asia; their influence extends to the China Seas, and about the changes of the monsoons these awful gales are experienced.

561. In like manner, the Mauritius hurricanes, or the cyclones of the Indian Ocean, occur during the unsettled state of the atmospheric equilibrium which takes place at that debatable period during the contest between the trade-wind force and the monsoon force (§ 477), and which debatable period occurs at the changing of the monsoon, and before either force has completely gained or lost the ascendency. At this period of the year, the winds, breaking loose from their controlling forces, seem to rage with a fury that would break up the very fountains of the deep.

562. So, too, with the West India hurricanes of the Atlantic. These winds are most apt to occur during the months of August and September. There is, therefore, this remarkable difference between these gales and those of the East Indies: the latter occur about the changing of the monsoons, the former during their height. In August and September, the southwest monsoons of Africa (§ 479) and the southeast monsoons of the West Indies (§ 474) are at their height; the agent of one drawing the northeast trade-winds from the Atlantic into the interior of New Mexico and Texas, the agent of the other drawing them into the interior of Africa.

Its two forces, pulling in opposite directions, assist now and then to disturb the atmospheric equilibrium to such an extent that the most powerful revulsions in the air are required to restore it.

563. Extra-tropical Gales.—In the extra-tropical regions of each hemisphere furious gales of wind also occur. One of these, remarkable for its violent effects, was encountered on the 24th of December, 1853, about three hundred miles from Sandy Hook, latitude 39° north, longitude 70° west, by the San Francisco, steam-ship (§ 72). That ship was made a complete wreck in a few moments, and she was abandoned by the survivors, after incredible hardships, exertions, and sufferings. Some months after this disaster, I received by the California mail the abstract log of the fine clipper ship "Eagle Wing" (Ebenezer H. Linnell), from Boston to San Francisco. She encountered the ill-fated steamer's gale, and thus describes it:

564. "*December 24th*, 1853. Latitude 39° 15′ north, longitude 62° 32′ west. First part threatening weather; shortened sail: at 4 P.M. close reefed the top-sails and furled the courses. At 8 P.M. took in fore and mizen top-sails; hove to under close-reefed main top-sail and spencer, the ship lying with her lee rail under water, nearly on her beam-ends. At 1 30 A.M. the fore and main top-gallant-masts went over the side, it blowing a perfect hurricane. At 8 A.M., moderated; a sea took away jib-boom and bowsprit-cap. In my thirty-one years' experience at sea, I have never seen a typhoon or hurricane so severe. Lost two men overboard—saved one. Stove sky-light, broke my barometer, &c., &c."

565. Severe gales in this part of the Atlantic—*i. e.*, on the polar side of the calm belt of Cancer—rarely occur during the months of June, July, August, and September. This appears to be the time when the fiends of the storm are most busily at work in the West Indies. During the remainder of the year, these extra-tropical gales, for the most part, come from the northwest. But the winter is the most famous season for these gales. That is the time when the Gulf Stream has brought the heat of summer and placed it (§ 71) in closest proximity to the extremest cold of the north. And there would, therefore, it would seem, be a conflict between these extremes; consequently, great disturbances in the air, and a violent rush from the cold to the warm.

566. In like manner, the gales that most prevail in the extra-

tropics of the southern hemisphere come from the pole and the west, *i. e.*, southwest.

567. Storm and Rain Charts for the Atlantic Ocean have already been published by the Observatory, and others for the whole seas are in process of construction. The object of such charts is to show the directions and relative frequency of gales in all parts of the sea, the relative frequency of calms, fogs, rain, thunder, and lightning.

These charts are very instructive.

CHAPTER XVII.

ROUTES.

How Passages have been shortened, § 568.—How closely Vessels follow each other's Track, 570.—The Archer and the Flying Cloud, 571.—The great Race-course upon the Ocean, 573.—Description of a Race, 575.—Present Knowledge of Winds enables the Navigator to compute his Detour, 582.

568. THE principal routes across the ocean are exhibited on Plate VIII.; the great end and aim of all this labor and research are in these, and consist in the shortening of passages—the improvement of navigation. Other interests and other objects are promoted thereby, but these, in the mind of a practical people, who, by their habits of thought and modes of action, mark the age in which we live as eminently utilitarian, do not stand out in relief half so grand and imposing as do those achievements by which the distant isles and marts of the sea have been lifted up, as it were, and brought closer together, for the convenience of commerce, by many days' sail.

569. We have been told in the foregoing pages how the winds blow and the currents flow in all parts of the ocean. These control the mariner in his course; and to know how to steer his ship on this or that voyage so as always to make the most of them, is the perfection of navigation. The figures representing the vessels are so marked as to show whether the prevailing direction of the wind be adverse or fair.

570. When one looks seaward from the shore, and sees a ship disappear in the horizon as she gains an offing on a voyage to India, or the Antipodes perhaps, the common idea is that she is bound over a trackless waste, and the chances of another ship, sailing with the same destination the next day, or the next week, coming up and speaking with her on the "pathless ocean," would, to most minds, seem slender indeed. Yet the truth is, the winds and the currents are now becoming to be so well understood, that the navigator, like the backwoodsman in the wilderness, is enabled literally "to blaze his way" across the ocean; not, indeed, upon trees, as in the wilderness, but upon the wings of the wind. The

results of scientific inquiry have so taught him how to use these invisible couriers, that they, with the calm belts of the air, serve as sign-boards to indicate to him the turnings, and forks, and crossings by the way.

571. Let a ship sail from New York to California, and the next week let a faster one follow after: they will cross each other's path many times, and are almost sure to see each other by the way. Thus a case in point happens to be before me. It is the case of the "Archer" and the "Flying Cloud" on their last voyage to California. They are both fine clipper ships, ably commanded. But it was not until the ninth day after the "Archer" had sailed from New York that the "Flying Cloud" put to sea, California bound also. She was running against time, and so was the "Archer," but without reference to each other. The "Archer," with "Wind and Current Charts" in hand, went blazing her way across the calms of Cancer, and along the new route, down through the northeast trades to the equator; the "Cloud" followed after, crossing the equator upon the trail of Thomas of the "Archer." Off Cape Horn she came up with him, spoke him, handed him the latest New York dates, and invited him to dine on board the "Cloud," which invitation, says he of the "Archer," "I was reluctantly compelled to decline."

572. The "Flying Cloud" finally ranged ahead, made her adieus, and disappeared among the clouds that lowered upon the western horizon, being destined to reach her port a week or more in advance of her Cape Horn consort. Though sighting no land from the time of their separation until they gained the offing of San Francisco—some six or eight thousand miles off—the tracks of the two vessels were so nearly the same, that, being projected on the Plate IX., they would appear almost as one.

573. This is the great race-course of the ocean; it is fifteen thousand miles in length. Some of the most glorious trials of speed and of prowess that the world ever witnessed have taken place over it. Here the modern clipper ship—the noblest work that has ever come from the hands of man—has been sent, guided by the lights of science, to contend with the elements, to outstrip steam, and astonish the world.

574. The most celebrated and famous race that has ever been run came off upon this course: it was in the autumn of 1852,

when navigators were beginning fully to reap the benefits of these researches with regard to the winds and currents, and other facts connected with the Physical Geography of the Sea, that four splendid new clipper ships put to sea from New York, bound for California. They were ably commanded, and, as they passed the bar at Sandy Hook, one by one, and at various intervals of time, they presented really a most magnificent spectacle. The names of these ships and their masters were, the "Wild Pigeon," Captain Putnam; the "John Gilpin," Captain Doane — alas! now no more; the "Flying Fish," Captain Nickels, and the "Trade Wind," Captain Webber. Like steeds that know their riders, they were handled with the most exquisite skill and judgment, and in such hands they bounded out upon the "glad waters" most gracefully. Each, being put upon her mettle from the start, was driven, under the seaman's whip and spur, at full speed over a course that it would take them three long months to run.

575. The "Wild Pigeon" sailed October 12; the "John Gilpin," October 29; the "Flying Fish," November 1; and the "Trade Wind," November 14. It was the season for the best passages. Each one was provided with the *Wind and Current Charts*. Each one had evidently studied them attentively; and each one was resolved to make the most of them, and do his best. All ran against time; but the "John Gilpin" and the "Flying Fish" for the whole course, and the "Wild Pigeon" for part of it, ran neck and neck, the one against the other, and each against all. It was a sweepstake with these ships around Cape Horn and through both hemispheres.

576. Wild Pigeon led the other two out of New York, the one by seventeen, the other by twenty days. But luck and chances of the winds seem to have been against her from the start. As soon as she had taken her departure, she fell into a streak of baffling winds, and then into a gale, which she fought against and contended with for a week, making but little progress the while; she then had a time of it in crossing the horse latitudes. After having been nineteen days out, she had logged no less than thirteen of them as days of calms and baffling winds; these had brought her no farther on her way than the parallel of 26° north in the Atlantic. Thence she had a fine run to the equator, crossing it between 33° and 34° west, the thirty-second day out. She was un-

avoidably forced to cross it so far west; for only two days before, she crossed 5° north in 30°—an excellent position.

In proof that the Pigeon had accomplished all that skill could do and the chances against her would permit, we have the testimony of the barque Hazard, Captain Pollard. This vessel, being bound to Rio at the same time, followed close after the Pigeon. The Hazard is an old hand with the Charts; she had already made six voyages to Rio with them for her guide. This was the longest of the six, the mean of which was twenty-six and a half days. She crossed the line this time in 34° 30′, also by compulsion, having crossed 5° north in 31°. But, the fourth day after crossing the equator, she was clear of Cape St. Roque, while the Pigeon cleared it in three days.*

577. So far, therefore, chances had turned up against the Pigeon, in spite of the skill displayed by Putnam as a navigator, for the Gilpin and the Fish came booming along, not under better management, indeed, but with a better run of luck and fairer courses before them. In this stretch they gained upon her—the Gilpin seven and the Fish ten days; so that now the abstract logs show the Pigeon to be but ten days ahead.

Evidently the Fish was most confident that she had the heels of her competitors; she felt her strength, and was proud of it; she was most anxious for a quick run, and eager withal for a trial. She dashed down southwardly from Sandy Hook, looking occasionally at the Charts; but, feeling strong in her sweep of wing, and trusting confidently in the judgment of her master, she kept, on the average, two hundred miles to leeward of the right track. Rejoicing in her many noble and fine qualities, she crowded on her canvas to its utmost stretch, trusting quite as much to her heels as to the Charts, and performed the extraordinary feat of crossing, the sixteenth day out from New York, the parallel of 5° north.

The next day she was well south of 4° north, and in the Doldrums, longitude 34° west.

Now her heels became paralyzed, for Fortune seems to have deserted her a while—at least her master, as the winds failed him, feared so; they gave him his motive power; they were fickle, and he was helplessly baffled by them. The bugbear of a northwest

* According to the received opinion, this was impossible. *Vide* § 276.

current off Cape St. Roque (§ 276) began to loom up in his imagination, and to look alarming; then the dread of falling to leeward came upon him; chances and luck seemed to conspire against him, and the mere possibility of finding his fine ship back-strapped filled the mind of Nickels with evil forebodings, and shook his faith in his guide. He doubted the Charts, and committed *the* mistake of the passage.

578. The *Sailing Directions* had cautioned the navigator, again and again, not to attempt to fan along to the eastward in the equatorial doldrums; for, by so doing, he would himself engage in a fruitless strife with baffling airs, sometimes re-enforced in their weakness by westerly currents. But the winds had failed, and so too, the smart captain of the Flying Fish evidently thought, had the *Sailing Directions*. They advise the navigator, in all such cases, to dash right across this calm streak, stand boldly on, take advantage of slants in the wind, and, by this device, make easting enough to clear the land. So, forgetting that the Charts are founded on the experience of great numbers who had gone before him, Nickels, being tempted, turned a deaf ear to the caution, and flung away three whole days, and more, of most precious time, dallying in the doldrums.

He spent four days about the parallel of 3° north, and his ship left the doldrums, after this waste of time, nearly upon the same meridian at which she entered them.

She was still in 34°, the current keeping her back just as fast as she could fan east. After so great a loss, her very clever master, doubting his own judgment, became sensible of his error. Leaving the spell-bound calms behind him, where he had undergone such trials, he wrote in his log as follows: "I now regret that, after making so fine a run to 5° north, I did not dash on, and work my way to windward to the northward of St. Roque, as I have experienced little or no westerly set since passing the equator, while three or four days have been lost in working to the eastward, between the latitude of 5° and 3° north, against a strong westerly set;" and he might have added, "with little or no wind."

In three days after this he was clear of St. Roque. Just five days before him, the Hazard had passed exactly in the same place, and gained two days on the Fish by cutting straight across the doldrums, as the *Sailing Directions* advised him to do.

The Wild Pigeon, crossing the equator also in 33°, had passed along there ten days before, as did also the Trade Wind twelve days after. The latter also crossed the line to the west of 34°, and in four days after had cleared St. Roque.

But, notwithstanding this loss of three days by the Fish, who so regretted it, and who afterward so handsomely retrieved it, she found herself, on the 24th of November, alongside of the Gilpin, her competitor. They were then both on the parallel of 5° south, the Gilpin being thirty-seven miles to the eastward, and of course in a better position, for the Fish had yet to take advantage of slants, and stand off shore to clear the land. They had not seen each other.

579. The Charts showed the Gilpin now to be in the best position, and the subsequent events proved the Charts to be right, for thence to 53° south the Gilpin gained on the Pigeon two days, and the Pigeon on the Fish one.

By dashing through the Straits of Le Maire, the Fish gained three days on the Gilpin; but here Fortune again deserted the Pigeon, or rather the winds turned against her; for as she appeared upon the parallel of Cape Horn, and was about to double round, a westerly gale struck her and kept her at bay for ten days, making little or no way, except alternately fighting in a calm or buffeting with a gale, while her pursuers were coming up "hand over fist," with fine winds and flowing sheets.

They finally overtook her, bringing along with them propitious gales, when all three swept past the Cape, and crossed the parallel of 51° south on the other side of the "Horn," the Fish and the Pigeon one day each ahead of the Gilpin.

The Pigeon was now, according to the Charts, in the best position, the Gilpin next, and the Fish last; but all were doing well.

From this parallel to the southeast trades of the Pacific the prevailing winds are from the northwest. The position of the Fish, therefore, did not seem as good as the others, because she did not have the sea-room in case of an obstinate northwest gale.

But the winds favored her. On the 30th of December the three ships crossed the parallel of 35° south, the Fish recognizing the Pigeon; the Pigeon saw only a "clipper ship," for she could not conceive how the ship in sight could possibly be the Flying Fish, as that vessel was not to leave New York for some three weeks after she did; the Gilpin was only thirty or forty miles off at the same time.

The race was now wing and wing, and had become exciting. With fair winds and an open sea, the competitors had now a clear stretch to the equator of two thousand five hundred miles before them.

The Flying Fish led the way, the Wild Pigeon pressing her hard, and both dropping the Gilpin quite rapidly, who was edging off to the westward.

The two foremost reached the equator on the 13th of January, the Fish leading just twenty-five miles in latitude, and crossing in 112° 17′;* the Pigeon forty miles farther to the east. At this time the John Gilpin had dropped two hundred and sixty miles astern, and had sagged off several degrees to the westward.

580. Here Putnam, of the Pigeon, again displayed his tact as a navigator, and again the fickle winds deceived him: the belt of northeast trades had yet to be passed; it was winter; and, by crossing where she did, she would have an opportunity of making a fair wind of them, without being much to the west of her port when she should lose them. Moreover, it was exactly one year since she had passed this way before; she then crossed in 109°, and had a capital run thence of seventeen days to San Francisco.

Why should she not cross here again? She saw that the 4th edition of *Sailing Directions*, which she had on board, did not discountenance it, and her own experience approved it. Could she have imagined that, in consequence of this difference of forty miles in the crossing of the equator, and of the two hours' time behind her competitor, she would fall into a streak of wind which would enable the Fish to lead her into port one whole week? Certainly it was nothing but what sailors call "a streak of ill luck" that could have made such a difference.

But by this time "John Gilpin" had got his mettle up again. He crossed the line in 116°—exactly two days after the other two—and made the glorious run of fifteen days thence to the pilot grounds of San Francisco.

Thus end the abstract logs of this exciting race and these remarkable passages.

* Twenty-five days after that, the Trade Wind clipper came along, crossed in 112°, and had a passage of sixteen days thence into San Francisco.

The Flying Fish beat: she made the passage in 92 days and 4 hours from port to anchor; the Gilpin in 93 days and 20 hours from port to pilot;* the Wild Pigeon had 118. The Trade Wind followed, with 102 days, having taken fire, and burned for eight hours on the way.

The result of this race may be taken as an illustration as to how well navigators are now brought to understand the winds and the currents of the sea.

581. Here are three ships sailing on different days, bound over a trackless waste of ocean for some fifteen thousand miles or more, and depending alone on the fickle winds of heaven, as they are called, to waft them along; yet, like travelers on the land, bound upon the same journey, they pass and repass, fall in with and recognize each other by the way; and what, perhaps, is still more remarkable, is the fact that these ships should each, throughout that great distance, and under the wonderful vicissitudes of climates, winds, and currents which they encountered, have been so skillfully navigated, that, in looking back at their management, now that what is past is before me, I do not find a single occasion, except the one already mentioned, on which they could have been better handled.

There is another circumstance which is worthy of notice in this connection, as illustrative of the accuracy of the knowledge which these investigations afford concerning the force, set, and direction both of winds and currents, and it is this:

582. I had computed the detour which these vessels would have to make, on account of adverse winds, between New York and their place of crossing the equator. The whole distance, including detour to be sailed to reach this crossing at that season of the year, was, according to calculation, 4115 miles. The "Gilpin" and the "Hazard" only kept an account of the distance actually sailed; the former reaching the equator after sailing 4099 miles, the latter, 4077; thus accomplishing that part of the voyage by sailing, the one within thirty-eight, the other within sixteen miles of the detour which calculation showed they would be compelled to make on account of head-winds. With his way blazed through the forest, the most experienced backwoodsman would have to make a detour greater than this on account of floods in the rivers.

* The abstract log of the Gilpin is silent after the pilot came on board.

Am I far wrong, therefore, when I say that the present state of our knowledge with regard to the physical geography of the sea has enabled the navigator to blaze his way among the winds and currents of the sea, and so mark his path that others, using his signs as finger-boards, may follow in the same track?

CHAPTER XVIII.

A LAST WORD.

Brussels Conference, § 584. — How Navigators may obtain a Set of Maury's Wind and Current Charts, 585.—The Abstract Log, 586.

583. I HAVE, I am aware, not done more in this little book than given only a table or two of contents from the interesting volume which the Physical Geography of the Sea is destined some day to open up to us. The subject is a comprehensive one: there is room for more laborers, and help is wanted.

Nations, no less than individuals; "stay-at-home travelers," as well as those who "go down to the sea in ships," are concerned in the successful prosecution of the labors we have in hand.

We are now about to turn over a new leaf in navigation, on which we may confidently expect to see recorded much information that will tend to lessen the dangers of the sea, and to shorten the passages of vessels trading upon it. (See Appendix L.)

We are about to open in the volume of Nature a new chapter, under the head of MARINE METEOROLOGY. In it are written the laws that govern those agents which "the winds and the sea obey." In the true interpretation of these laws, and the correct reading of this chapter, the planter as well as the merchant, the husbandman as well as the mariner, and states as well as individuals, are concerned. All have a deep interest in these laws; for with the hygrometrical conditions of the atmosphere, the well-being of plants and animals is involved. The health of the invalid is often dependent upon a dry or a damp atmosphere, a cold blast or a warm wind.

The atmosphere pumps up our rivers from the sea, and transports them through the clouds to their sources among the hills; and upon the regularity with which this machine, whose motions, parts, and offices we now wish to study, lets down that moisture, and the seasonable supply of rain which it furnishes to each region of country, to every planter, and upon all cultivated fields, depend the fruitfulness of this country, the sterility of that.

The principal maritime nations, therefore, have done well by agreeing to unite upon one plan of observation, and to co-operate with their ships upon the high seas with the view of finding out all that patient research, systematic, laborious investigation, may reveal to us concerning the winds and the waves; and philosophical travelers, and every sailor that has a ship under his foot, may do even better by joining in this system.

584. By the recommendations of the Brussels Conference, every one who uses the sea is commanded or invited to make certain observations; or, in other words, to propound certain queries to Nature, and to give us a faithful statement of the replies she may make.

Now, unless we have accurate instruments, instruments that will themselves tell the truth, it is evident that we can not get at the real meaning of the answers that Nature may give us.

An incorrect observation is not only useless of itself, but, when it passes undetected among others that are correct, it becomes worse than useless; nay, it is mischievous there, for it vitiates results that are accurate, places before us wrong premises, and thus renders the good of no value.

585. Those ship-masters who, entering this field as fellow-laborers, will co-operate in the mode and manner recommended by the Brussels Conference, and keep, voyage after voyage, and as long as required, a journal of observations and results according to a prescribed form—and which form is annexed, under the title of Abstract Log—are entitled, by sending the same, at the end of the voyage, to the Superintendent of the National Observatory, to a copy of my Sailing Directions, and such sheets of the Charts as relate to the cruising-ground of the co-operator.

586. There are two forms of abstract logs: one, the more elaborate, for men-of-war; the other for merchantmen. The observations called for by the latter are a *minimum*, the least which will entitle the co-operator to claim the proffered bounty. It must give, *at least*, the latitude and longitude of the ship daily; the height of the barometer, and the readings of both the air and the water thermometer, *at least* once a day; the direction and force of the wind three times a day—first, middle, and latter part—at the

hours eight P.M., four A.M., and noon; the variation of the compass occasionally; and the set of the current whenever encountered. These observations, to be worth having, must be accurately made; and as every thermometer and every barometer has its sources of error, consequently, every ship-master who undertakes hereafter to co-operate with us, and keep an abstract log, should have his barometer and thermometer accurately compared with standard instruments, the errors of which have been accurately determined.

These errors the master should enter in the log; the instruments should be numbered, and he should so keep the log as to show what instrument is in use. For instance, a master goes to sea with thermometers Nos. 4719, 1, 12, &c., their errors having been ascertained and entered on the blank page for the purpose in the abstract log. He first uses No. 12. Let it be so stated in the column of Remarks, when the first observation is recorded, thus: Thermometer No. 12. During the voyage, No. 12 gets broken, or for some reason is laid aside, and another, say 4719, is brought into use. So state when the first observation with it is recorded, and quote in the column of Remarks the errors both of Nos. 12 and 4719. Now, with such a statement of errors given in the log for each of the instruments, according to the number, the observations may be properly corrected when they come up here for discussion.

It is rare to find a barometer or a thermometer that has no error, as it is to find a chronometer without error. A good thermometer, the error of which the maker should guarantee not to exceed in any part of the scale one degree, will cost, in the United States, not less than $2, perhaps $2 50.

The errors of thermometers sometimes are owing to inequalities in the bore of the tube, sometimes to errors of division on the scale, &c. Therefore, in comparing thermometers with a standard, they should be compared, at least, for every degree between melting ice and blood heat.

MAN-OF-WAR LOG.

Abstract Log of United States.............................*Captain*................ *From*........*to*........185 .

1	2	*a*		*b*		*c*			*d*		*e*		*f*							*g*				
Date.	Hour.	3	4	5	6	7	8	9	10	11	12	13	14	15	16	17	18	19		20	21	22	23	REMARKS.
2d.	2																		Margin for Binding.					
	IV.*																							
	6																							
	8																							
	IX.*																							
	10																							
Noon.	XII.*																							
	2																							
	III.*																							
	4																							
	6																							
	VIII.*																							
	10																							
	12																							

EXPLANATION.

Headings and Breadth of Columns stated in Inches and Decimals of an Inch —(1.) Date, .5 in.—(2.) Hour, .3.—(*a*) LATITUDE BY.—(3.) Observation, .8.—(4.) D. R., .8.—(*b*) LONGITUDE BY.—(5.) Observation, .8.—(6.) D. R , .8.—(*c*) CURRENTS.—(7.) Direction, .8.—(8.) Rate, .3.—(9.) Magnetic variation observed, .6.—(*d*) WINDS.—(10.) Direction, .9.—(11.) Rate, .3.—(*e*) BAROMETER.—(12.) Height, .5.—(13.) Thermometer attached, .4.—(*f*) THERMOMETER.—(14.) Dry bulb, .3.—(15.) Wet bulb, .3.—(16.) Form and direction of clouds, .8.—(17.) Proportion of sky clear, .3.—(18.) Hours of fog, A ;† Rain, B ; Snow, C ; Hail, D., .3.—(19.) State of the sea, .3.—Margin for binding, one inch.—(*g*) WATER.—(20.) Temperature at surface, .3.—(21.) Specific gravity, .3.—(22.) Temperature at depth, .3.—(23.) State of the weather, .6.—Remarks, 8.5 inches.—Size of sheet, 11 by 14 inches.

* Observations at these hours are most important.

† State the hours of fog, rain, &c., in figures, thus: $\frac{A}{2}, \frac{B}{1}, \frac{C}{.5}$, meaning 2 hours of fog, 1 of rain, and half an hour of snow.

MERCHANT-SERVICE LOG.

Abstract Log of.................................*Captain*.................. *From*............*to*.............185 .

				c′		*e′*		*f′*						*d′*		
1′	2′	3′	5′	7′	8′	12′	13′	14′	20′	16′	17′	18′	9′	10′	11′	REMARKS.
2d.	9															
Noon.	XII.															
	3															
	VIII.															
3d.	IV.															
	9															
Noon.	XII.															

The headings *c′*, *e′*, *f′*, *d′*, correspond with the headings *c*, *e*, *f*, *d* ; and the columns 1′, 2′, 3′, 5′, 7′, 8′, 12′, 13′, 14′, 20′, 16′, 17′, 18′, 9′, 10′, 11′, with their breadths, to the same numbers in the man-of-war log, except (10′), 1.5 in. ; (14′), air ; (20′), water.

☞ The *prevailing* direction of the wind from noon to 8 P.M., from 8 P.M. to 4 A.M., and from 4 A.M. till noon, must be entered severally on the heavy lines opposite 8, 4, and noon. Observation for columns 12′, 13′, 14′, 20′, 16′, and 17′, also at 9 A.M. and 3 P.M.

APPENDIX

ADDITIONS AND CORRECTIONS FOR THE SECOND EDITION.

A.—Page 81, § 118.

MECHANICAL POWER OF EVAPORATION.

The mechanical power exerted by the air and the sun in lifting water from the earth, in transporting it from one place to another, and in letting it down again, is inconceivably great. The utilitarian who compares the water-power that the Falls of Niagara would afford if applied to machinery, is astonished at the number of figures which are required to express its equivalent in horse-power. Yet what is the horse-power of the Niagara, falling a few steps, in comparison with the horse-power that is required to lift up all the water that is discharged into the sea, not only by this river, but by all the other rivers in the world, as high as the clouds. The calculation has been made by engineers, and, according to it, the force for making and lifting vapor from each area of one acre that is included on the surface of the earth, is equal to the power of 30 horses; and, for the whole area of the earth, it is 800 times greater than all the water-power in nature.

B.—Page 125, § 236.

THE MAELSTROM.

The Maelstrom, that school-books make so much of, is a whirlpool, or rather an eddy, off the coast of Norway, supposed to be created by a conflict or meeting of the tides which have been divided by the British Islands.

C.—Page 128, § 247.

QUANTITY OF SOLID MATTER IN THE SEA.

It is difficult to form an adequate conception of the immense quantities of solid matter, in solution, which the current from the Atlantic carries into the Mediterranean. In the abstract log for March 8th, 1855, Mr. William Grenville Temple, master of the United States ship Levant, homeward bound, has described the indraught there:

"Weather fine; made 1¼ pt. lee-way. At noon, stood in to Almiria Bay, and anchored off the village of Roguetas. Found a great number of vessels waiting for a chance to get to the westward, and learned from them that at least a thousand sail are weather-bound between this and Gibraltar. Some of them have been so for six weeks, and have even got as far as Malaga, only to be swept back by the current. Indeed, no vessel has been able to get out into the Atlantic for three months past."

Now, suppose this current, which baffled and beat back this fleet for so many days, ran no faster than two knots the hour. Assuming its depth to be 400 feet only, and its width seven miles, and that it carried in with it the average proportion of solid matter—say one thirtieth—contained in sea water; and admitting these postulates into calculation as the basis of the computation, it appears that salts enough to make no less than 88 cubic miles of solid matter, of the density of water, were carried into the Mediterranean during these 90 days. Now, unless there were some escape for all this solid matter, which has been running into that sea, not for 90 days merely, but for ages, it is very clear that the Mediterranean would, ere this, have been a vat of very strong brine, or a bed of cubic crystals.

D.—Page 139, § 267.

THE DESOLATE REGION.

Between Humboldt's Current and the great equatorial flow there is an area marked as the "desolate region," Plate IX. It was observed that this part of the ocean was rarely visited by the whale, either sperm or right; why, it did not appear; but observations asserted the fact. Formerly, this part of the ocean was seldom whitened by the sails of a ship, or enlivened by the presence of man. Neither the industrial pursuits of the sea nor the highways of commerce called him into it. Now and then a roving cruiser or an enterprising whaleman passed that way; but to all else it was an unfrequented part of the ocean, and so remained until the gold-fields of Australia and the guano islands of Peru made it a thoroughfare. All vessels bound from Australia to South America now pass through it, and in the journals of some of them it is described as a region almost void of the signs of life in both sea and air. In the South Pacific Ocean especially, where there is such a wide expanse of water, sea-birds often exhibit a companionship with a vessel, and will follow and keep company with it through storm and calm for weeks together. Even those kinds, as the albatross and Cape pigeon, that delight in the stormy regions of Cape Horn and in the inhospitable climates of the Antarctic regions, not unfrequently accompany vessels into the perpetual summer of the tropics.

The sea-birds that join the ship as she clears Australia will, it is said, follow her to this region, and then disappear. Even the chirp of the stormy-petrel ceases to be heard here, and the sea itself is said to be singularly barren of "moving creatures that have life."

E.—Page 155, § 297.

MAGNESIA IN SEA WATER.

It is the chloride of magnesium which gives that damp, sticky feeling to the clothes of sailors that are washed or wetted with salt water.

F.—Page 170, § 343.

THE QUESTION "WHENCE COME THE SALTS OF THE SEA?" RECONSIDERED.

I once thought with Darwin and those other philosophers who hold that the sea derived its salts originally from the washings of the rains and rivers. I now question that opinion; for, in the course of the researches connected with the "Wind and Current Charts," I have found evidence, from the sea and in the Bible, which seems to cast doubt upon it. The account given in the first chapter of Genesis, and that contained in the hieroglyphics which are traced by the hand of Nature on the geological column as to the order of creation, are marvelously accordant. The Christian man of science regards them both as true; and he never overlooks the fact that, while they differ in the mode and manner as well as in the things they teach, yet they never conflict; and they contain no evidence going to show that the sea was ever fresh; on the contrary, they both afford circumstantial evidence sufficient for the belief that the sea was salt as far back as the morning of creation, or at least as the evening and the morning of the day when the dry land appeared.

That the rains and the rivers do dissolve salts of various kinds from the rocks and soil, and empty them into the sea, there is no doubt. These salts can not be evaporated, we know; and we also know that many of the lakes, as the Dead Sea, which receive rivers and have no outlet, are salt. Hence the inference that these inland water-basins received their salts from the washings of the soil; and consequently the conjecture arose that the great sea derived its salts from the same source and by the same process. But, and per contra, though these solid ingredients can not be taken out of the sea by evaporation, they can be extracted by other processes. We know that the insects of the sea do take out a portion of them, and that the salt ponds and arms which, from time to time in the geological calendar, have been separated from the sea, afford an escape by which the quantity of chloride of sodium in its waters—the most abundant of its solid ingredients—is regulated. The insects of the sea can not build their structures of this salt, for it would dissolve again, and as fast as they could separate it. But here the ever-ready atmosphere comes into play, and assists the insects in regulating the salts. It can not take them up from the sea, it is true, but it can take the sea away from them; for it pumps up the water from these pools that have been barred off, transfers it to the clouds, and they deliver it back to the sea as fresh water, leaving the solid matter it contained in a solid state behind.

These are operations that have been going on for ages; proof that they are still going on is continually before our eyes; for the "hard water" of our fountains, the marl-banks of the valleys, the salt-beds of the plains, and the coral islands of the sea, are monuments in attestation.

There is no proof, nor is there any reason for the belief, that the sea is growing salter or fresher. Hence we infer that the operations of addition and extraction are reciprocal and equal; that the effect of rains and rivers in washing down is compensated by the processes of evaporation and secretion in taking out

If the sea derived its salts originally from the rivers, the geological records of the past would show that river beds were scored out in the crust of our planet before the sea had deposited any of its fossil shells and infusorial remains upon it. If, therefore, we admit the Darwin theory, we must also admit that there was a period when the sea was without salt, and consequently without shells or animals either of the silicious or calcareous kind. If ever there were such a time, it must have been when the rivers were collecting and pouring in the salts which now make the brine of the ocean. But while the palæontological records of the earth, on one hand, afford no evidence of any such fresh-water period, the Mosaic account is far from being negative with its testimony on the other. According to it, we infer that the sea was salt as early, at least, as the fifth day, for it was on that day of creation that the waters were commanded to "bring forth abundantly the moving creature that hath life." It is in obedience to that command that the sea now teems with organisms; and it is marvelous how abundantly the obedient waters do bring forth, and how wonderful for variety as well as multitude their progeny is. All who pause to look are astonished to see how the prolific ocean teems and swarms with life. The moving creatures in the sea constitute in their myriads of multitudes one of the "wonders of the deep."

The last sentence had not been copied when I received an abstract log from one of that noble corps of mariners who are observing the phenomena of the sea for me, in which there is a very apposite remark. Captain Foster, of the American ship "Garrick," the keeper of the log, is one of my most patient of observers. It is his custom to amuse himself by making drawings in his abstract log of the curious animalculæ which, with the microscope, he finds in the surface water alongside; and though he has been following the sea for many years, he never fails to express his wonder and amazement at the immense numbers of living creatures that the microscope reveals to him in sea water. Hitherto his examinations related only to the surface waters, but in the log now before me he went into the depths, and he was more amazed than ever to see how abundantly the waters even there bring forth.

"January 28th, 1855. In examining animalculæ in sea water, I have," says he, "heretofore used surface water. This afternoon, after pumping for some time from the stern pump seven feet below the surface, I examined the water, and was surprised to find that the fluid was literally alive with animated matter, embracing beautiful varieties." Of some he says, "Numerous heads, purple, red, and variegated."

There is wonderful meaning in that word ABUNDANTLY, as it stands recorded in that Book, and is even at this day repeated by the great waters.

So far the two records agree, and the evidence is clear that the sea was salt when it received this command. Do they afford any testimony as to its condition previously? Let us examine.

On the second day of creation the waters were gathered together unto one place, and the dry land appeared. Before that period, therefore, there were no rivers, and consequently no washings of brine by mists, nor dew, nor rains from the valleys among the hills. The water covered the earth. This is the account of Revelation; and the account which Nature has written, in her own peculiar characters, on the mountain and in the plain, on the rock and in the sea, as to the early condition of our planet, indicates the same. The inscriptions on the geological column tell that there was a period when the solid parts of the earth's crust which now stand high in the air were covered by water. The geological evidence that it was so, with perhaps the exception of a solitary mountain peak here and there, is conclusive; and when we come to examine the fossil remains that are buried in the mountains and scattered over the plains, we have as much reason to say that the sea was salt when it covered or nearly covered the earth, as the naturalist, when he sees a skull or bone whitening on the wayside, has to say that it was once covered with flesh.

Therefore we have reason for the conjecture that the sea was salt "in the beginning," when "the waters under heaven were gathered together unto one place," and the dry land first appeared; for, go back as far as we may in the dim records which young Nature has left inscribed upon the geological column of her early processes, and there we find the fossil shell and the remains of marine organisms to inform us that when the foundations of our mountains were laid with granite, and immediately succeeding that remote period when the primary formations were completed, the sea was, as it is now, salt; for had it not been salt, whence could those creeping things which fashioned the sea-shells that cover the tops of the Andes, or those madrepores that strew the earth with solid matter that has been secreted from briny waters, or those infusorial deposits which astound the geologist with their magnitude and extent, or those fossil remains of the sea which have astonished, puzzled, and bewildered man in all ages—whence, had not the sea been salt when its metes and bounds were set, could these creatures have obtained solid matter for their edifices and structures? Much of that part of the earth's crust which man stirs up in cultivation, and which yields him bread, has been made fruitful by these "salts," which all manner of marine insects, aqueous organisms, and sea-shells have secreted from the ocean. Much of this portion of our planet has been filtered through the sea, and its insects and creeping things are doing now precisely what they were set about when the dry land appeared, viz., preserving the purity of the ocean, and regulating it in the due performance of its great offices. As fast as the rains dissolve the salts of the earth, and send them down through the rivers to the sea, these faithful and everlasting agents of the Creator elaborate them into pearls, shells, corals, and precious things; and so, while they are preserving the sea, they are also embellishing the land by imparting new adaptations to its soil, beauty and variety to its landscapes.

G.—PAGE 170, § 344.

FURTHER OBJECTS OF THE SALTS IN THE SEA.

"THERE has been another question raised which bears upon what has already been said concerning the offices which, in the sublime system of terrestrial arrangements, have been assigned to the salts of the sea.

"On the 20th of January last, Professor Chapman, of the University College, Toronto, communicated to the Canadian Institute a paper on the 'Object of the Salt Condition of the Sea,' which, he maintains, is '*mainly intended to regulate evaporation.*' To establish this hypothesis, he shows by a simple but carefully conducted set of experiments, that the salter the water, the slower the evaporation from it; and that the evaporation which takes place in 24 hours from water about as salt as the average of sea water, is 0.54 per cent. less in quantity than from fresh water.

"This suggestion and these experiments give additional interest to our investigations into the manifold and marvelous offices which, in the economy of our planet, have been assigned by the Creator to the salts of the sea. It is difficult to say what, in the Divine arrangement, was the *main* object of making the sea salt and not fresh. Whether it was to assist in the regulation of climates, or in the circulation of the ocean, or in re-adapting the earth for new conditions by transferring solid portions of its crust from one part to another, and giving employment to the corallines and insects of the sea in collecting this solid matter into new forms, and presenting it under different climates and conditions, or whether the main object was, as the distinguished professor suggests, to regulate evaporation, it is not necessary now or here to discuss. I think we may regard all the objects of the salts of the sea as *main* objects.

"But we see in the professor's experiments the dawn of more new beauties, and the appearance of other exquisite compensations, which, in studying the 'wonders of the deep,' we have so often paused to contemplate and admire. As the trade-wind region feeds the air with the vapor of fresh water, the process of evaporation is checked, for the water which remains, being salter, parts with its vapor less readily; and thus, by the salts of the sea, floods may be prevented. But again, if the evaporating surface were to grow salter and salter, whence would the winds derive vapor duly to replenish the earth with showers? for the salter the surface, the more scanty the evaporation. Here is compensation, again, the most exquisite; and we perceive how, by reason of the salts of the sea, drought and famine, if not prevented, may be, and probably are, regulated and controlled; for that compensation which assists to regulate the amount of evaporation, is surely concerned in adjusting also the quantity of rain. Were the salts of the sea lighter instead of heavier than the water, they would, as they feed the winds with moisture for the cloud and the rain, remain at its surface, and become more niggardly in their supplies, and finally the winds would howl over the sea in very emptiness, and instead of cool and refreshing sea breezes to fan the invalid and nourish the plants, we should have the gentle trade wind coming from the sea in frightful blasts of parched, and thirsty, and blighting air. But the salts, with their manifold and marvelous adaptations, come in here as a counterpoise, and, as the waters attain a certain degree of saltness, they become too heavy to remain longer in contact with the thirsty trade winds, and are carried down, because of their salts, into the depths of the ocean; and thus the winds are *dieted* with vapor in due and wholesome quantities.

"In this view of the subject, and for the purpose of carrying on the investigations which Professor Chapman's interesting paper suggests, observations upon the specific gravity of sea water become still more interesting. It is to be hoped, therefore, that my fellow-laborers at sea will not slight column 21 in the man-of-war abstract log."—MAURY's *Sailing Directions*, 7th ed., p. 857.

H.—PAGE 224, § 479.

EFFECTS OF ISLANDS UPON THE TRADE WINDS.

"THE islands, such as the Society and Sandwich, that stand far away from any large extent of land, have a very singular but marked effect upon the wind. They interfere with the trades very often, and turn them back; for westerly and equatorial winds are common at both these groups, in their winter time. Some hydrographers have taken those westerly winds of the Society Islands to be an extension of the monsoons of the Indian Ocean. Not so: they are local, and do not extend a great way either from the Sandwich or Society Islands.

"That they are local about the former group, an examination of sheet No. 5, Pilot Chart North Pacific, will instantly show.

"It is a curious thing is this influence of islands in the trade-wind region upon the winds in the Pacific. Every navigator who has cruised in those parts of that ocean has often turned with wonder and delight to admire the gorgeous piles of cumuli, heaped up and arranged in the most delicate and exquisitely beautiful masses that it is possible for fleecy matter to assume. Not only are these piles found capping the hills among the islands, but they are often seen to overhang the lowest islet of the tropics, and even to stand above coral patches and hidden reefs, 'a cloud by day,' to serve as a beacon to the lonely mariner out there at sea, and to warn him of shoals and dangers which no lead nor seaman's eye has ever seen or sounded out.

"These clouds, under favorable circumstances, may be seen gathering above the low coral island, and performing their office in preparing it for vegetation and fruitfulness in a very striking manner. As they are condensed into showers, one fancies that they are a sponge of the most exquisite and delicately elaborated material, and that he can see, as they 'drop down their fatness,' the invisible but bountiful hand aloft that is pressing and squeezing it out."—MAURY's *Sailing Directions*, 7th ed., p. 820.

I.—PAGE 248, § 541.

WHITENESS OF THE WATER.

CAPT. W. E. KINGMAN, of the American clipper ship the Shooting Star, reports in his last abstract log a remarkable white patch, in lat. 8° 46′ S., long. 105° 30′ E., and which, in a letter to me, he thus describes:

"*Thursday*, July 27, 1854. At 7h. 45m. P.M., my attention was called to notice the color of the water, which was rapidly growing white. Knowing that we were in a much frequented part of the ocean, and having never heard of such an appearance being observed before in this vicinity, I could not account for it. I immediately hove the ship to and cast the lead; had no bottom at 60 fathoms. I then kept on our course, tried the water by thermometer, and found it to be 78½°, the same as at 8 A.M. We filled a tub, containing some 60 gallons, with the water, and found that it was filled with small luminous particles, which, when stirred, presented a most remarkable appearance. The whole tub seemed to be alive with worms and insects, and looked like a grand display of rockets and serpents, seen at a great distance in a dark night; some of the serpents appeared to be six inches in length, and very luminous. We caught, and could feel them in our hands, and they would emit light until brought within a few feet of a lamp, when, upon looking to see what we had, behold, nothing was visible; but, by the aid of a sextant's magnifier, we could plainly see a jelly-like substance without color. At last, a specimen was obtained of about two inches in length, and plainly visible to the naked eye; it was about the size of a large hair, and tapered at the ends. By bringing one end within about one fourth of an inch of a lighted lamp, the flame was attracted toward it, and burned with a red light; the substance crisped in burning something like a hair, or appeared of a red heat before being consumed. In a glass of the water there were several small, round substances (say $\frac{1}{16}$th of an inch in diameter), which had the power of expanding to more than twice their ordinary size, and then contracting again; when expanded, the outer rim appeared like a circular saw, only that the teeth pointed toward the centre.

"This patch of white water was about 23 miles in length, north and south, divided near its centre by an irregular strip of dark water half a mile wide; its east and west extent I can say nothing about.

"I have seen what is called white water in about all the known oceans and seas in the world, but nothing that would compare with this in extent or whiteness. Although we were going at the rate of nine knots, the ship made no noise either at the bow or stern. The whole appearance of the ocean was like a plain covered with snow. There was scarce a cloud in the heavens, yet the sky, for about ten degrees above the horizon, appeared as black as if a storm was raging; the stars of the first magnitude shone with a feeble light, and the 'milky way' of the heavens was almost entirely eclipsed by that through which we were sailing.

The scene was one of awful grandeur; the sea having turned to phosphorus, and the heavens being hung in blackness, and the stars going out, seemed to indicate that all Nature was preparing for that last grand conflagration which we are taught to believe is to annihilate this material world.

"After passing through the patch, we noticed that the sky, for four or five degrees above the horizon, was considerably illuminated, something like a faint aurora borealis. We soon passed out of sight of the whole concern, and had a fine night, without any conflagration (except of midnight oil in trying to find out what was in the water). I send you this, because I believe you request your corps of 'one thousand assistants' to furnish you with all such items, and I trust it will be acceptable. But, as for its furnishing you with much, if any, information relative to the insects or animals that inhabit the mighty deep, time will only tell; I can not think it will."—Maury's *Sailing Directions*, 7th ed., p. 174.

K.—Page 249, § 541.

NUMBER AND SIZE OF THE INHABITANTS OF THE SEA.

"We dive into the liquid crystal of the Indian Ocean, and it opens to us the most wondrous enchantments of the fairy tales of our childhood's dreams. The strangely branching thickets bear living flowers. Dense masses of Meandrinas and Astræas contrast with the leafy, cup-shaped expansions of the Explanarias, the variously-ramified Madrepores, which are now spread out like fingers, now rise in trunk-like branches, and now display the most elegant array of interlacing branches. The coloring surpasses every thing: vivid green alternates with brown or yellow; rich tints of purple, from pale red-brown to the deepest blue. Brilliant rosy, yellow, or peach-colored Nullipores overgrow the decaying masses, and are themselves interwoven with the pearl-colored plates of the Retipores, resembling the most delicate ivory carvings. Close by wave the yellow and lilac fans, perforated like trellis-work, of the Gorgonias. The clear sand of the bottom is covered with the thousand strange forms and tints of the sea-urchins and star-fishes. The leaf-like Flustras and Escharas adhere like mosses and lichens to the branches of the corals; the yellow, green, and purple-striped Limpets cling like monstrous cochineal insects upon their trunks. Like gigantic cactus-blossoms, sparkling in the most ardent colors, the Sea Anemones expand their crowns of tentacles upon the broken rocks, or more modestly embellish the flat bottom, looking like beds of variegated Ranunculuses. Around the blossoms of the coral shrubs play the humming-birds of the ocean, little fish sparkling with red or blue metallic glitter, or gleaming in golden green, or in the brightest silvery lustre.

"Softly, like spirits of the deep, the delicate milk-white or bluish bells of the jelly-fishes float through this charmed world. Here the gleaming violet and gold-green Isabelle, and the flaming yellow, black, and vermilion-striped Coquette, chase their prey; there the band-fish shoots, snake-like, through the thicket, like a long silver ribbon, glittering with rosy and azure hues. Then come the fabulous cuttle-fish, decked in all colors of the rainbow, but marked by no definite outline, appearing and disappearing, intercrossing, joining company and parting again, in most fantastic ways; and all this in the most rapid change, and amid the most wonderful play of light and shade, altered by every breath of wind, and every slight curling of the surface of the ocean. When day declines, and the shades of night lay hold upon the deep, this fantastic garden is lighted up in new splendor. Millions of glowing sparks, little microscopic Medusas and Crustaceans, dance like glow-worms through the gloom. The sea-feather, which by daylight is vermilion-colored, waves in a greenish, phosphorescent light. Every corner of it is lustrous. Parts which by day were perhaps dull and brown, and retreated from the sight amid the universal brilliancy of color, are now radiant in the most wonderful play of green, yellow, and red light; and to complete the wonders of the enchanted night, the silver disk, six feet across, of the moon-fish,* moves, slightly luminous, among the crowd of little sparkling stars.

"The most luxuriant vegetation of a tropical landscape can not unfold as great wealth of form, while in the variety and splendor of color it would stand far behind this garden landscape, which is strangely composed exclusively of animals, and not of plants; for, characteristic as the luxuriant development of vegetation is of the sea bottom of the temperate zones, the fullness and multiplicity of the marine Fauna is just as prominent in the regions of the tropics. Whatever is beautiful, wondrous, or uncommon in the great classes of fish and Echinoderms, jelly-fishes and polypes, and the molluscs of all kinds, is crowded into the warm and crystal waters of the tropical ocean—rests in the white sands, clothes the rough cliffs, clings, where the room is already occupied, like a parasite, upon the first comers, or swims through the shallows and depths of the elements—while the mass of the vegetation is of a far inferior magnitude. It is peculiar in relation to this, that the law valid on land, according to which the animal kingdom, being better adapted to accommodate itself to outward circumstances, has a greater diffusion than the vegetable kingdom; for the Polar seas swarm with whales, seals, sea-birds, fishes, and countless numbers of the lower animals, even where every trace of vegetation has long vanished in the eternally frozen ice, and the cooled

* Orthagoriscus mola.

sea fosters no sea weed—that this law, I say, holds good also for the sea, in the direction of its depth; for when we descend, vegetable life vanishes much sooner than the animal, and, even from the depths to which no ray of light is capable of penetrating, the sounding-lead brings up news at least of living infusoria."—SCHLEIDEN'S *Lectures*, p. 403–406.

"Besides great numbers of individuals, and great rapidity of development, we come to absolute corporeal size. So far as we know, every group of animals has its largest representatives in water. The largest mammal, and, indeed, the largest animal now living upon the globe, is the whale, which, when full grown, is at least five times as long as the largest elephant. Among birds, the albatross, which sails almost exclusively over the sea, has the greatest expansion of wings (15 feet*); the most terrible of the lizard group, the crocodile, lives in the water. * * * * The largest of all known serpents, the Brazilian anaconda, lives, at all events, principally in the water, and the East India water-snakes seem to be among the most terrible of the poisonous kinds."—*The Plant*, by M. J. SCHLEIDEN, M.D., p. 395, 396.

L.—PAGE 271, § 583.

MORAL INFLUENCE OF THE WIND AND CURRENT CHARTS.

THE labor, I am encouraged to believe, is profitable to the seafaring man in more ways than one. Old seamen sometimes encourage me by telling of the wholesome effects which the Wind and Current Charts are having in improving and advancing the moral condition of sailor-men. I quote the following letter, received while these pages are going through the press, in illustration of what I mean:

"Callao, January 10th, 1855.

"SIR,—Having to proceed from this to the Chincha Islands and remain three months, I avail myself of the present opportunity to forward to you abstracts of my two passages over your southern routes, although not required to do so until my own return to the United States next summer, knowing that you are less amply supplied with abstracts of voyages over these regions than of many other parts of the ocean; and, such as it is, I am happy to contribute my mite toward furnishing you with material to work out still farther toward perfection your great and glorious task, not only of pointing out the most speedy routes for ships to follow over the ocean, but also of teaching us sailors to look about us, and see by what wonderful manifestations of the wisdom and goodness of the great God we are continually surrounded.

* I once caught one, off Cape Horn, which measured sixteen feet from tip to tip. —MAURY.

"For myself, I am free to confess that, for many years, I commanded a ship, and, although never insensible to the beauties of nature upon the sea or land, I yet feel that, until I took up your work, I had been traversing the ocean blindfolded. I did not think; I did not know the amazing and beautiful combination of all the works of Him whom you so beautifully term 'the Great First Thought.'

"I feel that, aside from any pecuniary profit to myself from your labors, you have done me good as a man. You have taught me to look above, around, and beneath me, and recognize God's hand in every element by which I am surrounded. I am grateful for this personal benefit. Your remarks on this subject, so frequently made in your work, cause in me feelings of the greatest admiration, although my capacity to comprehend your beautiful theory is very limited.

"The man of such sentiments as you express will not be displeased with, or, at least, will know how to excuse, so much of what (in a letter of this kind) might be termed irrelevant matter. I have therefore spoken as I feel, and, with sentiments of the greatest respect, remain your obedient servant,

"WILLIAM L. PHINNEY, *Ship 'Gertrude.'*

"Lieutenant M. F. Maury."

JUN 9 - 1916

110° East — 115° — 120° E.

20° N. — 20° North

North | N.N.E. | N.E. | E.N.E. | East | E.S.E. | S.E. | S.S.E. | South | S.S.W. | S.W. | W.S.W. | West | W.N.W. | N.W. | N.N.W.

B D

173 164 128 78 102 180 126 56 72 13 117 119 136 83 137 236 195 70 140 118 116 73 168 76

15° North

Dec. | Jan. | Feb. | March | April | May | June | July | Aug. | Sept. | Oct. | Nov. | Dec. | Jan. | Feb. | March | April | May | June | July | Aug. | Sept. | Oct. | Nov.

10° N. — 10° North

North | N.N.E. | N.E. | E.N.E. | East | E.S.E. | S.E. | S.S.E. | South | S.S.W. | S.W. | W.S.W. | West | W.N.W. | N.W. | N.N.W.

A C

148 93 23 70 105 92 85 131 73 64 121 13 79 12 103 18 221 36 124 279 132 249 175 205

5° North

105° East — 110° — 115° E.

D. M'Clelland, Sc.

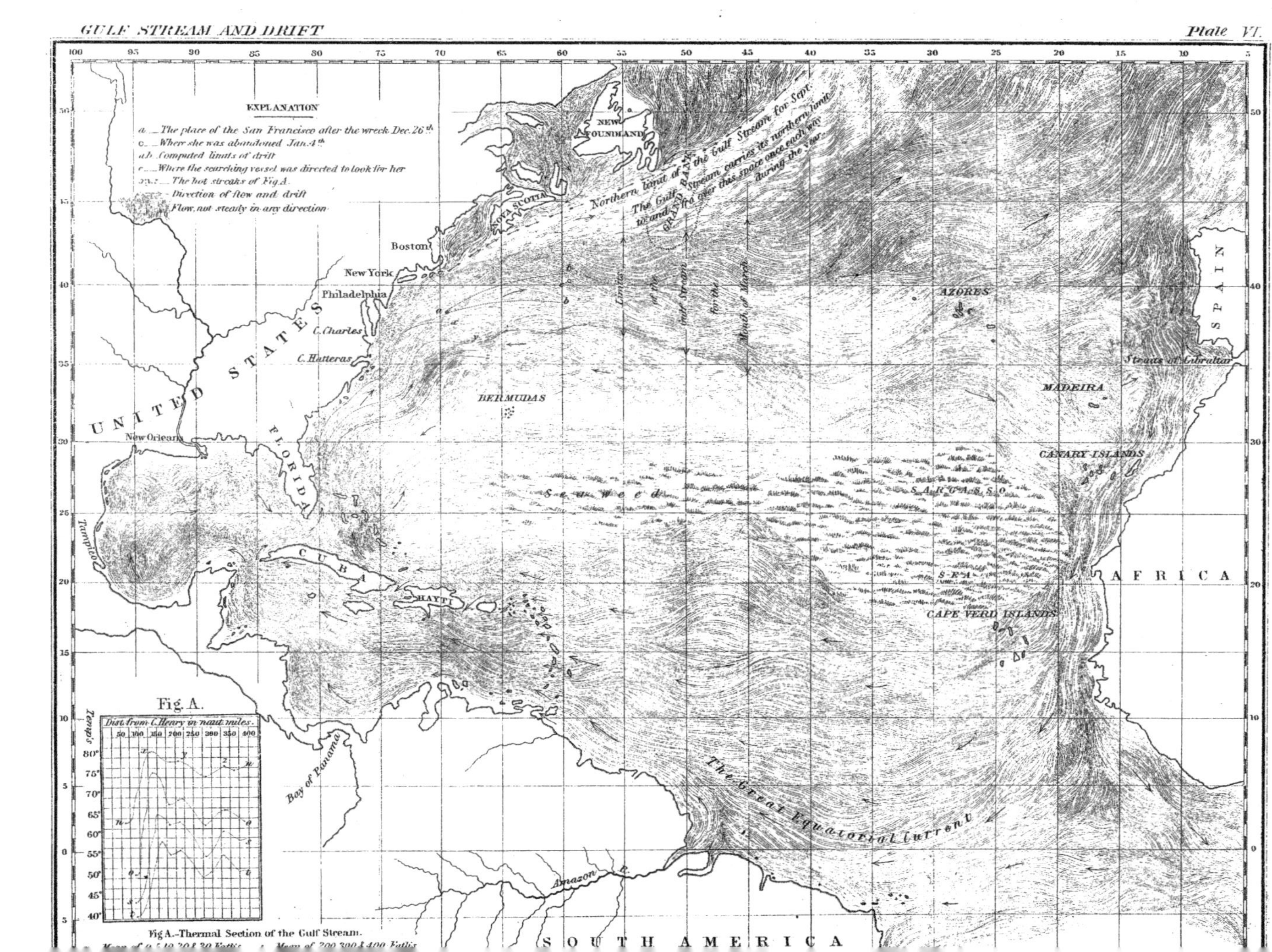

Fig. A.–Thermal Section of the Gulf Stream.

GEOLOGICAL AGENCY OF THE WINDS

Plate VII.

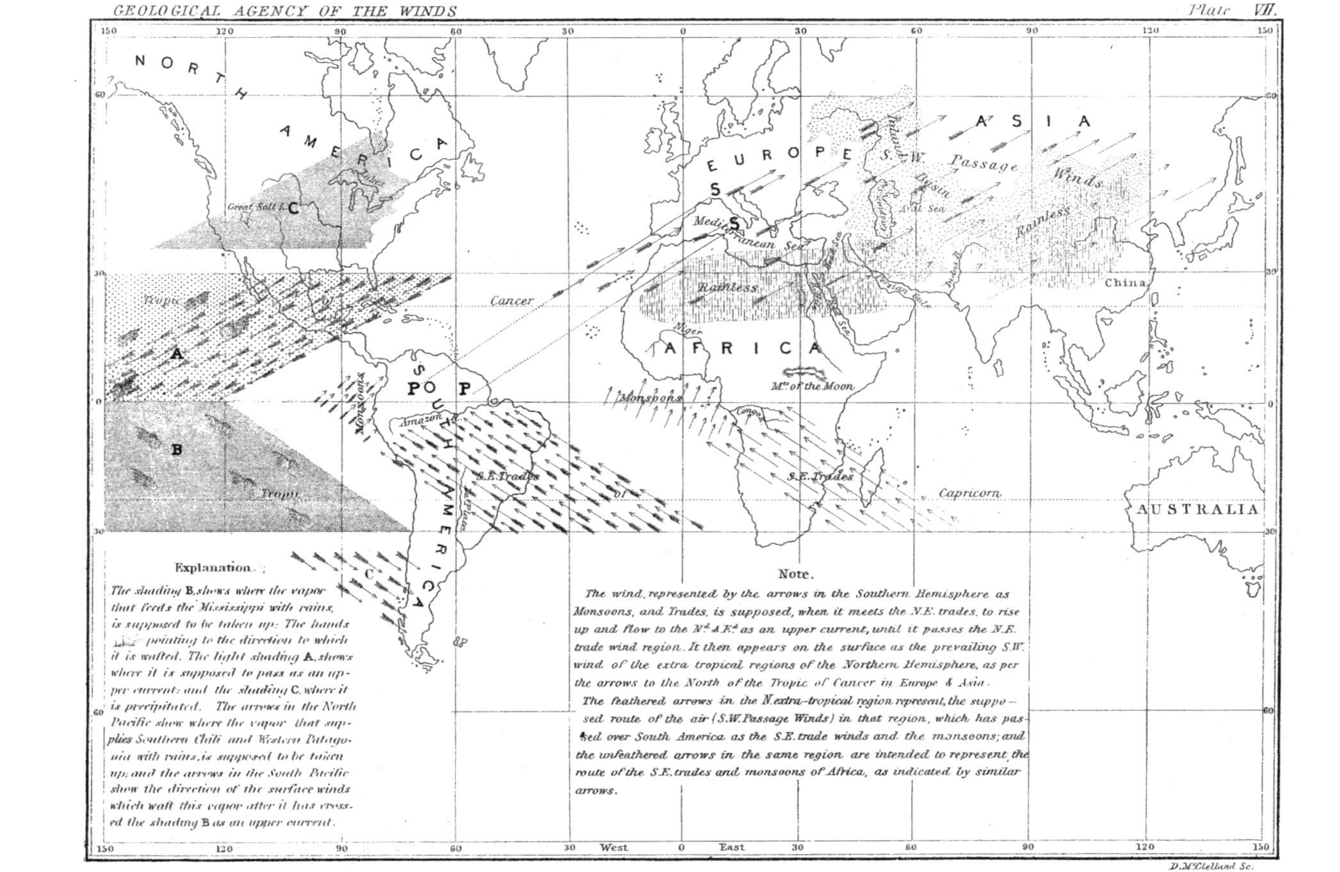

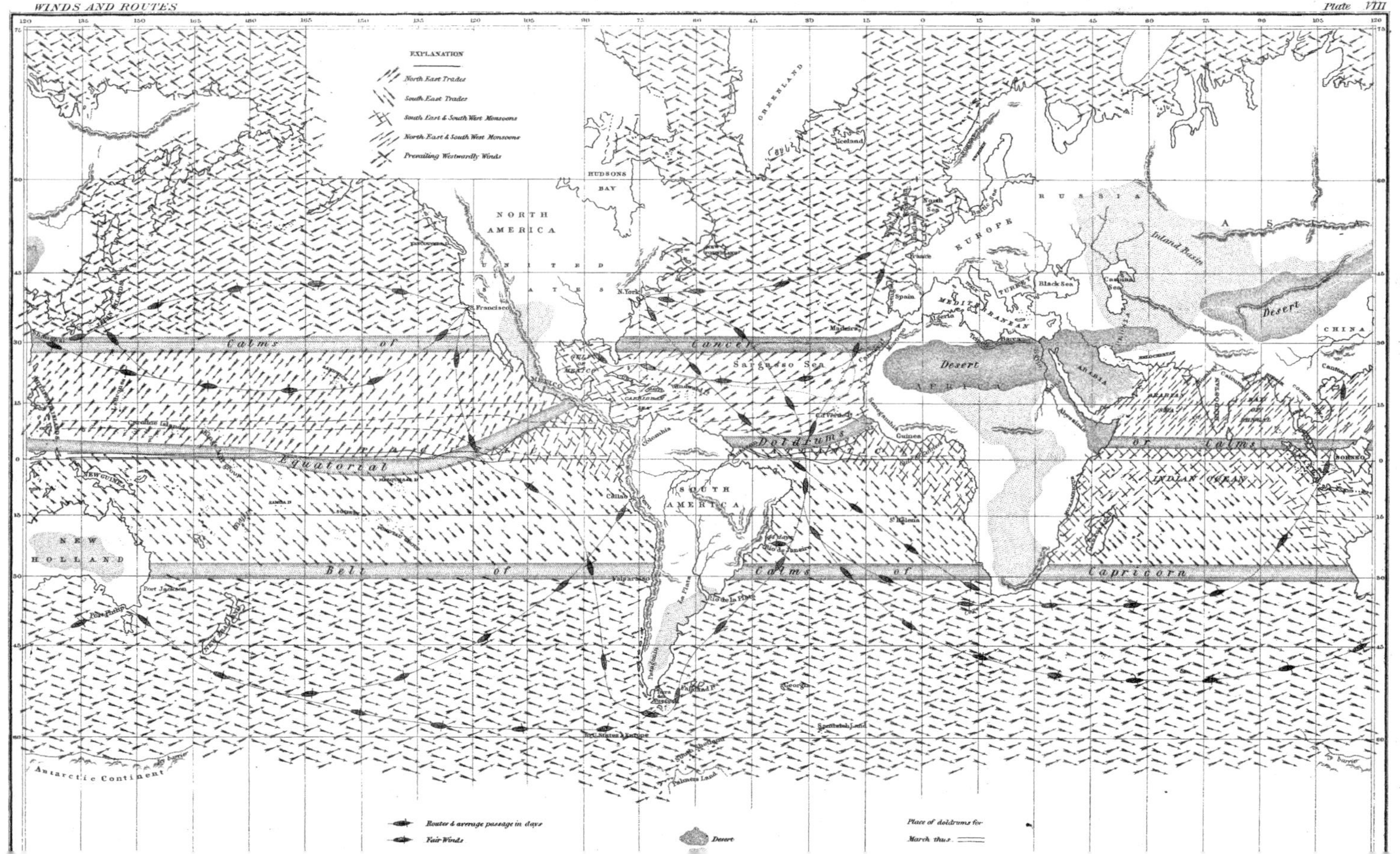

WINDS AND ROUTES
Plate VIII
EXPLANATION
North East Trades
South East Trades
South East & South West Monsoons
North East & South West Monsoons
Prevailing Westwardly Winds
NORTH AMERICA
UNITED STATES
HUDSONS BAY
GREENLAND
Iceland
EUROPE
RUSSIA
ASIA
Inland Basin
Desert
CHINA
Black Sea
Caspian Sea
MEDITERRANEAN
TURKEY
Spain
France
North Sea
Baltic Sea
Madeira
ARABIA
AFRICA
Desert
Guinea
St Helena
INDIAN OCEAN
BORNEO
SOUTH AMERICA
Colombia
Callao
Valparaiso
Rio de Janeiro
Rio de la Plata
La Plata
Patagonia
NEW HOLLAND
Port Jackson
Port Philip
NEW GUINEA
S. Francisco
N. York
Sargasso Sea
Calms of Cancer
Equatorial
Doldrums
Calms
Belt of Calms of Capricorn
Antarctic Continent
Palmers Land
Routes & average passage in days
Fair Winds
Desert
Place of doldrums for March thus

SEA DRIFT AND WHALES. on which the movements of the sea as indicated by the THERMOMETER are shewn.

Plate IX

August and September Hurricane of 1848.

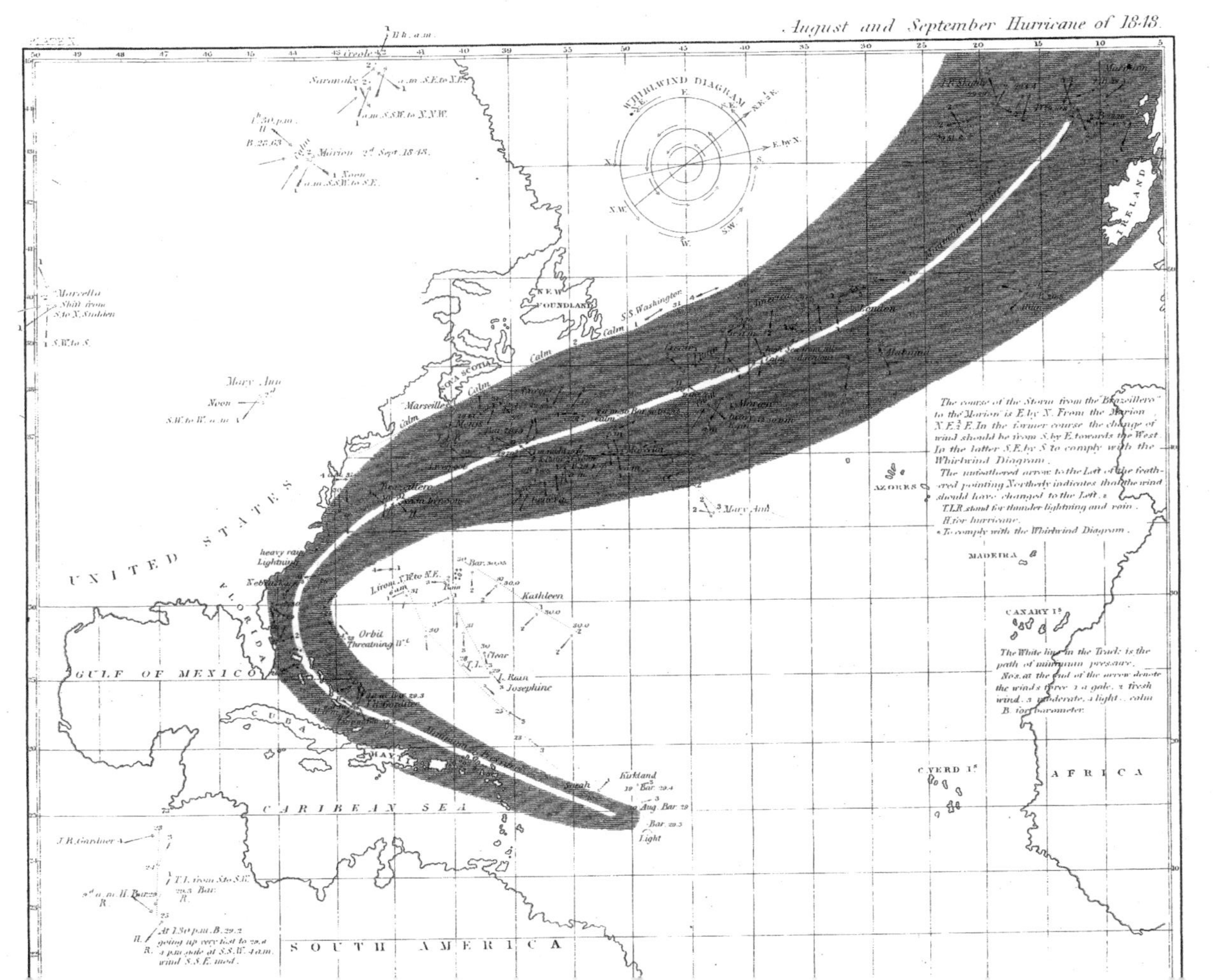

Basin of the North Atlantic Ocean. Plate XI.

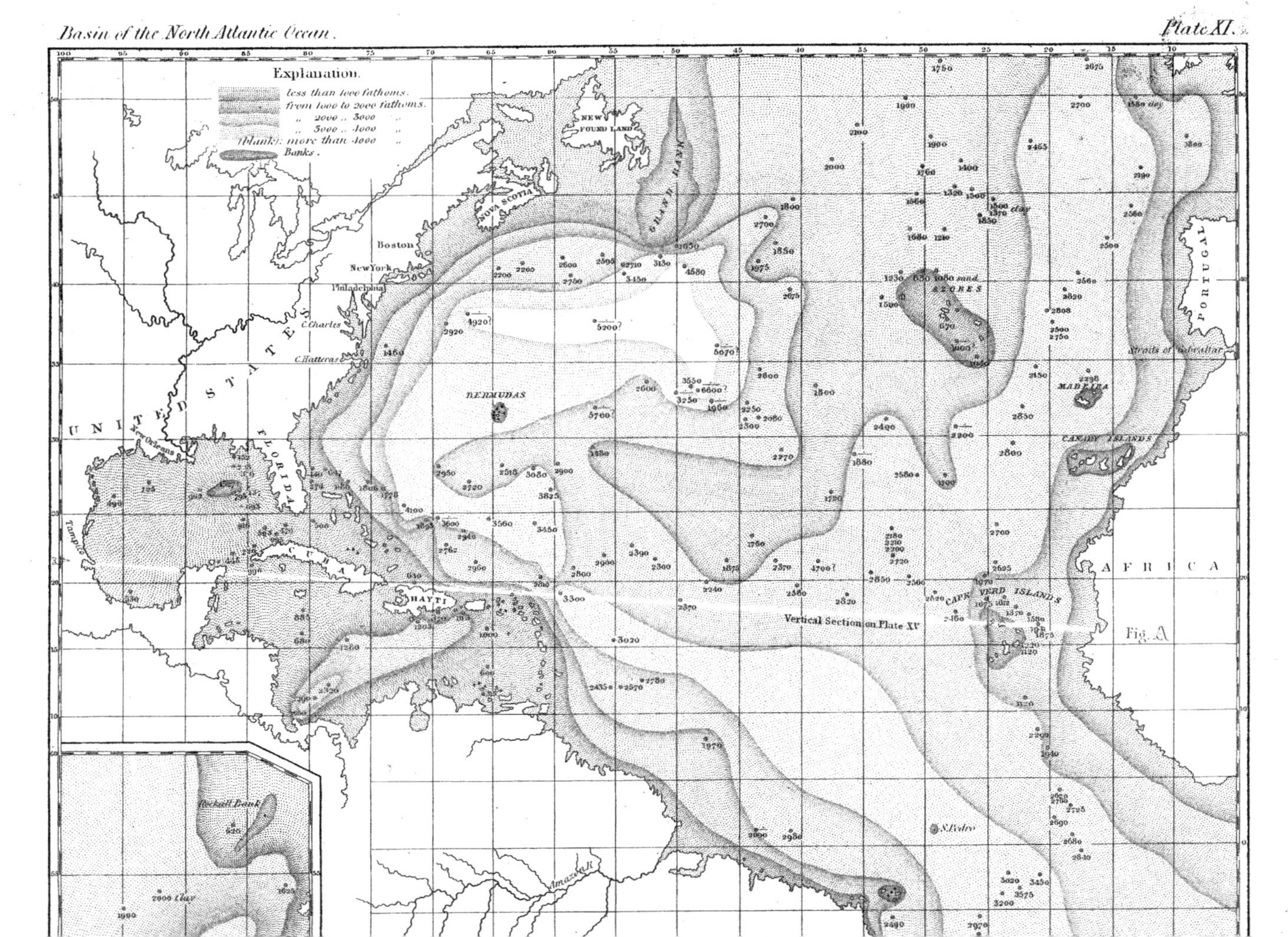

VERTICAL SECTION—NORTH ATLANTIC

PLATE [illegible].

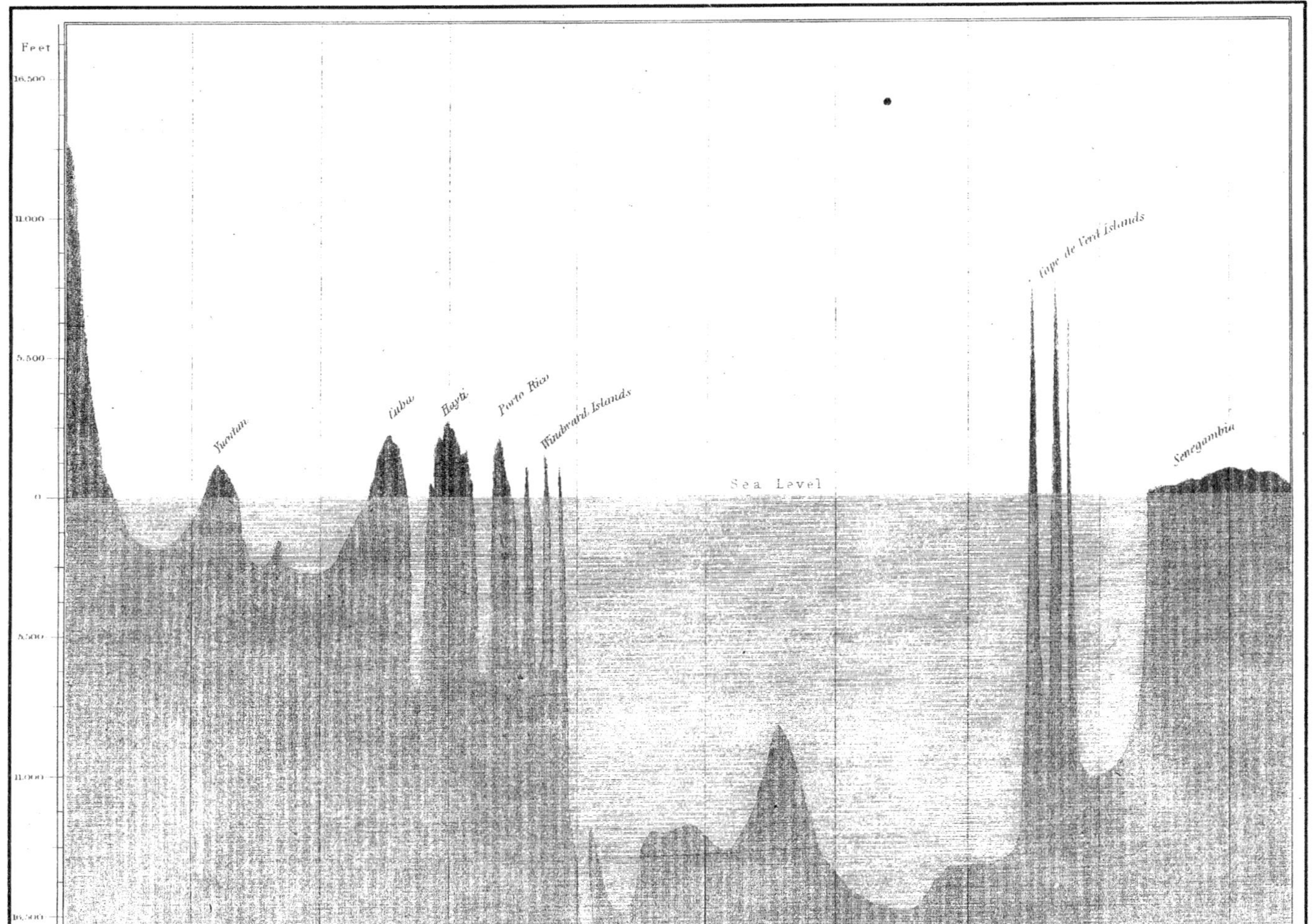